FIND OUT
ABOUT

FIND OUT ABOUT

Neil Grant

TREASURE PRESS

First published in Great Britain in 1985 by
The Hamlyn Publishing Group Limited

This edition published in 1990 by
Treasure Press
Michelin House
81 Fulham Road
London SW3 6RB

ISBN 1-85051-598-0

Printed in Czechoslovakia
52099/3

Introduction

Use *Find Out About* to amaze your friends and impress your teachers with the vast range of general knowledge questions you can ask and answer!

Do ferns have flowers?
Who were the Fascists?
When did the Space Age begin?
Where is the world's largest waterfall?

These are just a tiny sample of the many fascinating questions answered and explained here. Every question is illustrated in colour, demonstrating over and over again the truth of the Chinese saying that a picture is worth a thousand words.

The quick quizzes scattered throughout the book are a good test of general knowledge – try them out on your family and friends. Whether you dip into *Find Out About* at random or use the comprehensive index to look up certain information, you will find it a constant source of interest and enjoyment.

Best of all, this book is a valuable stimulus to further research. One fascinating fact discovered here may well spark off a life-long interest in a particular subject. Use your school or local library to find out more about those subjects which interest you. It is always a good idea to tell the librarian what you are looking for because he or she will know where to find the information you want.

Have lots of fun finding out!

When did *Great Britain* go to sea?

Isambard Kingdom Brunel (above right) was an English ship designer of the 19th century; the *Great Britain* (above) was his most successful ship.

In 1838 Brunel's steamer, the *Great Western*, broke the record for crossing the Atlantic. Like nearly all large ships then, she was built of wood. In the same year there was a violent storm which wrecked many ships. The only ship which survived without serious damage was built of iron. So, Brunel decided his next great ship had to have an iron hull.

The *Great Britain* was launched in 1843. She was the first large, iron-hulled, steam-driven ship to cross the Atlantic. She had a screw propeller (instead of paddle wheels like the *Great Western*) and was the largest ship afloat. Brunel's *Great Eastern* (1858) was even bigger, but less successful.

Why are New Zealanders called Kiwis?

The kiwi (left) is a bird which cannot fly and lives only in New Zealand. It is related to the moa, a bird even larger than the ostrich which is now extinct. The kiwi, named after its shrill call, is about the size of a chicken.

The kiwi has soft, slender feathers, almost like hair. With its long beak it probes for worms and insects, which it finds by smell. Because it is active mainly at night, roaming the forest on powerful feet, New Zealand's national emblem is not a very common sight.

10

What is an astrolabe?

Over a thousand years ago, astronomers in Arabia and Persia made quite accurate measurements of the stars. One of their instruments was the astrolabe. The Arabian astrolabe above measures the number of degrees (marked around the rim) the sun or a star is above the horizon.

Another, later kind of astrolabe is the armillary sphere (below), a model of the universe with Earth at the centre.

Where would you find domes rather than steeples?

Today the Christian religion is divided into many different churches, but in the Middle Ages there were only two organized Christian churches, Roman Catholic in Western Europe and Orthodox in Eastern Europe and Asia Minor. Among many differences, they adopted different styles for church building. Western churches usually had towers or spires, but Eastern churches had domes (below). The religion of Islam also adopted the dome for its mosques. Mosques also have minarets (bottom), spires from which the people are called to prayer.

Why is a starfish prickly?

Those little spines (below) are the tube-feet which help the starfish move about. The common starfish has tube-feet which end in small suckers. To move, the starfish pumps water into the spines it wants to use, making them stronger. Although it moves slowly, about 15 cm (6 in) a minute, it can climb over any surface and squeeze through the smallest crack in search of food. When it finds a tasty oyster, for example, it fastens its arms to both sides of the shell with the suckers and pulls it open. The burrowing starfish (bottom) has tube-feet which end in a point and are ideal for burrowing. It swallows small prey whole and doesn't need to open shellfish.

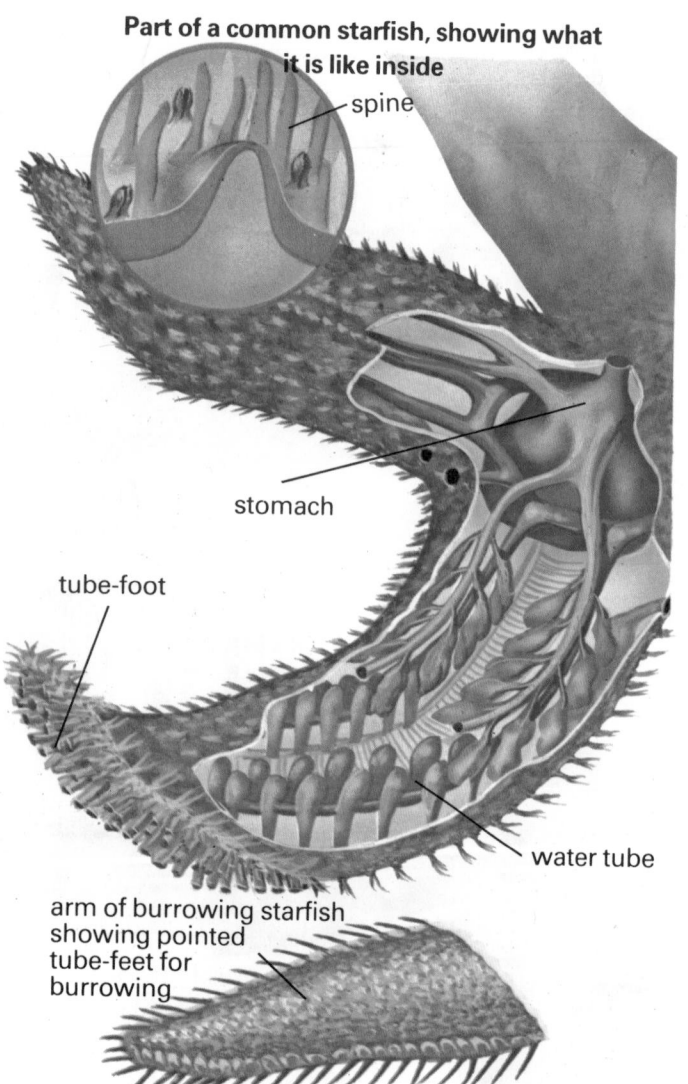

Part of a common starfish, showing what it is like inside

spine

stomach

tube-foot

water tube

arm of burrowing starfish showing pointed tube-feet for burrowing

Who was JFK?

John Fitzgerald Kennedy (above) was the 35th president of the United States of America. Elected in 1960, when he was 43, he was the youngest man ever elected president. He was also the first Roman Catholic.

He came from a rich Boston family, went to university at Harvard and (in spite of a weak back) was a naval officer in the Second World War – earning medals for bravery. He was a senator, representing Massachusetts, before his election as president.

As president, JFK proclaimed a 'new frontier' in US politics. He and his associates were young, intelligent, full of vigour (one of his favourite words), and optimistic. They planned new laws to help the poor, the old, the sick and racial minorities. They offered help and hope to the poor in other countries, especially in Latin America. Foreign affairs caused many problems, but Kennedy's diplomacy averted a crisis when the Soviet Union built missile bases in Cuba. Another of his successes was the international treaty banning nuclear tests (1963). He was also responsible for increasing military aid to South Vietnam, at the beginning of a terrible war.

His presidency showed great promise but the new age (as it seemed to many people) was cut short when Kennedy was shot dead in Dallas, Texas, on 22 November 1963.

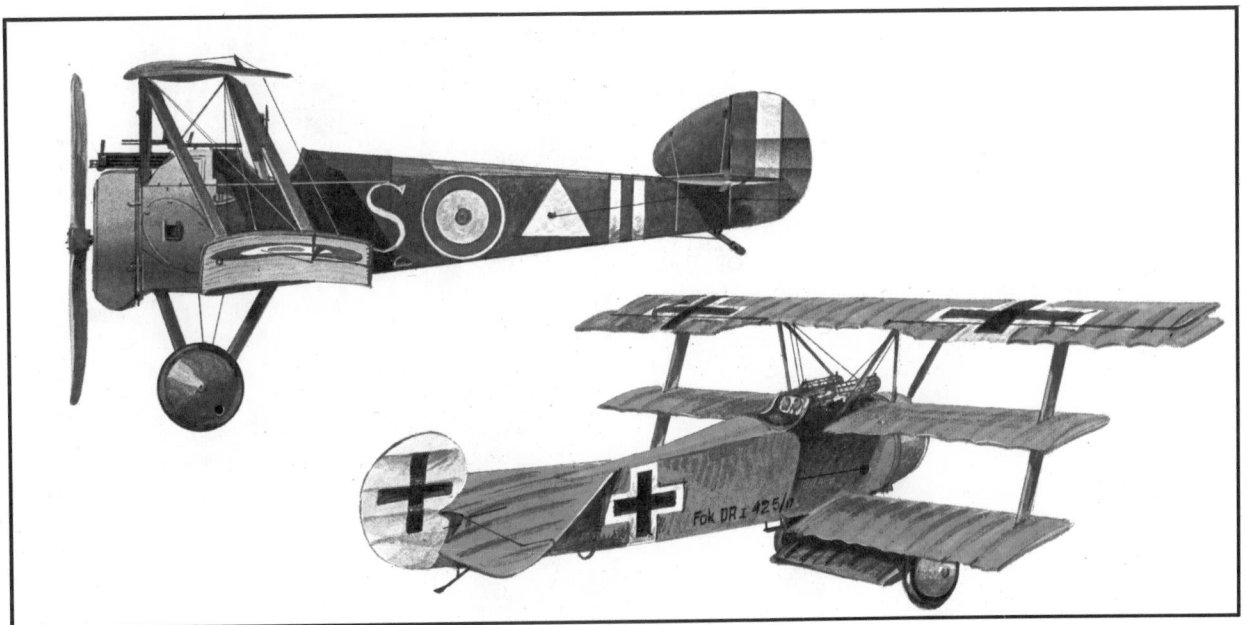

What is a biplane?

A biplane is an aeroplane with two sets of wings, or mainplanes. Although the aircraft which Louis Blériot flew across the English Channel in 1909 was a monoplane (single wings), most aeroplanes were biplanes until the 1920s.

Although the aeroplane was such a recent invention in 1914, aircraft design made rapid progress during the First World War. The first fighters were in the air by 1915, though air warfare had hardly been thought of two years earlier. At first it was carried on in an almost 'sporting' manner, like medieval knights jousting in a tournament. When the German ace, Baron von Richtofen, was killed in 1918 the British sent an unarmed plane to his base with a letter of regret.

Richtofen's aircraft (above) was a Fokker triplane (three mainplanes), painted red (hence his nickname, the Red Baron). The Royal Flying Corps (later the Royal Air Force) had, among other aircraft, the Sopwith Camel (top) which had a top speed of 180 km/h (112 mph).

Where would you find a sextant?

A sextant (left) measures the angle between the sun or a star and the horizon, the degrees of altitude being read from the curved part. Along with other information, the navigator of a boat or aircraft can then work out the craft's position when it is out of sight of land.

Who carried a boat through the jungle?

The expedition of the British explorer Henry M Stanley across Africa, from Zanzibar to the mouth of the River Zaire (or Congo, as it was then called), in 1874–77, was one of the toughest and strangest journeys in African

Can a lake be hot?

Spring water is usually very cold, but there are some places in the world where the springs are hot. They are usually in areas where volcanoes have erupted, places where deep in the earth the magma (very hot, liquid rock) has been cooling to form solid rock. Water circulating through these areas is heated, and reaches the surface as hot springs.

history. Over 200 people, mainly Zanzibaris, started out; very few finished the journey.

Among Stanley's equipment was a portable boat which he named the *Lady Alice*, after a girl he was hoping to marry (she grew tired of waiting for him and married someone else).

When they were only 80 km (50 miles) from the end of their 11 000-km (6800-mile) journey, Stanley decided to leave the river, whose rapids had drowned so many of his men, and march overland. The *Lady Alice* was dragged up to a high rock by the tired men and left to bleach and slowly rot away in the sun.

The most spectacular kind of hot spring is a geyser (the name comes from one particular geyser in Iceland). This is a hot fountain, which spouts steam and hot water at regular intervals. A famous geyser in Yellowstone National Park in the USA is known as 'Old Faithful' because it performs on such a strict timetable. Old Faithful sometimes spouts nearly 50 m (165 ft) into the air, but some geysers only rise a few centimetres. The gigantic geysers of Rotorua, New Zealand are the greatest. One, Waimanga, which is no longer active, sometimes let loose a jet of boiling water which went up nearly 500 m (1650 ft) into the air. Some also expel stones and mud.

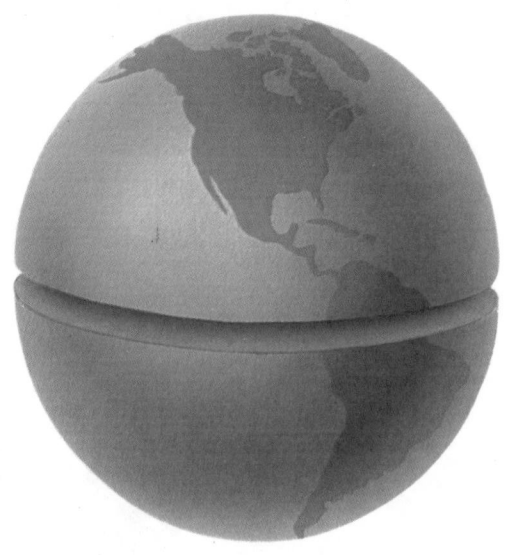

How big is a hemisphere?

A hemisphere is half (*hemi-*) of a globe or sphere. Hemispheres usually refer to sections of the planet Earth.

The Earth can be divided into halves in two ways: northern and southern hemispheres (above), which are divided by the equator; or eastern and western hemispheres (below), which are divided by a line which joins the North and South Poles and passes through the Atlantic and Pacific Oceans. America is in the Western hemisphere, whereas Europe and Africa are in the eastern hemisphere.

Who were the Suffragettes?

In January 1908 Mrs Emmeline Pankhurst, a small, slight Englishwoman, spoke at a political meeting in the quiet Devon town of Newton Abbot. She was pelted with stones buried inside snowballs and showered with rotten vegetables. Two men attacked her and knocked her unconscious. One of her supporters was killed.

What was it about? The right of women to vote in elections for government.

At that time no women were allowed to vote in elections in Britain (or most other countries). Many people, men as well as women, believed this was unfair and said so, but Mrs Pankhurst went further. She was the leader of the Suffragettes (the word suffrage means 'the right to vote'), who were prepared to break the law in order to draw attention to their demand. They were the extremists of the women's suffrage movement (above, one is being arrested). They invaded the House of Commons, chained themselves to railings and smashed shop windows. 'I am what you call a hooligan', Mrs Pankhurst told an American audience.

When they were sent to prison they refused to obey the rules, wear prison clothes – or eat. So they were fed by force, a painful and dangerous business.

During the First World War women took over the industrial jobs which had been done by the men who joined the army. They gained new respect for themselves as independent citizens, and in 1918 women over the age of 30 gained the vote.

Quick Quiz

What animal are you eating when you eat (1) mutton, (2) veal, (3) pork, (4) beef, (5) venison?

Answers: (1) sheep, (2) calf, (3) pig, (4) bullock, (5) deer.

Who wrote stories about (1) Alice, (2) Mowgli, (3) Peter Pan, (4) Noddy, (5) the Hobbit?

Answers: (1) Lewis Carroll, (2) Rudyard Kipling, (3) J. M. Barrie, (4) Enid Blyton, (5) J. R. R. Tolkien.

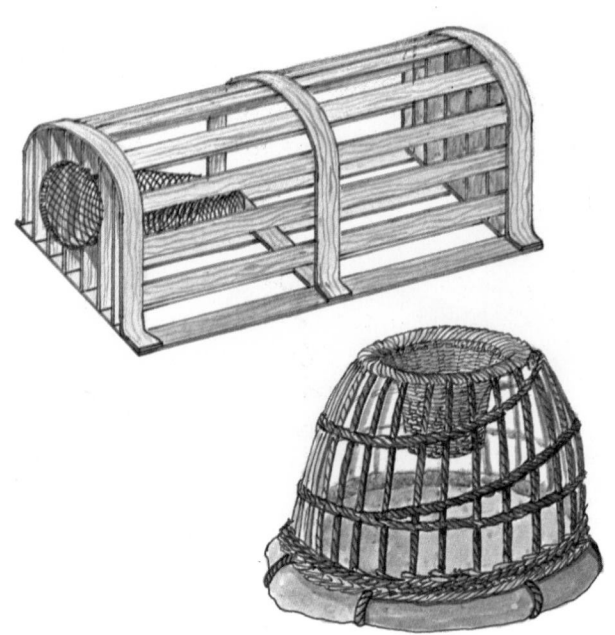

Could you ride a penny-farthing?

The first sensible bicycle was made by Kirkpatrick Macmillan in Dumfries, Scotland, in 1839. Many strange machines resembling bicycles had been made much earlier, but this was the first that could be both steered and pedalled. It had pedals like a modern child's pedal car, going to and fro, not round in a circle. The French took the lead in bicycle-making after that, producing the *vélocipède*, which had a front wheel slightly larger than the back wheel.

But the father of the cycle industry was James Starley, a foreman at the Coventry Sewing Machine Company. In 1870, when he was 67, he invented his Ariel bicycle, with a very large front wheel and a very small rear wheel trailing behind (above). This was the 'ordinary' bicycle or 'penny-farthing'. (The old English penny was a very large coin; the farthing, or quarter-penny, was a very small one.) It was easy to fall off a penny-farthing. All the same, they were still in use long after the appearance of the 'safety' bicycle, with equal wheels and a chain, in 1874.

Are lobsters cooked in pots?

Usually they are, but lobsters are also *caught* in pots. A lobster pot is a trap made of wickerwork (left below), like a basket, or of wooden strips or hoops (left above). The fisherman baits the trap with scraps of fish and lowers it into the water. The lobster, attracted by the bait, enters through a funnel-shaped opening. But once inside, it can't get out again.

What kind of people live in tents?

In earlier times a great many people, especially in Asia and northern Africa, were nomads. Nomadic people have no permanent home, but travel from place to place, stopping wherever there is water and grazing for their animals. In hot countries, the nomad's home is usually a tent like the one below, which can be rolled up easily and carried on the back of a camel. The only furniture nomadic peoples of the Middle East have is their carpets.

In the far distant past, long before people discovered how to work metals or grow crops, all people were nomadic. They lived on what nature provided, and were forced to follow the herds they hunted. Today, nomads everywhere are beginning to settle down, even those in desert countries like Saudi Arabia or Iran. However, there are still many who prefer the old, wandering way of life. There are even some nomads left in Europe – the gypsies – though they drive cars and live in modern caravans.

What is the biggest flower in the world?

In the hot, wet forests of Malaysia, in South-east Asia, there grows a plant called rafflesia. It is a parasite, living on the roots of vines; it has no leaves, and its flowers smell like rotten meat. But the flowers of one kind of rafflesia (botanists have discovered six species), though smelly and ugly, may be nearly 1 m (3 ft 3 in) in width, which makes them the largest flowers in the world (above).

Can you see a living cell?

Every living thing is made up of tiny organisms called cells. They are far too small for a human eye to see, but they can be seen under a microscope. The microscope is one of the most valuable instruments scientists have. Without it, many of the great discoveries in science would have been impossible.

A compound microscope like this one can magnify up to about 2500 times, making a human hair look like a tree trunk. (A double-page spread of this book magnified 2500 times would be larger than a tennis court!)

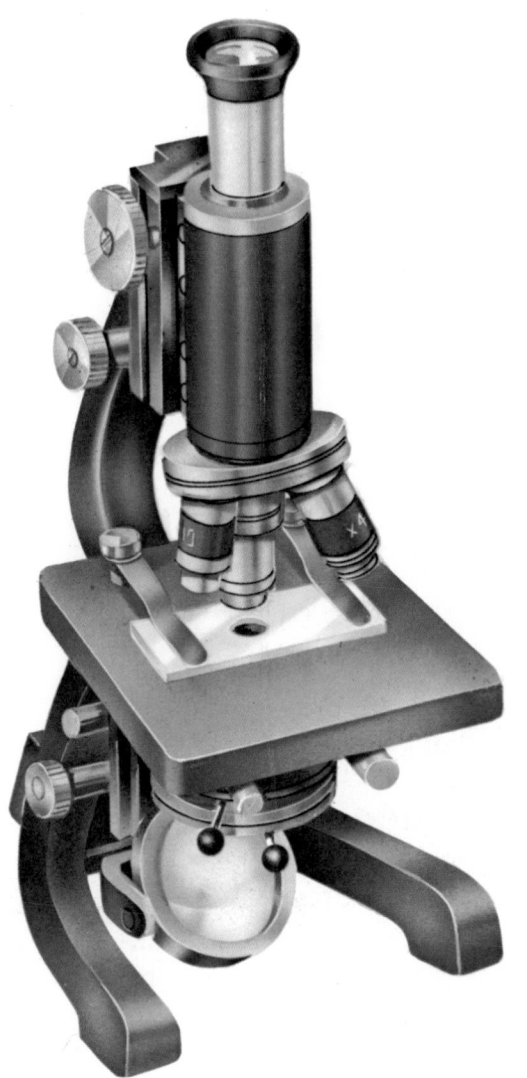

Have you ever been battered by a ram?

Before guns and explosives were invented, wars were often decided by sieges. A losing army could take refuge behind a city's stone walls. However, there were some weapons for attacking stone defences, like the ancient Greek battering ram above (note the ram's head) and the siege catapult below.

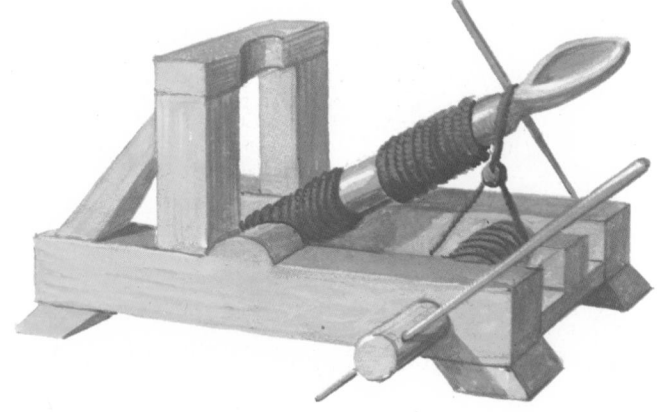

19

Can a jumbo fly?

This kind of 'jumbo' can! It is a Boeing 747 airliner, 70 m (231 ft) long with a wingspan of 60 m (197 ft). The first of the big jumbo jets, it can carry more than 500 passengers. It has a maximum speed of nearly 1000 km/h (600 mph) and can travel more than 11 000 km (7000 miles) without refuelling.

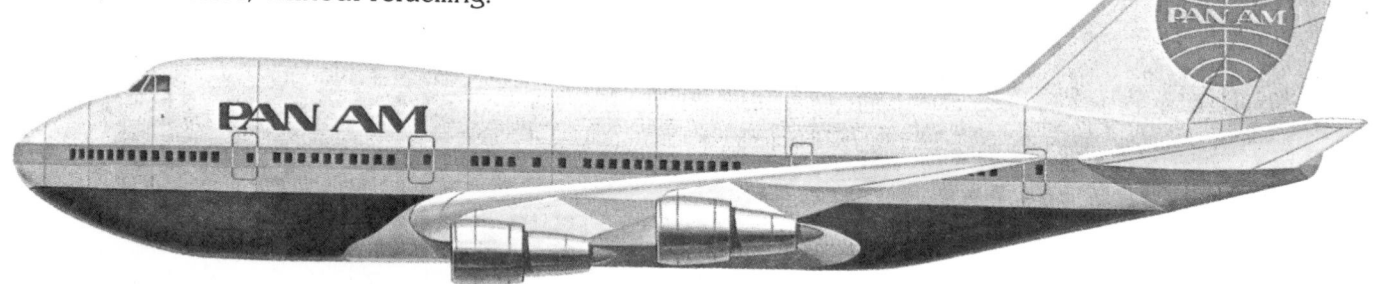

Can you count the stars?

On a very clear night it may be possible to see over 1000 stars without a telescope. No one knows how many stars there are in the universe. The photograph below shows one cluster of stars in one constellation (Hercules), which is visible to the naked eye as a tiny. misty patch.

Where does china come from?

China clay, or kaolin, is usually mined from pits like this, for making pottery, or china, as well as other things such as plastics. To make porcelain (the finest kind of china) it is fused with china stone, or petuntse, at very high temperature.

Brown pelican

Flamingo

Skimmer

Great spotted woodpecker

Hawaiian honeycreeper

Common kingfisher

Hummingbird

Why do birds have beaks?

A bird's beak is a nose as well as a mouth, and it may also be a pair of hands, or a knife and fork, or a hammer, a vice, or many other useful things. It all depends on the shape.

The pelican traps fish in its pouched bill, while the kingfisher spears them. Woodpeckers chip away at trees to catch wood-boring insects. The flamingo's bill contains a filter, which catches tiny animals as water is passed through it. The skimmer uses its bill like a scoop as it flies over the surface of a lake or river, and snaps it shut when it touches food. The Hawaiian honeycreeper and this South American hummingbird have long beaks to sip nectar from flowers.

Who wore greaves and a cuirass?

The soldiers below, called hoplites, were Greeks in the army of Alexander the Great, who conquered a great area stretching from Egypt to India in the 4th century BC. They carry spears and short swords, and wear simple armour made of bronze. The chest protector is called a cuirass and the shinguards are greaves. They were away from home for 12 years during Alexander's conquests.

How big is an eagle?

The eagle is the Rolls Royce of birds. The soaring, stately flight of this rare creature is a wonderful sight. This is the golden eagle, which is about 80 cm (2 ft 7 in) long with a wingspan of about 220 cm (7 ft 3 in) – some eagles are bigger. Eagles have been hunted by people and are now rare.

Why put a horse in a box?

Racehorses usually travel to races in special vans called horseboxes. Because horses are such nervous creatures, transporting them can be difficult. Vehicles like this often have compartments so that riders and grooms can accompany their horses.

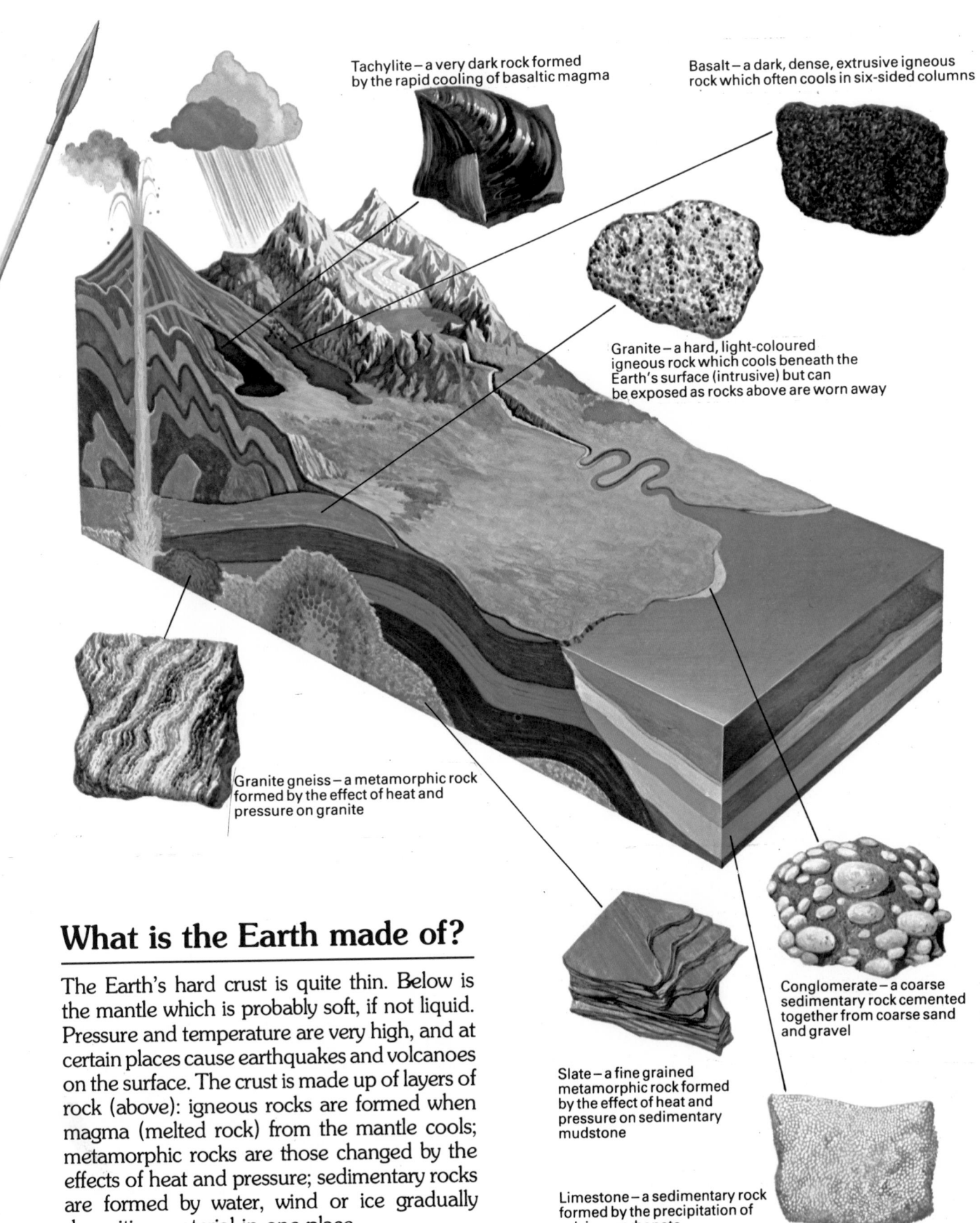

Tachylite – a very dark rock formed by the rapid cooling of basaltic magma

Basalt – a dark, dense, extrusive igneous rock which often cools in six-sided columns

Granite – a hard, light-coloured igneous rock which cools beneath the Earth's surface (intrusive) but can be exposed as rocks above are worn away

Granite gneiss – a metamorphic rock formed by the effect of heat and pressure on granite

Conglomerate – a coarse sedimentary rock cemented together from coarse sand and gravel

Slate – a fine grained metamorphic rock formed by the effect of heat and pressure on sedimentary mudstone

Limestone – a sedimentary rock formed by the precipitation of calcium carbonate

What is the Earth made of?

The Earth's hard crust is quite thin. Below is the mantle which is probably soft, if not liquid. Pressure and temperature are very high, and at certain places cause earthquakes and volcanoes on the surface. The crust is made up of layers of rock (above): igneous rocks are formed when magma (melted rock) from the mantle cools; metamorphic rocks are those changed by the effects of heat and pressure; sedimentary rocks are formed by water, wind or ice gradually depositing material in one place.

What is a desert?

A desert is land where very little grows and human beings find it hard to live. The usual reason is lack of useable water. About one-fifth of the land in the world is desert, or semi-desert. There are large deserts in every continent except Europe.

We think of deserts as hot, flat and sandy, but that describes only a few places. Many deserts are mountainous, and rocky or stony rather than sandy. The icy Antarctic, where nothing lives, might be called a desert too, because all the water is frozen. Even in hot deserts, nights are often cold, because the sky is normally clear and there is no 'blanket' of clouds to keep the land warm.

lanner falcon

coral snake

rattlesnake

thorny devil

horned lizard

shovel-nosed snake

gila monster

scorpion

tarantula

Though desserts may look barren, they often conceal valuable minerals below the surface. Yet the real treasure in the desert is water. Although there is a place in Chile where *no rain has ever been recorded*, all deserts have a little water somewhere. Most deserts contain oases, places where water can be found at all times, and in these little green patches human settlements grow. Even where water is very scarce, the desert is not lifeless. Many plants and – as you can see in this picture – animals can live there. Desert plants can store water when it rains to last them many months – until the next shower. The saguaro cactus, which looks something like huge green fingers, grows as big as a large tree in the Californian desert, and can store several litres of water.

The desert animals pictured here could not all be found in the same desert. But they are all types which can live in very dry conditions. Turn the page to find out more about them.

barbary falcon

camel

mourning wheatear

gerbil

sandgrouse

jerboa

ground squirrel

fennec fox

kangaroo rat

gerbil

beetle

Desert animals

Some animals are able to live very well in the desert, and true desert-dwellers have special ways of dealing with the lack of water or the extreme heat. Reptiles, whose body temperatures change with the temperature outside, are especially common. You seldom see large animals (except camels) in the desert, but though they are usually small, desert animals are surprisingly numerous.

Birds

Birds have one great advantage over other kinds of animals: they can fly, and therefore cover much greater distances at much greater speed than animals that depend on their feet. The sandgrouse will fly hundreds of kilometres each day to a water hole. Some birds migrate enormous distances and many of the birds seen in gardens in northern Europe in the summer, like swallows and martins, spend the winter in Africa. So does the wheatear, which may be seen as far north as Iceland and Norway in summer. Another member of the wheatear family, the desert or 'mourning' wheatear, is a desert bird which breeds only in Africa and Asia. The odd one does sometimes venture as far north as Britain, but probably by mistake!

Perhaps the most typical desert bird is the falcon. The ancient sport of falconry (see page 49) began in the Middle East and is still a favourite sport of the sheikhs of Arabia. The saker, or Barbary falcon is the falcon mostly used by the Arabs for this sport and a game bird called the bustard is its favourite prey.

Falcons hunt by eye, scanning the ground below them. They like open country with few plants or trees to conceal the small animals they hunt. Today, falcons are rare. Even the peregrine falcon, once common throughout Europe, is scarce now. True desert falcons like the saker, although very rare, may have a better chance of surviving because they suffer less interference from human beings. The lanner falcon also flies in desert skies, though it may be seen in parts of southern Italy and Greece as well as in North Africa.

Reptiles and Insects

Some reptiles and insects have adapted very well to life in the desert. They have various methods of avoiding the extreme heat. The brilliantly-coloured American coral snake, for example, is a burrower. It spends most of the time underground (where its bright colours cannot be seen) and so avoids the direct heat of the sun. The shovel-nosed snake, as its name suggests, is another burrower. Several forms of the rattlesnake (another American snake) prefer dry plains or desert, especially the sidewinder, whose peculiar sideways wriggle leaves tell-tale tracks in the the sand. Some biologists believe that the rattlesnake's rattle, which is made by rapid shaking of the loose, horny segments in its tail, was developed as a warning to larger animals of the plains which might otherwise tread on it by mistake.

Like the rattlesnake, some desert insects, spiders and scorpions, have a bad reputation which they do not really deserve. Nobody wants to find a scorpion or a tarantula in the bed, but

peregrine falcon

rattlesnake attacking prairie dog

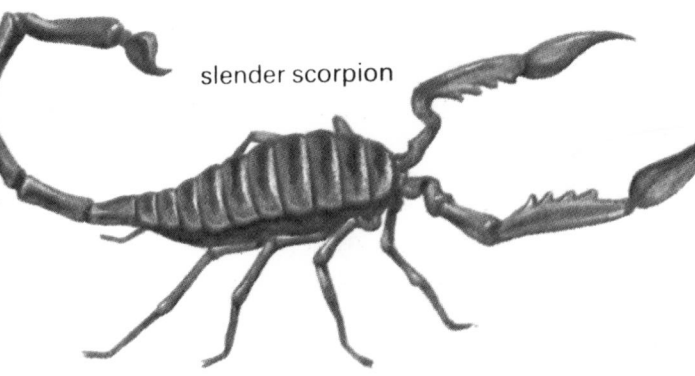

slender scorpion

these creatures, like the rattlesnake, will not attack a human being except in self-defence. The wind scorpion (actually a member of the spider family), which lives in the deserts of Africa and Arabia, is a savage hunter, but its bite is not poisonous. True scorpions have a sting in their tail, however, which is best avoided!

Tarantulas too are not a pretty sight. They are large, hairy spiders. Often any such spider is called a tarantula, though the name is not scientifically correct. Their bite may be unpleasant but otherwise tarantulas are harmless. Some that live in the dry south-west of the USA can be tamed as pets (though it's not difficult to think of nicer pets!).

The Australian desert contains some strange-looking reptiles. One of the strangest is the thorny devil, a lizard whose fierce appearance is designed to frighten its enemies. Despite its name, the thorny devil is shy and harmless. The gila monster, unlike other lizards, does have a poisonous bite. It lives in the American south-west and in Mexico and hunts at night, lying quietly in a burrow during the day.

Mammals

Human beings like animals that look pretty and dislike those that look ugly. This is unfair: a gila monster does not look like a monster to another gila monster! The desert contains several small animals, mainly rodents, that are especially attractive to us. Gerbils are now popular pets. They are more interesting than hamsters, and better-tempered! However, the ancestral home of the gerbil is not a warm cage in a house, but the harsh Mongolian desert.

Another charming Asian rodent is the jerboa, which hops along on its long hind legs and holds its food in its 'hands'. The kangaroo rat of North America also gets about on its hind legs. This is one of the most successful desert animals because it seldom needs to drink, getting enough moisture from fats in the food it eats. Kangaroo rats can even live in Death Valley, California, one of the harshest deserts in the world. Like camels and most desert mammals, they cannot sweat. Sweating means, of course, losing moisture from the body, which is just what desert creatures must avoid.

There are many varieties of the American ground squirrel. One form, the Mojave ground squirrel, 'aestivates', which is the opposite of hibernating: it sleeps in the summer months.

Other desert mammals include the golden mole of south-west Africa and the Sahara fox, or fennec fox, of North Africa and Arabia. With its soft, creamy fur and enormous ears, which help to get rid of body heat as well as pick up the sounds of the small animals it hunts, this desert fox is a very attractive animal. It hunts at night, resting in a shady burrow during the day.

The largest desert animal, and the one most people know best, is the camel. Nearly all camels, however, are domestic animals, like cattle. Wild camels lived on the borders of the Sahara and Arabian deserts rather than the central desert regions. The bactrian camel comes from the Gobi Desert in eastern Asia, where, in winter at least, it is very cold. It has two humps instead of the single hump of the Arabian camel. Camels have broad feet which do not sink into sand or snow. They can close both their nostrils and their eyes tightly against blowing sand, and, thanks to their humps, they can go for a long time without drinking. The camel's hump is a kind of larder, a store of fat which provides extra food and water when needed.

camel

Where does cotton come from?

Nowadays, many of our clothes are of artificial materials such as nylon or polyester, which are made in factories by chemical processes. But the best jumpers, sweaters and suits are made of wool, which comes from sheep, and many other clothes (jeans, T-shirts, etc) are made from another natural material called cotton.

Cotton comes not from an animal but from a plant (above). Cotton plants grow in hot countries like India, parts of Africa, the southern USA and the West Indies. The cotton plant is a shrub-like annual which flowers quickly. The seeds within the seedpods (bolls) grow a mass of fine fibre hairs. Finally the bolls burst to reveal a soft ball of white fibre. The cotton which is woven into material for making clothes is made from this fibre.

Today the cotton bolls are picked by machines and the seeds are removed from the bolls by another machine called a 'gin'. The soft fibre is pressed into large bales, to be sold to the spinning mills where it is spun into yarn, then woven into cloth.

How much wood would a woodpecker peck . . . ?

As everyone knows, woodpeckers can make holes in trees with their beaks, but not all woodpeckers do it for the same reason. In the USA, the acorn woodpecker (below) selects a tree to act as a larder. Working in small groups, these birds make holes in the tree in which they store acorns. As many as 50 000 acorns may be stored in one tree.

Most woodpeckers use their strong beaks and long extendible tongues (which often have harpoon-like tips) to extract insect larvae from wood.

Was this the first cartoon strip?

The Bayeux tapestry is a strip of embroidery about 70 m (230 ft) long. In a series of pictures, with words, it tells the story of the Norman Conquest of England, in 1066. It was probably made soon after that date, and is now in the Museum of Bayeux, France.

Quick Quiz

What are the following materials made from?
(1) mohair, (2) linen, (3) sacking, (4) leather, (5) silk, (6) cashmere.

Answers: (1) fleece of Angora goats, (2) flax, (3) jute or hemp, (4) skins of animals, (5) cocoons of silkworms, (6) fine downy wool at the roots of the hair of Kashmir goats.

Is it a boat, is it a plane?

Below is a type of boat called a hydrofoil, which travels with its hull lifted clear of the water. Unlike a hovercraft, which rides on a cushion of air, the hydrofoil is raised by foils which produce 'lift' in a similar way to the wings of an aeroplane. When it stops, it sinks down into the water and looks like an ordinary boat. Hydrofoils like this are used as passenger ferries. They are faster and use less fuel than normal ferries. Their only drawback is that they cannot sail in very rough seas.

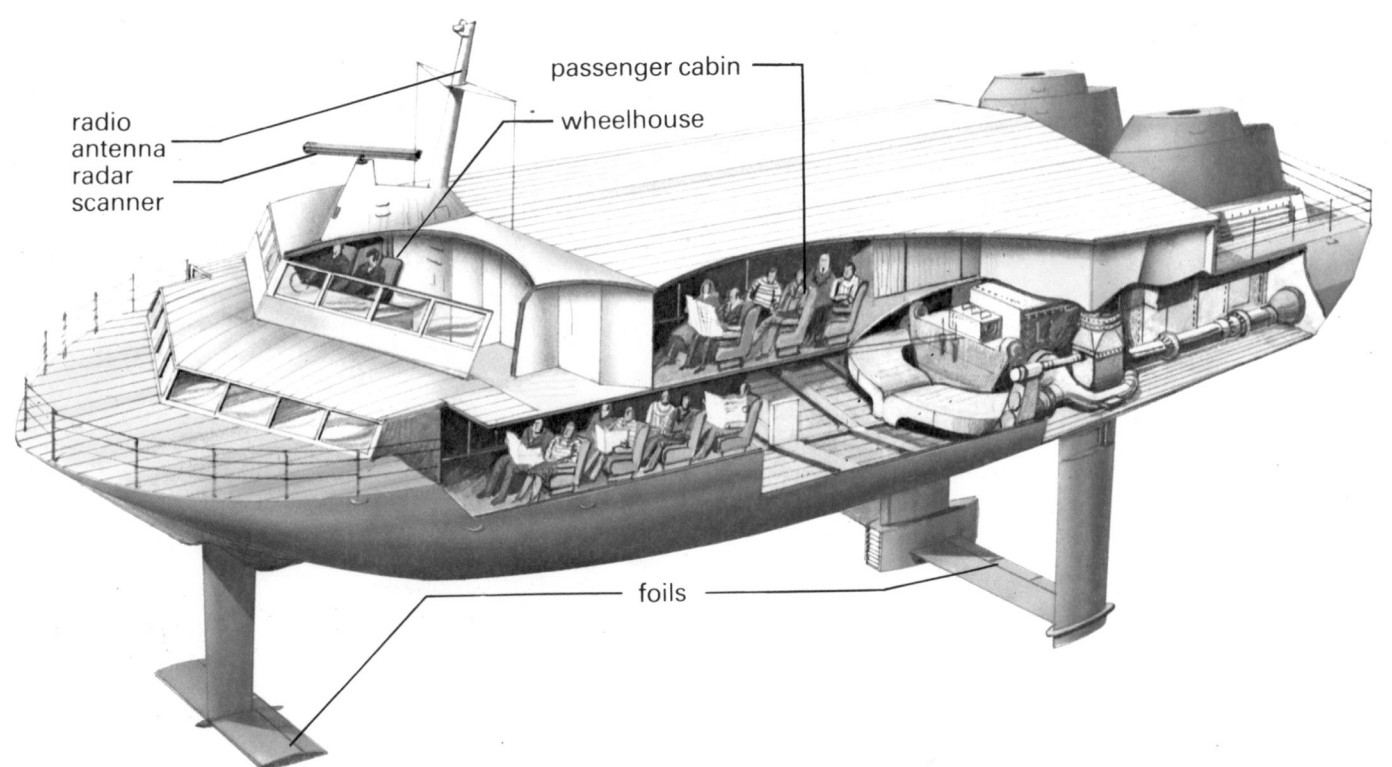

radio antenna
radar scanner
wheelhouse
passenger cabin
foils

Who swallowed the Sun?

When the Moon blocks the Sun from view, it is called an eclipse of the Sun (a total eclipse is, in fact, a rare event). In ancient times, when Sun and Moon were worshipped as gods, an eclipse was terrifying. One ancient Chinese explanation was that a dragon had swallowed the Sun (below).

How can tanks cover their tracks?

Tanks have tracks instead of wheels to bear their enormous weight over rough or soft ground. So, for long journeys by road, it is quicker and easier to transport them on trucks like the one above.

Quick Quiz

What animals are known by these nicknames?
(1) Reynard, (2) Polly, (3) Jumbo, (4) Bruin, (5) Brock.

Answers: (1) fox, (2) parrot, (3) elephant, (4) bear, (5) badger.

What kind of animals are the following?
(1) Kermit, (2) Basil Brush, (3) Tarka, (4) Mrs Tiggy-winkle, (5) Donald.

Answers: (1) frog, (2) fox, (3) otter, (4) hedgehog, (5) duck.

velvet stem

death cap

cup fungus

fly agaric

verdigris agaric

scaly wood mushroom

Can you eat fungus?

A walk in the woods early on a damp morning in autumn is the best time and place for spotting fungi – toadstools and mushrooms. They come in great variety, in all shapes and sizes and in many different colours. On weekends in eastern Europe many people go walking in the woods looking for edible fungi. However, although many kinds are edible, others are highly poisonous. So don't try eating any without expert advice.

dryad's saddle

tinder bracket

orange-peel fungus

stinkhorn

horn of plenty

blewit

sulphur tuft

hanterelle

parasol mushroom

milk cap

the sickener

fairy ring mushroom

puff ball

What makes the lights go on?

When you turn on a light switch in the house, a light comes on. The bulb lights up because it is connected to an electric current. The electricity is supplied by a system of cables called the national grid. The advantage of a national system is that when the supply runs low in one region, it can be supplemented by power from another region. All Western Europe will soon belong to the same system.

Most of the power lines are carried by steel pylons, which are spread out across the countryside like alien giants. Some cables are laid underground.

Electricity is generated in power stations, where large amounts of fuel are needed to drive the generators. In Britain, the largest source of energy for power stations like the one above is coal, and the second largest is oil. They share one drawback. They are fossil fuels, formed in the Earth over millions of years. They cannot be replaced and will one day run out.

In Norway nearly all electricity comes from hydro-electric power stations. They use the power of Norway's many fast-flowing rivers ('hydro' means water). But few countries can generate much electricity in this way.

A small amount of our electricity already comes from nuclear power stations. Many people are frightened of nuclear power because it makes use of a very dangerous process and, if an accident happened, thousands of people could be killed by radiation. However, nuclear power seems to be the main solution to the energy problems of the future.

Where is Java?

The modern republic of Indonesia is made up of over 3000 islands. Sumatra, Java, Sulawesi, Bali and Timor are the chief ones. Indonesia also includes part of Borneo (Kalimantan) and New Guinea (Irian Jaya). These islands are very warm, wet and rich, especially Java, which is one of the most heavily populated places in the world. Although it is only about 1000 km (620 miles) long and 300 km (185 miles) wide, Java has about 70 million people. Its soil is so rich that farmers can grow two or even three crops of rice in one year.

Human civilizations have existed in these islands for a very long time. One of Man's ancestors, known as Java Man, lived here, and a Buddhist kingdom was centred on Sumatra between the 7th and 9th centuries.

Java

Javanese dancer

Bali

Traditional costumes from different Indonesian islands

Sumatra

CHINA

Salween

Hanoi

LAOS
Vientiane

Irrawaddy

Mekong

THAILAND   VIETNAM

Bangkok

Luzon

Manila

South China
Sea

PHILIPPINES

KAMPUCHEA
Phnom-
Penh

Ho Chi Minh City
(Saigon)

Mindanao

Sabah

BRUNEI

Kuala
Lumpur   MALAYSIA

Malaya   Sarawak

SINGAPORE   Kalimantan

Sumatra

Sulawesi
(Celebes)

Irian Jaya

INDONESIA

Jakarta

Java   Bali

Timor

0   1000 kilometres

0   600 miles

33

When was the Age of Steam?

Two hundred years ago very few factories, as we know them, existed anywhere. Western Europe and North America became industrialized very quickly in the 19th century. In a few years, goods which had been made by hand were being made – in huge numbers – by large machines in noisy factories.

All this progress was powered by the steam engine, which drove the machines for over a century. Today we have different sources of power, though steam engines are still used in a few places.

The most famous steam-driven machines were the railway locomotives, which revolutionized public transport. The early ones looked quite different from the *Duke of Gloucester* (below), but worked in practically the same way. Water was heated by burning fuel, usually coal, although wood and oil were sometimes used, to make steam. The steam was used to drive a piston which was connected to the driving wheels.

The *Duke of Gloucester* was the last mainline steam locomotive used by British Rail. It started work in 1952 and was retired only 10 years later. It is now at the Great Central Steam Trust in Loughborough, England.

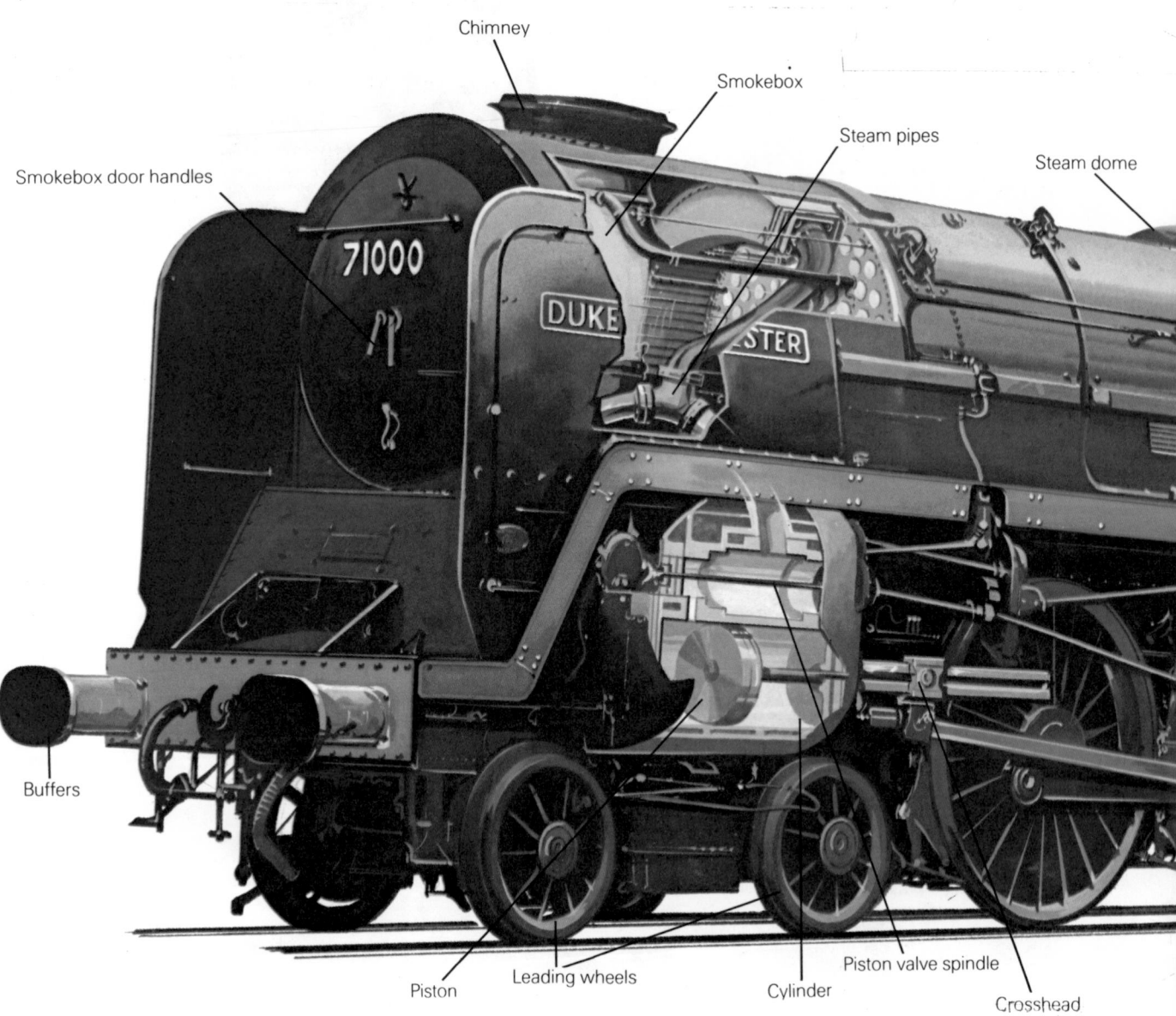

Chimney

Smokebox

Steam pipes

Steam dome

Smokebox door handles

71000

DUKE ... STER

Buffers

Piston

Leading wheels

Cylinder

Piston valve spindle

Crosshead

Is there anything in outer space?

The American *Pioneer* spacecraft (below) was one of the first to travel beyond the Earth's atmosphere. Astronomers wanted to know if outer space was completely empty. *Pioneer* discovered that there are hydrogen atoms very thinly scattered in space.

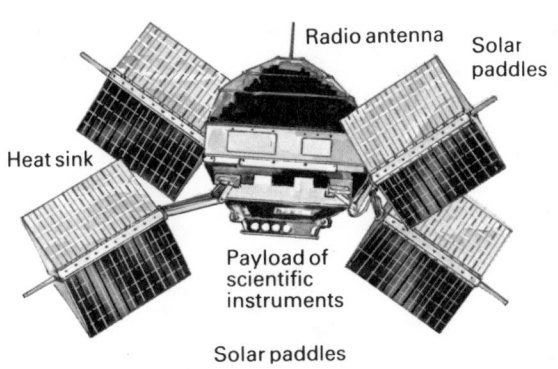

Radio antenna

Solar paddles

Heat sink

Payload of scientific instruments

Solar paddles

How does a boa take a nap?

Above is an Amazonian tree boa resting. Often called the emerald tree boa, it inhabits tropical South America. When resting in this characteristically coiled position it is almost impossible to see. It feeds mainly on birds, squirrels and iguana lizards. Like all boas, this 2-m (6.5-ft)-long snake constricts (squeezes) its prey to death.

Safety valve

Boiler tubes

Firebox

Cab

Coal

Tender

71000

Driving wheels

Coupling rod

Connecting rod

Trailing wheels

Bogie

Track

35

What is the largest animal that ever lived?

Whales are not only the largest animals in the world today, but the blue whale (below) is the largest animal that has ever lived on Earth. Whales are mammals which breathe air, though they live in the sea, and give birth to live young which they feed with their own milk. Whales provide many valuable products and in the past so many blue and sperm whales were killed that the whole race nearly died out. Today, these rare whales are protected.

The blue whale grows to a length of 30 m (90 ft) and can weigh as much as 112 tonnes. We know very little about these serene and stately animals. Their lives are probably more complicated, and their intelligence greater, than we know.

What happens in a silo?

Modern farm buildings are often less attractive, though more efficient, than old ones. In this steel silo (below), grain for feeding animals is stored and dried by currents of warm air.

What colour is a chameleon?

A chameleon (below) is a kind of lizard which lives in hot countries, particularly Madagascar, Africa and Asia. Famous for its use of camouflage, it can change its own colour to match its background. Thus, almost invisible, it waits, very still, for insects, which it catches with its long, sticky tongue. It flicks out its tongue very rapidly, in $\frac{1}{25}$ of a second.

Who lives in the Arctic?

This Inuit (or Eskimo) woman carrying her baby on her back is well wrapped up against the cold of the Arctic. The Inuit, who share the same distant ancestors as American Indians, live in Alaska, northern Canada and Greenland. In lands where farming is impossible, the Inuit depend on hunting for a living, although some now live in modern towns. They rely on sea mammals, particularly seals, for food, tools, clothes and oil, and also catch reindeer and fish.

Quick Quiz

Where would you find all these?
The archer, the crab, the twins, the lion.

Answer: In the night sky – they are names of
constellations (groups of stars).

Who are these planets named after?
Mars, Venus, Jupiter, Pluto, Mercury.

Answer: They are the names of ancient
Roman gods. Mars was god of war, Venus
goddess of love, Jupiter the father of the gods,
Pluto the god of hell, Mercury the messenger
god.

Can you hear the stars?

The planets, the Sun and many other stars give off radio signals. A radio telescope is designed to collect these radio waves (which are invisible) from beyond the Earth. A normal telescope 'collects' light waves. Because radio waves are much longer than light waves, radio telescopes have to be much larger than optical telescopes to see the sky in as much detail. Below is the big radio telescope at Jodrell Bank, England, whose dish is 76 m (250 ft) in diameter. Many important discoveries have been made by radio telescopes. Some years ago astronomers were puzzled by faint interference for which no source could be discovered. One theory is that this far, far distant chatter is the echo of a big bang when the universe was created.

Can you see the man in the Moon?

There is no man in the Moon of course (though one or two astronauts have been there), and if there were one, you would need a really powerful telescope to see him! The huge telescopes used by astronomers cost millions of pounds, and even small ones like that below are expensive. Binoculars are usually better than a very cheap telescope.

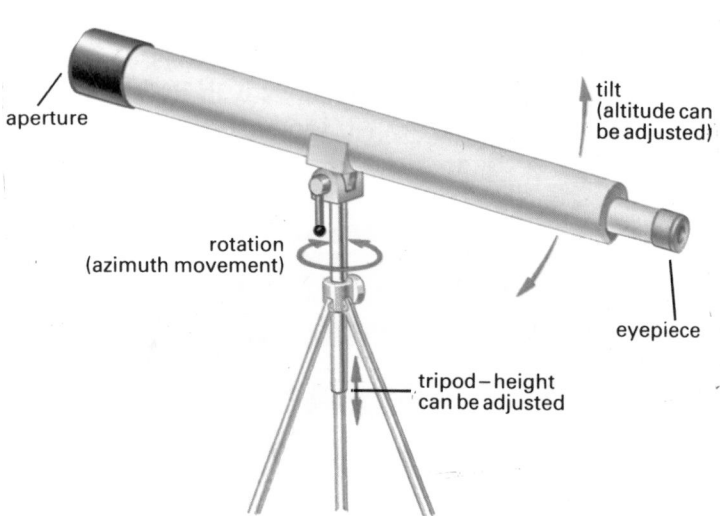

aperture

rotation
(azimuth movement)

tilt
(altitude can
be adjusted)

eyepiece

tripod – height
can be adjusted

Who was inspired by an apple?

According to an old story, Isaac Newton (1642–1727), an English scientist (left), was sitting in an orchard when an apple fell on his head, and that started him thinking about gravity. He showed that gravity works in a similar way to a magnet pulling or 'attracting' pieces of iron to it. The Earth's gravitational field pulls everything heavier than air down towards the Earth's surface. It also keeps our Moon from drifting off into space.

Who travelled inside a horse?

According to Homer's *Iliad*, the first story in ancient literature, the city of Troy fell when the Greeks got into it hidden inside a huge wooden horse (below).

Butter, cheese or milk?

Cows are very valuable animals to human beings. They give us milk, from which we make butter and cheese. The commonest dairy (milk-giving) cows are Friesians, like the ones above. Europeans drink an average of nearly 3 l (5 pt) of milk per week each.

Why does this road have a hole in it?

Many animals will not walk across a grating because they see space below their feet. Below is a cattle grid – bars laid over a hole – which prevents farm animals straying.

What is basalt?

The Earth's crust is made up of many different kinds of rocks. Some were formed when magma (very hot, liquid rock in the crust) cooled and became solid. These are called igneous rocks. One of the commonest is granite, and another is basalt. As a rule, basalt is the main type of rock in lava flows, which means it was produced by some type of volcanic eruption. If it solidified quickly it has a glassy appearance. Sometimes it forms as giant, six-sided columns – a spectacular sight. The basalt columns above are in the Auvergne, southern France.

B June — the North Pole is tilted towards the Sun and it is summer in the Northern Hemisphere, winter in the Southern Hemisphere

A March — it is spring in the Northern Hemisphere and autumn in the Southern Hemisphere

B   N

A

S

D   N

N

C

S

S

The Seasons

C September — it is autumn in the Northern Hemisphere and Spring in the Southern Hemisphere

D December — the South Pole is tilted towards the Sun and it is summer in the Southern Hemisphere and winter in the Northern Hemisphere

Why is the summer hot?

The Earth takes one year to circle around the Sun. But the Earth is tilted, so that at different times of year some parts receive more sunlight than others (above). These changes give us the seasons. On the equator, the Earth's tilt makes little difference, and there is no great change in the seasons.

Who said the Earth moves?

We cannot feel the Earth moving, but we do see the Sun move in the sky every day. Naturally, people used to think the Earth was still and the Sun travelled around it. The man who showed that the Earth actually moves around the Sun was Nicolaus Copernicus (right), a Polish astronomer, in his book *On the Revolutions of Heavenly Bodies* (1543).

Who won the Battle of Britain?

In 1940 the Nazi government of Adolf Hitler in Germany had defeated all its enemies except Britain. The conquest of Britain was planned, but before it could invade, Germany had to gain control of the air. No German soldiers could be landed on the coast of England until the Royal Air Force had been defeated.

The Battle of Britain, which lasted from July to September 1940, was entirely an air battle. The RAF's Fighter Command had 55 squadrons of Spitfires (far right) and Hurricanes. The Luftwaffe (German air force) had a slightly larger number of fighters like this Messerschmitt 109 (right), besides thousands of bombers which, Hitler hoped, would bomb the British into surrender. The Spitfire was probably the most successful fighter of the war. Though no faster than a Messerschmitt, it could turn and climb more sharply. The RAF was very short of experienced pilots, but it had other advantages. The chief of them was radar. Because the enemy planes could be tracked by radar, the British pilots could take off when they approached, instead of flying constant patrols to look for them.

The Germans tried to destroy the British fighter bases in south-east England, and nearly

42

Douglas Bader was a great ace of the Battle of Britain.

Adolf Galland, the Luftwaffe's Inspector-General of Fighters.

How fast is this car going?

It looks as if it is standing still, but it is travelling at about 130 km/h (80 mph). A high shutter speed is needed to 'stop' fast-moving subjects, but high-speed film must be used to achieve a good result.

The amount of light entering the camera can be controlled by the aperture and shutter speed. The aperture, which is the hole in the front of the camera, can be increased or decreased in size to vary the amount of light reaching the film. The shutter can also be varied to control the length of time which the film is exposed to the light.

The speed of the film affects how *much* light needs to enter the camera. Film speed is usually expressed in the form of ASA (American Standards Association) numbers. The higher the ASA speed rating, the faster the film – that is, the faster it reacts to light, and therefore the less light it needs to produce a good result.

succeeded. Some historians believe that if they had continued this plan, they would have won the battle. But on 7 September they changed their target to London. Many Londoners were killed, and life in the capital became difficult, but the fighter bases remained in action.

The Germans were losing aircraft in large numbers. On one day, 15 September, they lost about 60 while the British lost only 26. That proved to be the last great German attack. Two days later, Hitler told his generals that the invasion of Britain would be delayed. It never took place.

Quick Quiz

What do these have in common?
Mosquito, Hurricane, Mustang, Stuka, Zero.

Answer: They are names of aircraft in the Second World War.

What do these have in common?
Sierra, Metro, Thunderbird, Imp, Maxi.

Answer: They are names of motor cars.

Do continents move?

Most geologists (scientists who study how the Earth was made) agree that hundreds of millions of years ago, the continents were joined together (below left). Many geological clues support this idea. For example, on the east coast of South America there is a belt of ancient rocks which matches the rocks on the west coast of Africa, on the opposite side of the Atlantic.

To add to the geological evidence, biologists have found that the same species of some animals live on different continents, separated by thousands of miles of ocean. How could this happen unless the two continents were once much closer?

The maps below show the way the continents have drifted apart. They are still doing so. Every year, New York moves about 2 cm ($\frac{3}{4}$ in) farther from London!

Why do continents move?

The drift of the continents is probably caused by the division of the Earth's crust into a number of gigantic 'plates'. These plates move very, very slowly but with tremendous power. The edges of the plates, called margins, appear as lines of weakness in the Earth's crust and cause upsets on the surface. For example, the ring of volcanoes around the Pacific Ocean marks the margins of one plate, which is pushing up against its neighbours. The Himalayan Mountains were probably formed when the plate under India crashed against the plate to the north of it. (This movement is probably not yet finished, in which case, the Himalayas are growing higher!) The three main types of crustal plate margin and the features produced by them on the Earth's surface are shown at the bottom of the page.

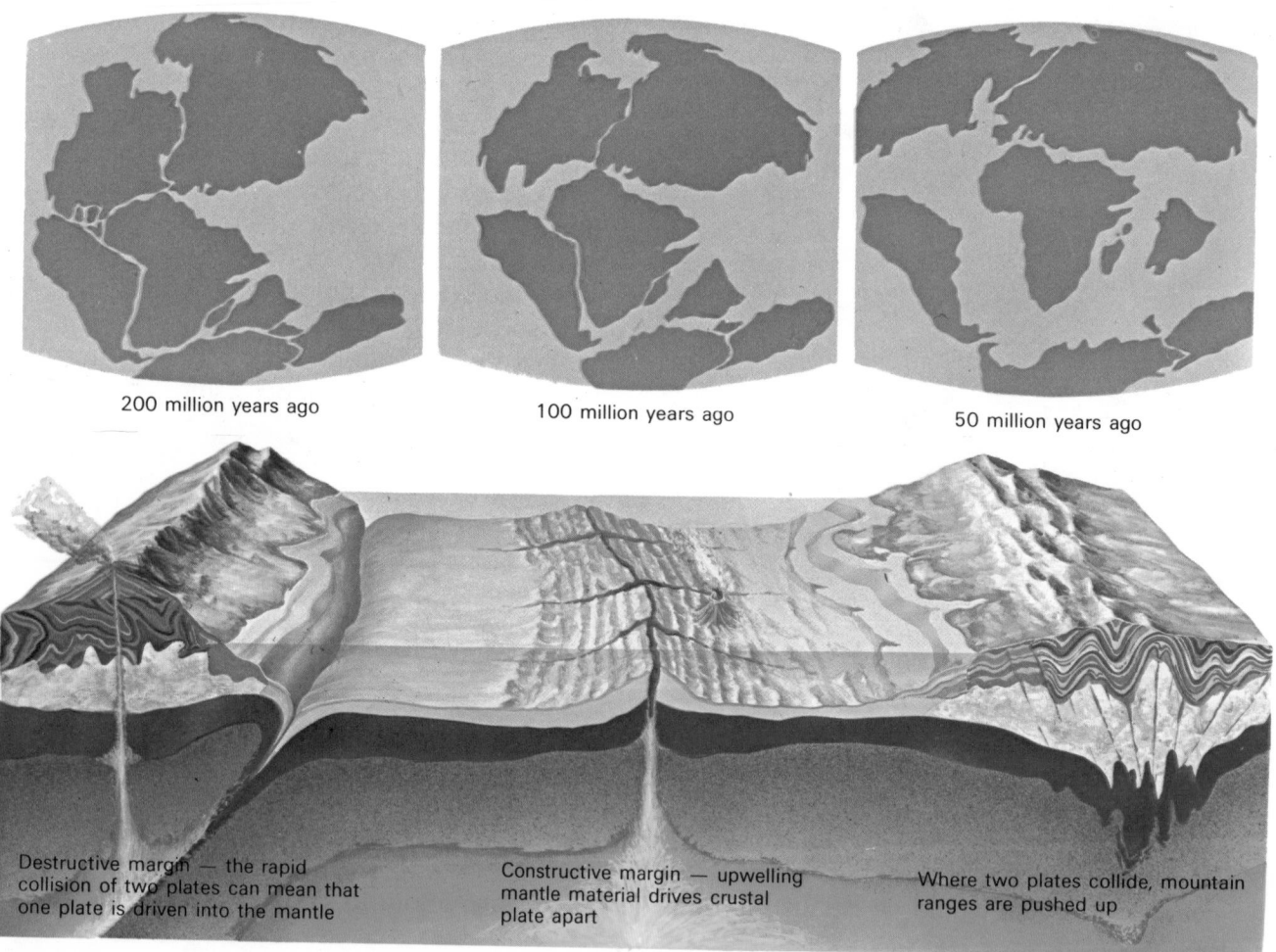

200 million years ago

100 million years ago

50 million years ago

Destructive margin — the rapid collision of two plates can mean that one plate is driven into the mantle

Constructive margin — upwelling mantle material drives crustal plate apart

Where two plates collide, mountain ranges are pushed up

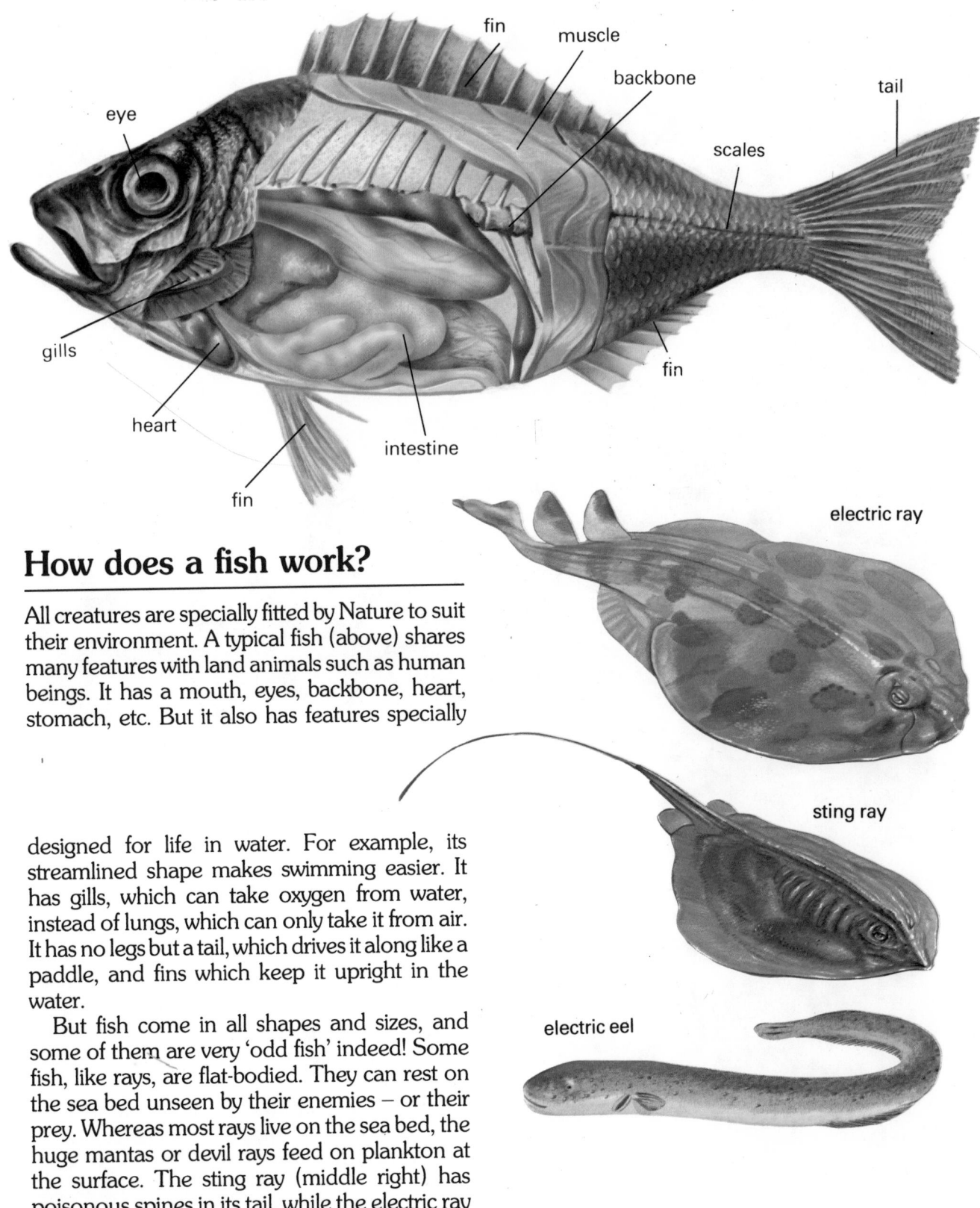

eye

fin

muscle

backbone

tail

scales

gills

heart

fin

intestine

fin

electric ray

sting ray

electric eel

How does a fish work?

All creatures are specially fitted by Nature to suit their environment. A typical fish (above) shares many features with land animals such as human beings. It has a mouth, eyes, backbone, heart, stomach, etc. But it also has features specially designed for life in water. For example, its streamlined shape makes swimming easier. It has gills, which can take oxygen from water, instead of lungs, which can only take it from air. It has no legs but a tail, which drives it along like a paddle, and fins which keep it upright in the water.

But fish come in all shapes and sizes, and some of them are very 'odd fish' indeed! Some fish, like rays, are flat-bodied. They can rest on the sea bed unseen by their enemies – or their prey. Whereas most rays live on the sea bed, the huge mantas or devil rays feed on plankton at the surface. The sting ray (middle right) has poisonous spines in its tail, while the electric ray (above right) and the electric eel (below right) can stun their prey with an electric shock.

Who painted the Mona Lisa?

The *Mona Lisa*, now in the Louvre museum in Paris, is probably the most famous painting in the world. It is a portrait, painted about 1500–1504, of a lady of Florence who wears a mysterious smile.

The painter was the great Italian genius, Leonardo da Vinci (above). Leonardo was a man full of curiosity and ideas. Besides painting pictures he made drawings of his ideas for machines, including things that look like a tank and a helicopter, which were not to appear for another 400 years.

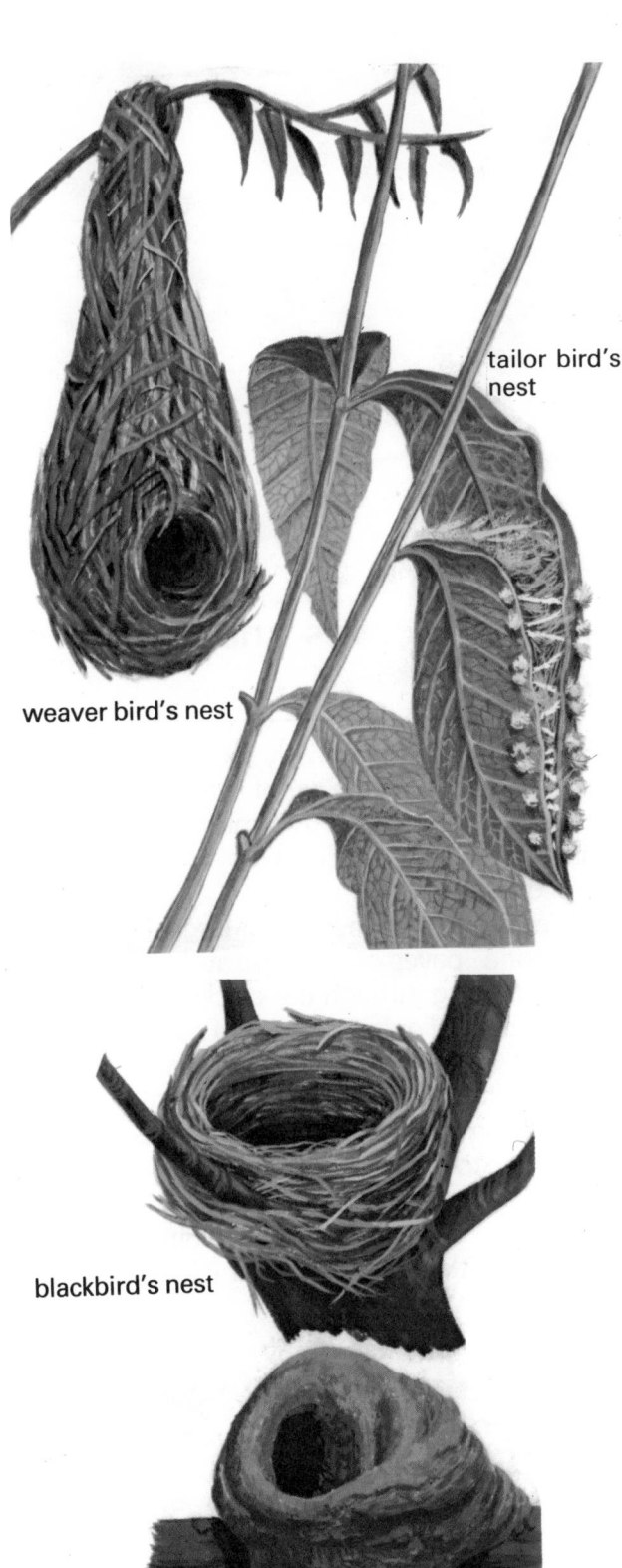

tailor bird's nest

weaver bird's nest

blackbird's nest

ovenbird's nest

Why do birds build nests?

Birds, like human beings, spend much time and energy looking after their young. Most birds build a nest where their eggs and then their babies will be protected, but as those on the left show, there are many different ways of doing it.

How can the Sun reduce fuel bills?

The solar (Sun) panels in the roof of this house (above) collect and store the energy in the Sun's rays. This can be used to heat all the household's hot water. In very sunny countries, it may even be enough to provide central heating too.

Quick Quiz

Who were the following Renaissance figures? (1) Michelangelo, (2) Martin Luther, (3) William Shakespeare, (4) the Medici family.

Answers: (1) Italian painter and sculptor, (2) German monk who founded the first Protestant church, (3) English dramatist, (4) rulers of Florence who gained enormous wealth and power in Italy and France.

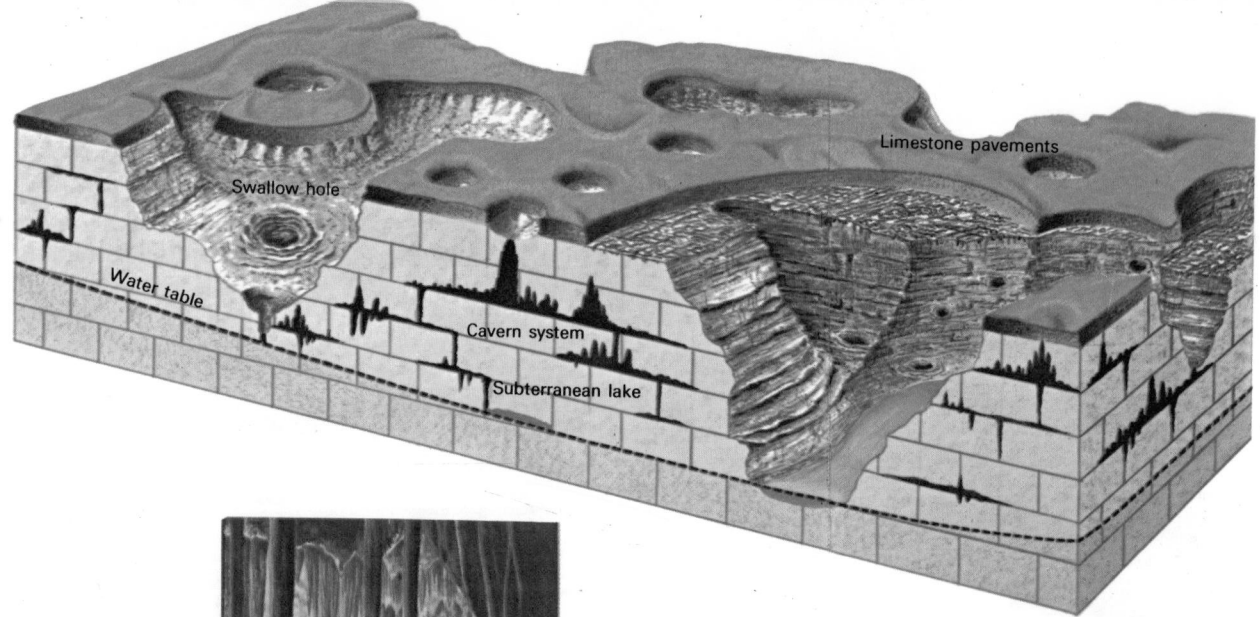

Swallow hole
Limestone pavements
Water table
Cavern system
Subterranean lake

How are caves and potholes formed?

Limestone is a sedimentary rock which consists largely of the remains of hard-shelled sea creatures, compressed over millions of years. Its main ingredient is calcium, which can be dissolved by water.

Limestone is often found as large slabs, called limestone pavements, separated by cracks. Water flowing through the cracks dissolves the limestone and enlarges them to make potholes (above). If the pothole has water flowing through it, it is called a swallow hole. Underground streams may gradually dissolve the limestone to make caverns and lakes. Stalactites (pointing down) and stalagmites (pointing up) are formed by dripping water containing calcium which is left as a solid deposit (illustrated left).

Who said, 'All the world's a stage'?

Everyone agrees that William Shakespeare (1564–1616), pictured on the left, was England's greatest playwright and poet. In Shakespeare's plays the stage does become the world, for he had what seems an unlimited understanding of all kinds of people. (The quotation comes from *As You Like It*.)

48

Did the dinosaurs eat each other?

Long ago, when the Earth was much younger, it was ruled by an extraordinary race of reptiles which we call dinosaurs. They included huge, placid plant-eaters like the 80-tonne Brachiosaurus; fearsome hunters like Tyrannosaurus with teeth 15 cm (6 in) long; and weirdly horned and armoured creatures like Triceratops. There were even flying dinosaurs.

Skeletons of one type of dinosaur, *Coelophysis* (above), were found in New Mexico, USA. Inside two of the skeletons were bones of its babies. As dinosaurs laid eggs, this discovery suggests that *Coelophysis* was a cannibal.

What wears jesses and a hood?

Hunting with a trained hawk or falcon is an ancient sport, well over 3000 years old and still practised by a few people. The hood, like blinkers on a horse, prevents the gyrfalcon on the right being distracted. The jesses are leather straps attached to its leg.

How does a space rocket work?

All rockets work in the same way, whether they are fireworks whizzing a few metres above the trees or mighty space launchers like the Saturn Moon rocket, 111 m (364 ft) long, on the opposite page. The force that makes the rocket go is called thrust. The escape, at high speed, of hot gases from the rocket's exhaust creates a pressure, or thrust, in the opposite direction, that is, forwards. A common mistake about rockets (and jet engines) is to believe that the vehicle is driven forwards by the hot gases pushing against the air. (If that were so, rockets could not move in space, where there is no air to push against.)

Space rockets are only carriers. The actual spacecraft or satellite is carried by the rocket until it reaches a point where it can go into orbit around the Earth or, in the case of the Saturn rocket, reach the Moon. The rocket is much larger than the space vehicle because it needs gigantic engines and enormous amounts of fuel (the Saturn rocket carried 3000 tonnes of fuel). Most of this power is required in the early stages of the flight to escape the pull of the Earth's gravity. It would be very wasteful to carry empty fuel tanks and unwanted engines into space, so space rockets are made in sections, or stages, which can be cast off when they have done their work (see below). The Saturn rocket is a three-stage rocket – really, three rockets stacked on top of each other, with the spacecraft at the tip. (The rocket which carries the American space shuttle has extra stages attached to the *sides* of the main rocket.)

In the Saturn rocket, the third stage

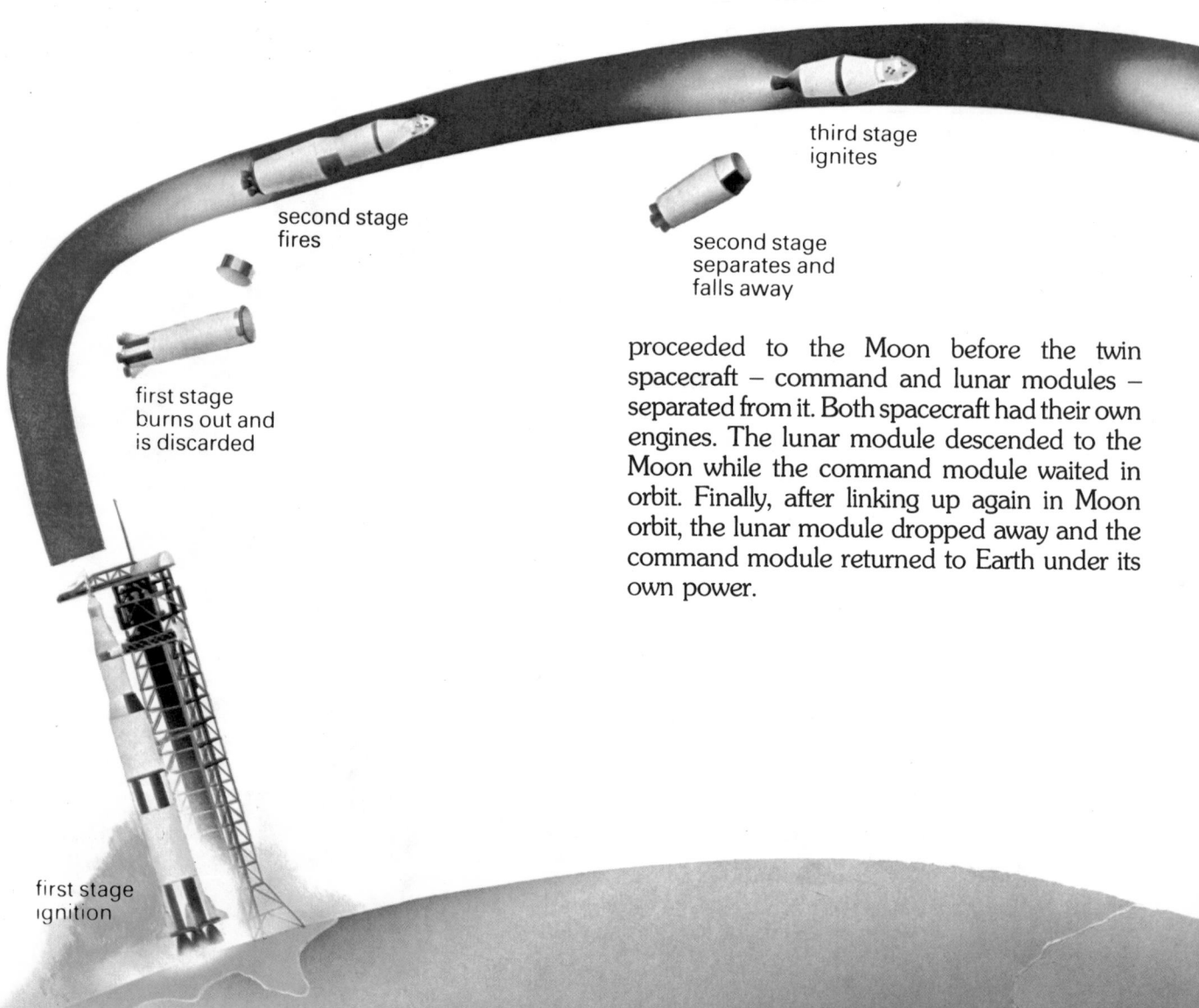

second stage
fires

first stage
burns out and
is discarded

third stage
ignites

second stage
separates and
falls away

first stage
ignition

proceeded to the Moon before the twin spacecraft – command and lunar modules – separated from it. Both spacecraft had their own engines. The lunar module descended to the Moon while the command module waited in orbit. Finally, after linking up again in Moon orbit, the lunar module dropped away and the command module returned to Earth under its own power.

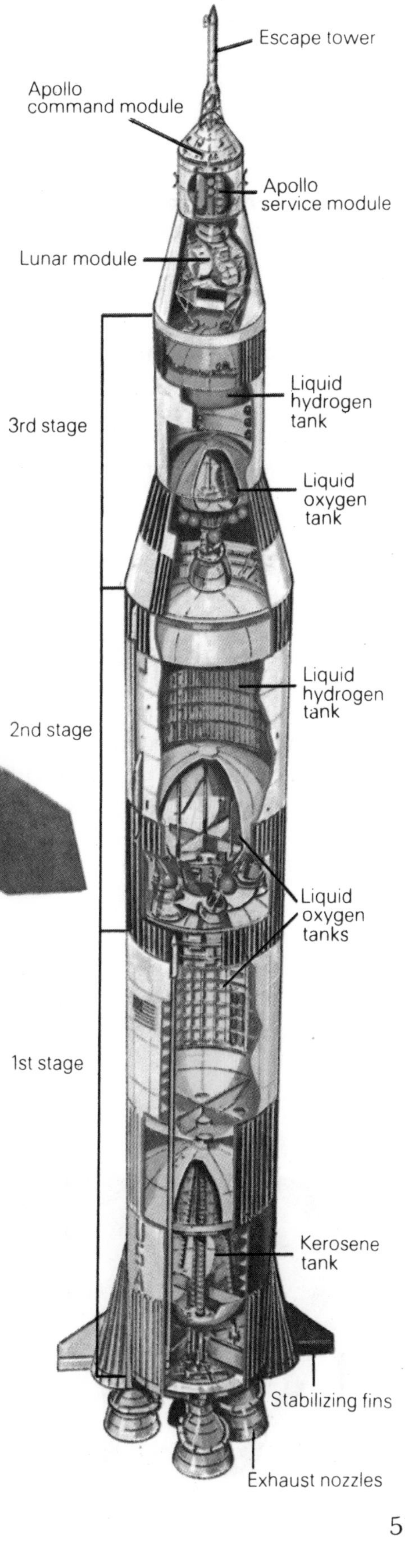

Escape tower

Apollo
command module

Apollo
service module

Lunar module

3rd stage

Liquid
hydrogen
tank

Liquid
oxygen
tank

2nd stage

Liquid
hydrogen
tank

Liquid
oxygen
tanks

1st stage

Kerosene
tank

Stabilizing fins

Exhaust nozzles

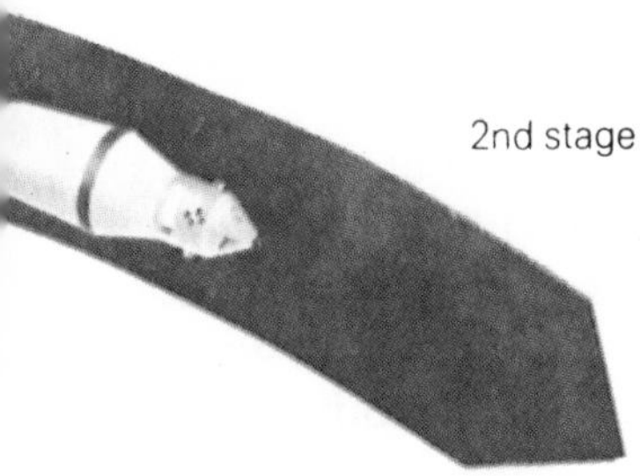

Are there ships in the desert?

Its ability to travel steadily across sandy wastes earned the camel the nickname 'ship of the desert' (see page 27).

What is a lens?

A lens is a piece of glass or other transparent material with a curved surface which can 'bend' light. This magnifying glass (above) is a lens which 'spreads out' the rays of light so that, when it is correctly focussed, objects seem larger. A lens can also concentrate light rays. If you focus the Sun's rays into a small spot of light on a piece of paper, the heat is so intense that the paper may burn. (Be very careful if you do this.)

Where is Lapland?

The Lapps live in a very cold region, almost entirely within the Arctic Circle, which stretches into four countries: northern Norway, Sweden, Finland, and the Soviet Union. They are quite different from their Scandinavian neighbours, and no one knows for certain where their ancestors came from. Their language however is related to Finnish and other Eastern European languages.

The land is mountainous in Norway and Sweden and there are extensive forests. In the north-east much of it is tundra, where the soil is frozen below the surface and few plants grow, except mosses and lichens. Farming is only possible in certain valleys and in the past, the Lapps of the mountainous regions were a nomadic people who followed the reindeer herds. Reindeer gave them food, in the form of meat and milk, transport (everyone knows that reindeer will pull a sleigh), and their skins provided clothing and shelter. Like most nomadic people they lived in tents.

A few Lapps still live in that way, but most now live in houses. The old Lapp culture, even the Lapp language, are in danger of being lost forever. The points on the traditional hat worn by the man on the left, represent the four winds.

What is a caribou?

Caribou is the North American name for reindeer (right). One of the largest of the deer family, it ranges across the Arctic lands, living on moss, which it finds beneath the snow, in winter, and on grass and saplings in the summer. It has broad hoofs which help it to walk on soft snow. The Lapps keep them in herds for food and for carrying loads.

What did the first aeroplanes look like?

Early experimental aeroplanes were fragile-looking machines, a mass of thin struts and wires. The idea was to make them as light as possible, and they crumpled up all too easily at the slightest stress. This triplane, which had three sets of tailplanes as well as wings, did manage to get into the air in 1909 but crashed soon afterwards. In the same year, though, Blériot made the first long, successful flight – across the English Channel.

How can you do the work of four people?

With a pulley containing only one wheel (above left), it takes four people to lift a heavy load. But by using a system with four wheels (above right), one person can raise the load on his or her own. This is because a four-wheel pulley increases the force applied by four times. Pulleys and gears, which work in a similar way, are simple machines. The amount by which they multiply forces depends on the number and size of the pulley and gear wheels.

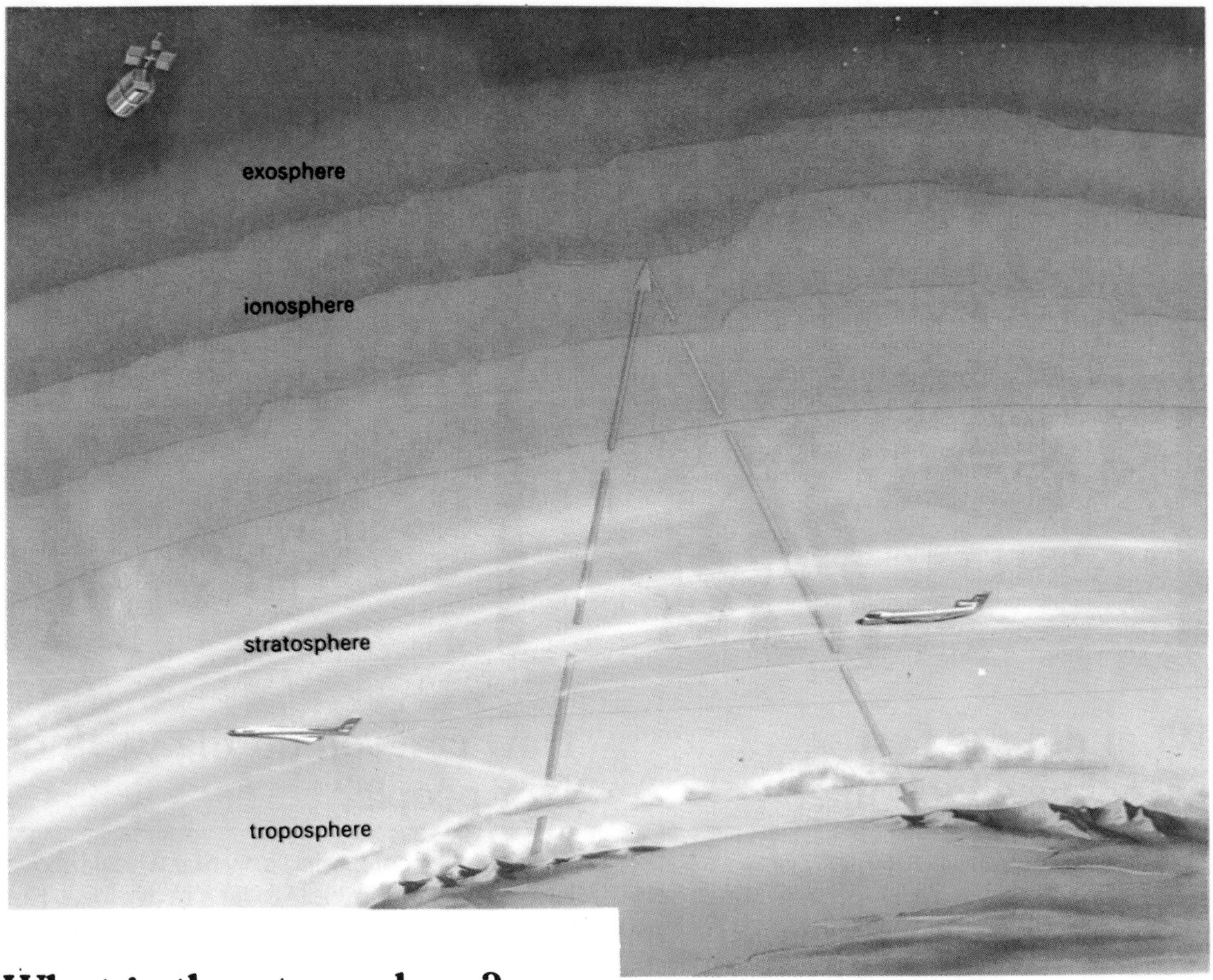

exosphere

ionosphere

stratosphere

troposphere

What is the atmosphere?

The atmosphere is the belt of air around the Earth. Without it, the Earth would be like the Moon – a large, dead globe of rock.

The atmosphere reaches hundreds of miles above the Earth, but the air gradually gets thinner. Scientists have divided the atmosphere into four layers (above). We live in the troposphere, which contains most of the weather and clouds. Above, in the stratosphere, the air is too thin to breathe, and it is calmer, so airliners fly at this level. The next layer is the ionosphere which extends to about 500 km (300 miles) above the ground. It helps long-distance radio communications by bouncing radio waves from one part of the Earth to another. The final layer is the exosphere, where spacecraft can go into orbit and the atmosphere gradually dwindles into outer space.

When did a tortoise go to war?

The formation above, called a 'tortoise', was adopted by soldiers of ancient Rome when they were attacking a fort. The barrier of shields warded off missiles.

Who were the Shang?

The civilization of China is the oldest in the world. It goes back at least as far as the Shang, or Yin, dynasty (ruling family), which probably began in the 18th century BC and lasted about 700 years. As the picture of a Shang warrior on the left shows, the Chinese at that distant time were skilful workers in bronze, and could also make silk. Moreover, the design of the armour and clothes was already similar to that which today we recognize as Chinese. In the Shang period the Chinese language already existed in a written form. According to tradition, the *I-Ching* or 'Book of Changes', the earliest work in Chinese literature, was compiled at the end of the Shang period.

Does a cactus flower?

Nearly all cacti have spines or prickles. In Latin America people grow hedges of cacti – they are better than barbed-wire fences! Another unusual feature of cacti is that most have no leaves. Their woody skeletons are covered with thick, juicy flesh, which holds a lot of water. Cacti can grow in deserts because of this internal water supply.

Many small cacti can be easily grown indoors, in pots. They do need water, though their roots must not be soaked. Cacti do flower, but many of them only produce flowers at long intervals. As you can see on the right, some cactus flowers are very beautiful.

Do all spiders spin webs?

The huge variety of spiders make up one of the most fascinating animal groups in all Nature. Although spiders look like insects, scientists insist they are not. The reason is that spiders have eight legs; to be an insect you must have only six. Scorpions, which also have eight legs, belong to the same biological group as spiders. This group, which also includes the mainly parasitic mites and ticks, is called the arachnids.

Everyone has seen a spider's web, a beautifully made net of silk threads. Garden spiders (usually the females) spin them from a fluid in their bodies which hardens in air, and insects that collide with the web are caught by sticky threads. The spider, hiding close by, feels the vibrations of the struggling insect and rushes out to seize its prey.

Not all spiders spin webs. Some live in burrows with carefully made lids or trapdoors. Others, such as the various wolf spiders, are simply hunters depending on sheer speed to catch their victims. There are spiders so large that they will attack birds, small reptiles, and rodents. Most spiders use poison to kill their prey when they have caught it, but only a few spiders have a bite dangerous to human beings. Spiders do not eat their prey, but suck out its juices.

Some spiders have very peculiar habits. The female black widow spider, after mating, proceeds to eat the much smaller male.

Scorpions are also hunters. They catch their prey in their powerful claws and stun it with the sting in their tail, which they carry curved over their backs. Some live in rain forests, while others prefer deserts.

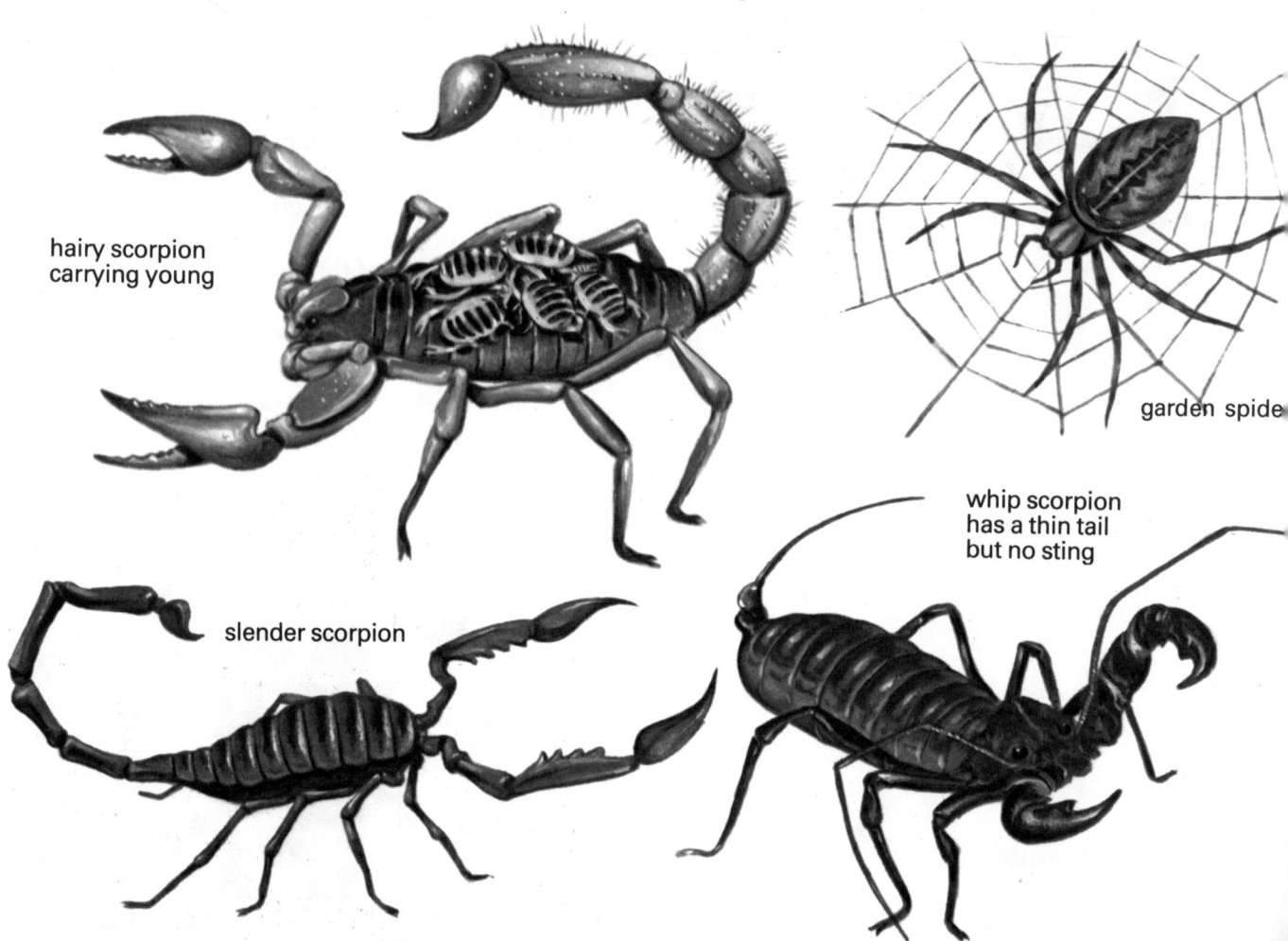

hairy scorpion carrying young

garden spider

slender scorpion

whip scorpion has a thin tail but no sting

Who killed the moa?

It is a sad fact that many animals have become – or will become – extinct because of humans. The moa (below) was a flightless bird in New Zealand. Larger than an ostrich, it was easy prey for Maori hunters. But European settlers were far more deadly, causing the destruction of 30 or 40 species of birds, including the huia (bottom).

Who made the first trans-Atlantic flight?

In the early days of flying, large prizes were offered by the London newspaper the *Daily Mail* for various flying feats. The £10 000 prize for crossing the Atlantic non-stop was won in 1919 by the English aviators Alcock and Brown, flying a converted bomber (above).

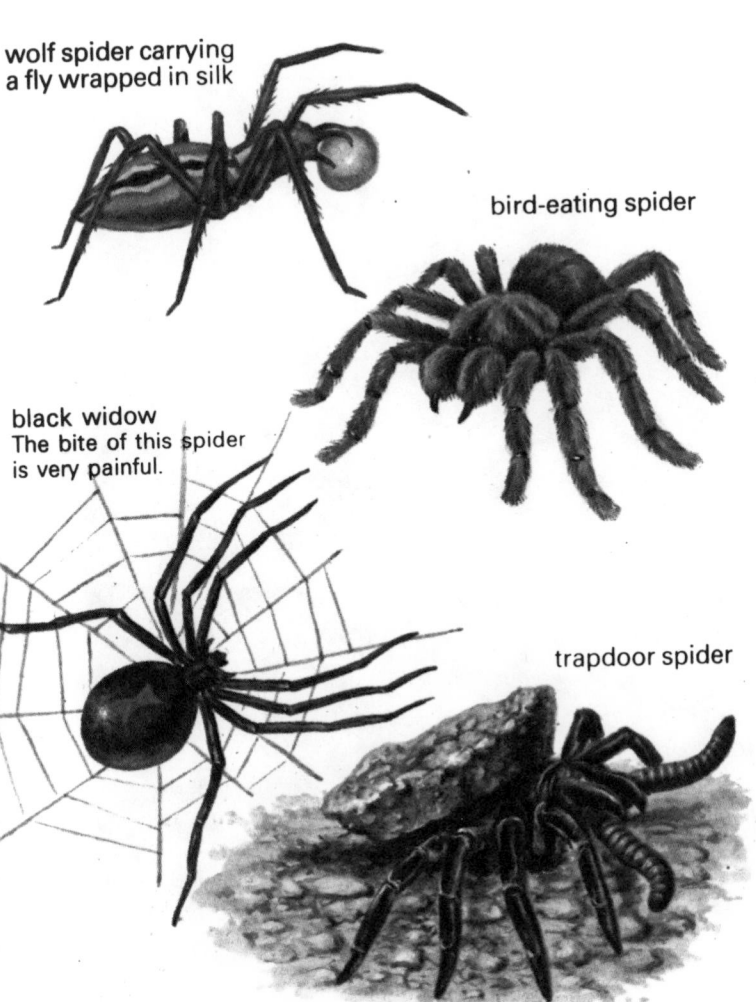

wolf spider carrying a fly wrapped in silk

bird-eating spider

black widow
The bite of this spider is very painful.

trapdoor spider

57

What is a volcano?

A volcano is a hole, or vent, in the Earth's crust from which molten lava (magma) – rock so hot that it is liquid – pours up from deep in the Earth. A volcano often forms a cone-shaped hill as the lava builds up around the central vent. Other volcanoes have several vents, and some have cracks, or fissures, from which lava pours in a sheet.

Volcanoes are either active, dormant or extinct. An active volcano may erupt at any moment. If it is dormant, which means 'sleeping', it is quiet at present but may become active in future. If it is extinct, it is 'dead'; it will not erupt again.

In earlier periods of the Earth's history volcanoes have been active almost everywhere. Today, they are mostly found in two regions. One belt runs around the Pacific Ocean, taking in the west coast of North and South America. This is known as the 'Ring of Fire'. Another belt runs roughly west to east, from the Caribbean across the Atlantic, through the Mediterranean region and on to Indonesia.

Earthquakes often happen in the same regions as volcanoes. The probable reason is that these are weak points in the Earth's crust, where the edges of the giant plates (see page 44) are moving against, or away from, each other.

Volcanoes erupt in different ways. Sometimes the pressure of hot gases builds up until the volcano literally explodes. When Krakatoa, a small volcanic island in Indonesia, erupted in this way in 1883, the noise was heard 5000 km (3000 miles) away. About two-thirds of the island was blown away or sank beneath the sea. Over 30 000 people were killed – many by tidal waves created by the explosion. The clouds of dust caused by the explosion were carried by the winds to all parts of the world.

There are about 500 active volcanoes in the world. A large eruption can often be detected in advance, and a watch is kept on most volcanoes likely to be dangerous to human life.

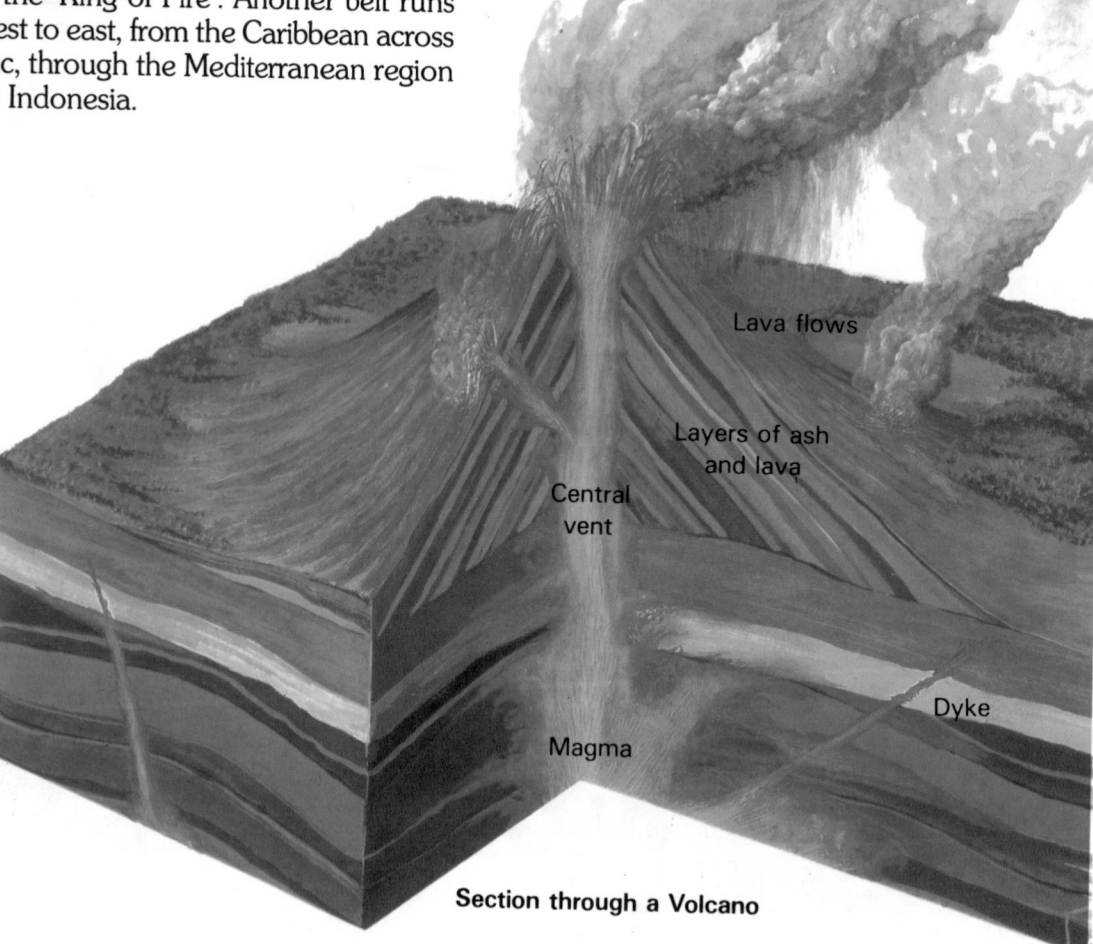

Lava flows

Layers of ash and lava

Central vent

Dyke

Magma

Section through a Volcano

Do ferns have flowers?

The class of plant known as ferns (right) has no flowers, fruit or seeds. They reproduce themselves through spores, which are tiny growths (so small you cannot see one except through a microscope) produced on the underside of the leaf. The wind may blow the spores a long way. If they settle somewhere damp, sheltered and shady, they grow into tiny plants. But these young plants, strange to say, look nothing like full-grown ferns. They are little, heart-shaped, green patches lying flat on the ground. From them new ferns will grow.

Although they do not flower, most ferns have very attractive leaves, which makes them popular as house plants. They usually like conditions indoors, not needing a lot of sunlight, and they are hardy – easy to grow.

Ferns were very common in an earlier period of the Earth's history, about 250 million years ago. The name of that period is Carboniferous ('coal-producing'), but it is sometimes called the 'Age of Ferns'. The plants that grew then helped to form the beds of what became, over millions of years, the coal we mine today.

Where would you find a hammer, anvil and stirrup?

You might find them in a blacksmith's shop, of course, but these are also the names of tiny bones in your ear (see right).

Most animals have ears, and the human ear is typical of most mammals. Ears are not only for hearing. They also help you keep your balance (fish use them solely for that purpose). The ear is divided into three parts – the outer ear (the part you can get hold of), the middle ear and the inner ear (the part that stops you falling over). The ear drum is made to vibrate by sound waves reaching it. The hammer, anvil and stirrup carry these vibrations from the ear drum to the cochlea, a snail-like tube filled with fluid and containing the organ of Corti, the actual organ of hearing. From the organ of hearing, sound waves are converted into nerve impulses and sent to the brain.

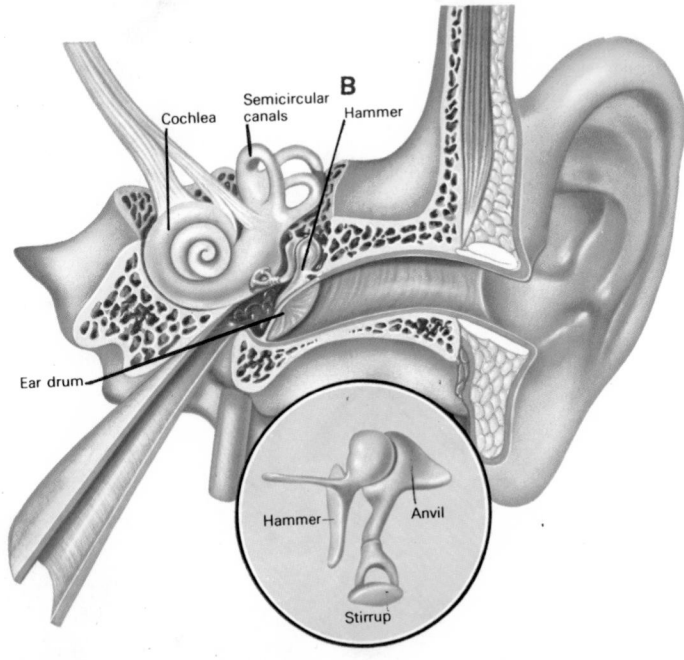

The mechanics of hearing are complicated. So far, biologists have not been able to explain exactly how the whole hearing system works.

Where are biomes?

This is a new word you may not find in your dictionary. Geographers use it to describe a region on Earth which contains its own typical kinds of plant and animal life (bio- means 'connected with life'). The different biomes or regions are caused by the climate and the type of soil.

The land surface of the Earth can be divided into nine main biomes (below). At the extreme north and south are regions of ice where there is little plant or animal life. In the tundra, mainly in the far north, the ground a few inches below the the surface is often frozen throughout the year. The mountain region, at its highest, may merge into ice. Three regions are wooded: coniferous forests (fir trees) occur in the coldest region; temperate forest, with many varieties of trees, is found in most of Europe; and tropical forest, or 'jungle', is found where it is always hot and damp. The regions of grassland, semi-desert and desert sometimes come between the temperate and tropical forest regions.

The water surface of the Earth can be divided into three main biomes: fresh water (lakes and rivers), salt water (seas and oceans), and the seashore, the narrow strip along the coasts where so many plants and animals have their own special way of life.

Unfortunately, the balance of the natural communities of the biomes is being upset by modern agriculture, pollution from cities and the destruction of forests.

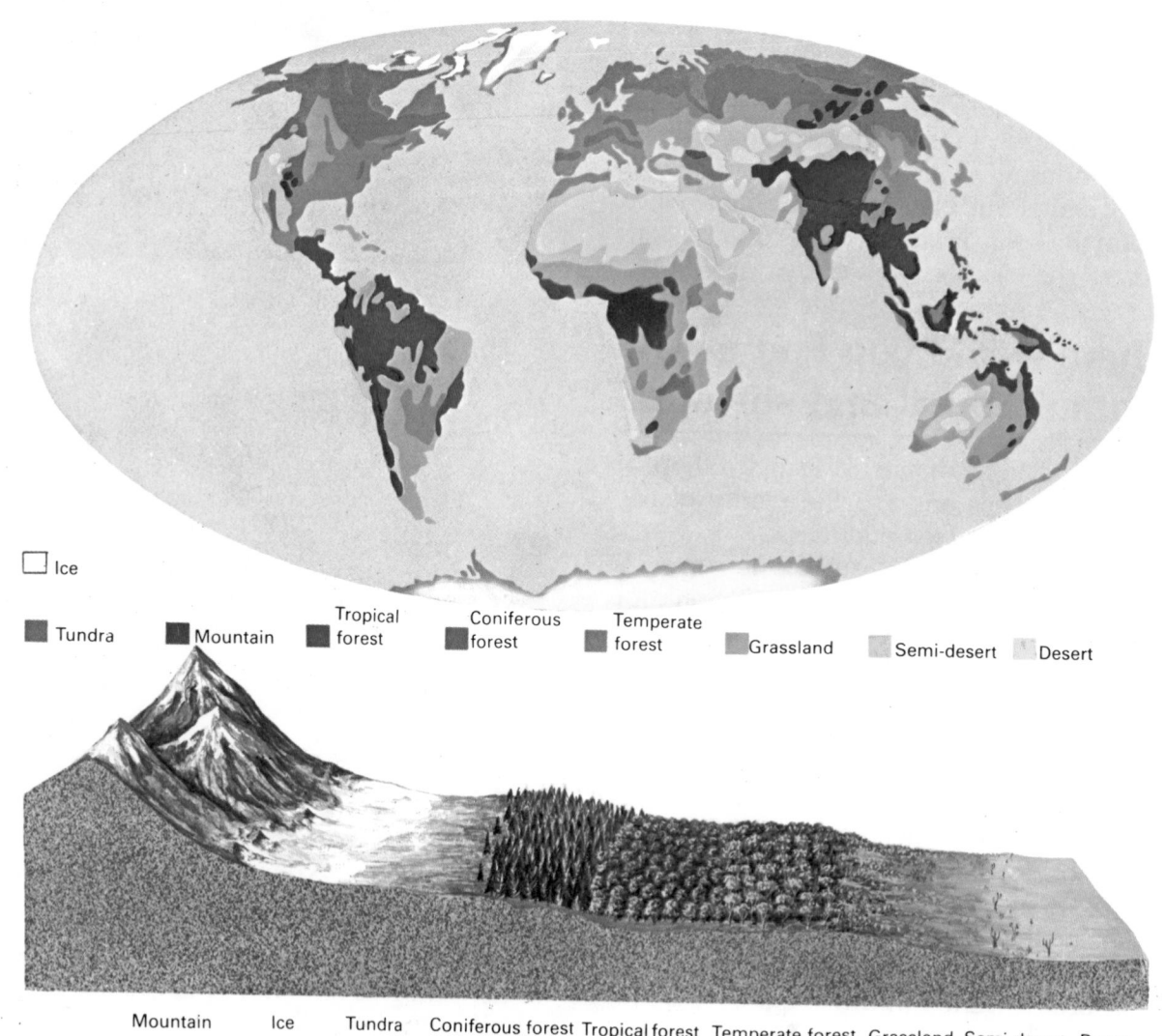

☐ Ice

🟦 Tundra   🟦 Mountain   🟦 Tropical forest   🟦 Coniferous forest   🟦 Temperate forest   🟩 Grassland   ⬜ Semi-desert   ⬜ Desert

Mountain   Ice   Tundra   Coniferous forest   Tropical forest   Temperate forest   Grassland   Semi-desert   Desert

native green

domestic blue

Who was the first Communist?

The German-born philosopher, Karl Marx (1818–83), is regarded by communist countries as the founder of their political system. Marx (below right) saw that the industrial revolution of the 19th century had produced much wealth, but that the working class, who produced the goods that made the wealth, were no better off than before.

He saw life as a struggle between capitalists (those who owned the machines and factories) and proletariat (the workers). He forecast that the outcome of this struggle would be a world-wide revolution which would bring the workers to power. The workers would then control the factories and farms (Marx called these 'the means of production') and use them for the benefit of everyone.

Marx's thinking inspired the Communist revolution in Russia in 1917, and subsequently many other similar revolutions in the 20th century. His writings continue to have great influence on the way people, both in communist and capitalist countries, think about how modern society is made up and operates, and what causes it to change.

What colour is a budgerigar?

'Budgies' are among the most popular pets. They are easy to keep, pretty to look at, and will become very tame. They can even be taught to speak.

Today, budgies come in all kinds of colours – blue, grey, violet, yellow and white. But these colours are the result of breeding experiments. The wild budgerigar, an Australian member of the parrot family, is always bright green (above).

Who was the first French emperor?

The ancient monarchy of France was overthrown by the revolution of 1789. But the revolution proved that, monarchy or not, France needed strong leadership. It was provided by Napoleon Bonaparte (below), the son of a lawyer in Corsica who became a brilliant general and, in 1804, Emperor of France. He represented many of the good ideas of the French revolutionaries and introduced reforms which made France one of the best governed countries in the world. He also gained control over much of Europe, making members of his family rulers of Spain, Naples and Holland. Defeated at Waterloo (1815), he went into exile.

Who was the Sun King?

Louis XIV (left) was king of France for 72 years (1643–1715). At that time France was the grandest, richest, and strongest state in Europe. And the French monarchy was its grandest institution. The royal palaces were the most magnificent, the royal court the most gorgeous ever seen. Louis took the Sun as his personal emblem. He was not just the king, he was 'France'.

Away from all this splendour, Louis's wars were helping to make France bankrupt. Yet revolution (see page 106) still lay a lifetime away.

Are nuts fruit?

Many trees produce nuts. Some, like the hazel or 'cob' nut, the chestnut and the walnut, are very good to eat; others, like the acorn and the beechnut, are edible but not so tasty. They are important, however, for many animals, such as squirrels, because they can be stored and eaten when food is scarce. Some nuts, like the Brazil nut, are simply seeds. Others, such as the almond, are stones in the fruit, like the stones in plums or cherries.

Hazel

Spanish chestnut

Common beech

Walnut

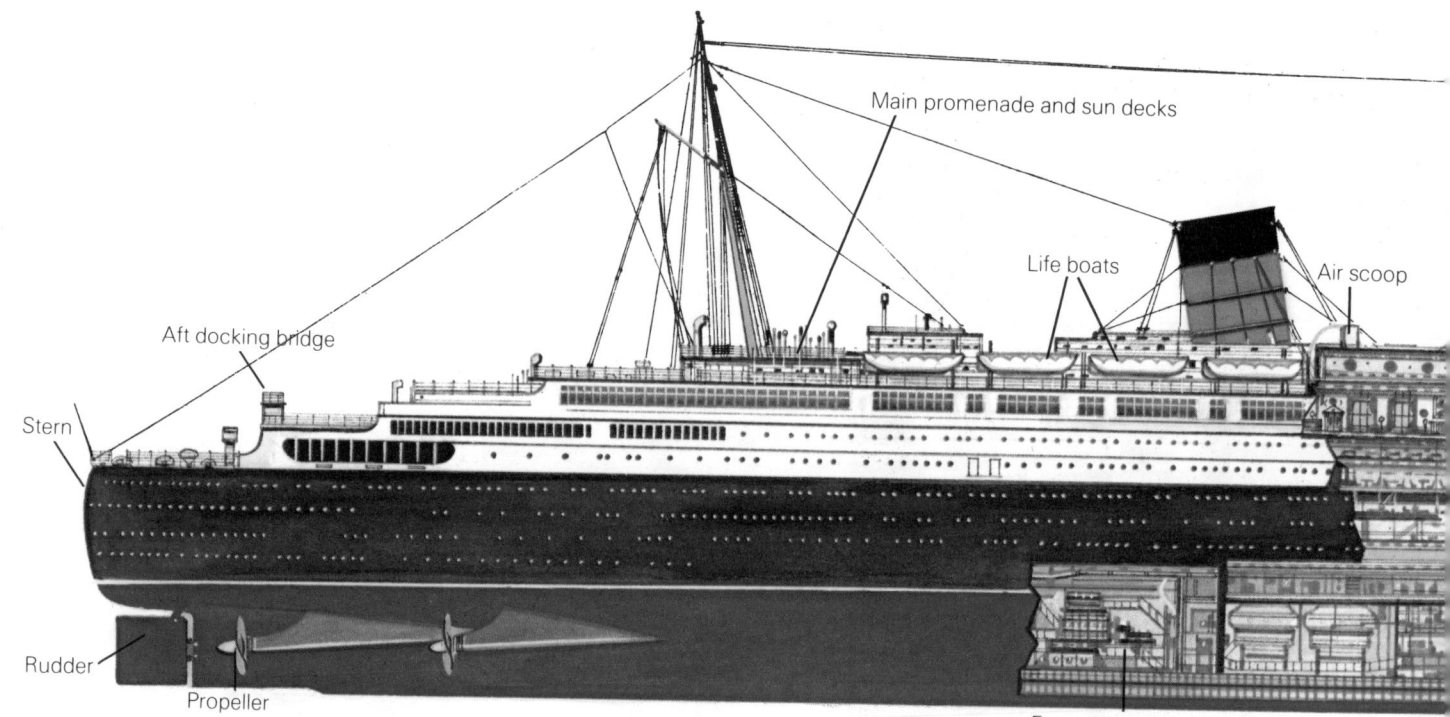

Main promenade and sun decks

Life boats

Air scoop

Aft docking bridge

Stern

Rudder

Propeller

Forward engine room containing 4 engines

Where could you find a floating swimming pool?

The greatest days of ocean liners were the 1930s. Today, airliners are much quicker and cheaper. Swimming pools were only one of the luxuries on a ship like the *Queen Mary* (above), launched in 1934. She was one of the last four great transatlantic liners, the others being Queen Elizabeth 1, United States and France.

What is inside your chest?

The diagram on the right shows the vital organs of the human body which are protected by the ribs. Most of the space inside the chest is taken up by the lungs. They recieve air from the trachea (windpipe) and feed oxygen to the bloodstream. The heart pumps the blood through the body, carrying oxygen and food to all parts. Below the lungs is the diaphragm, a sheet of muscle which divides the thorax, or chest, from the stomach. The diaphragm also controls breathing.

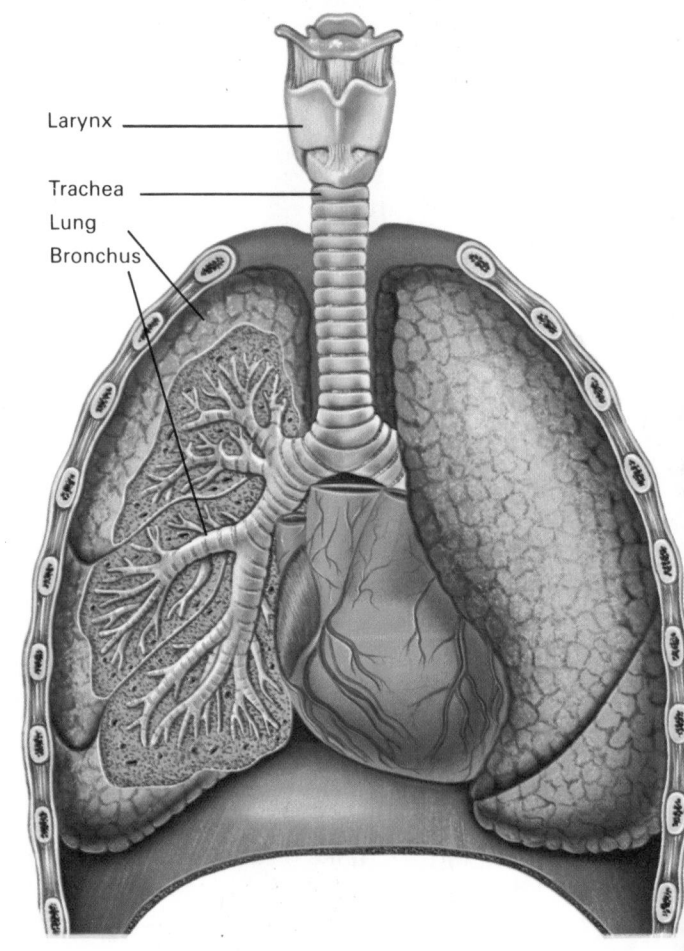

Larynx

Trachea

Lung

Bronchus

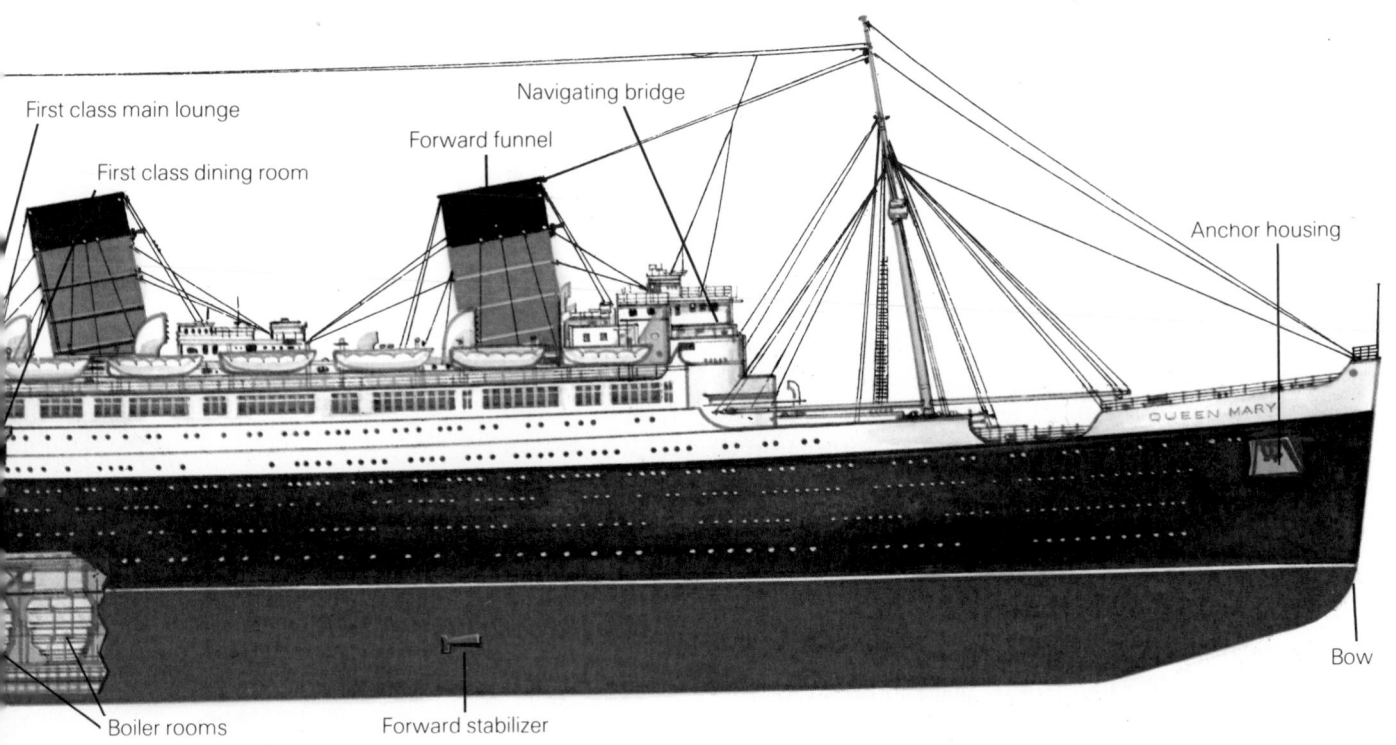

First class main lounge

First class dining room

Forward funnel

Navigating bridge

Anchor housing

QUEEN MARY

Bow

Boiler rooms

Forward stabilizer

Who invented submarines?

The first submarine was probably a leather-covered rowing boat built about 1620 by the Dutch engineer Cornelius van Diebbel. Not until the First World War (1914–18) did submarines become a powerful arm of the navy. The *Porpoise* (left) is a British patrol submarine launched in 1958. Some modern submarines are nuclear-powered, enabling them to remain submerged indefinitely. The engines do not need air and the air in the boat is constantly regenerated.

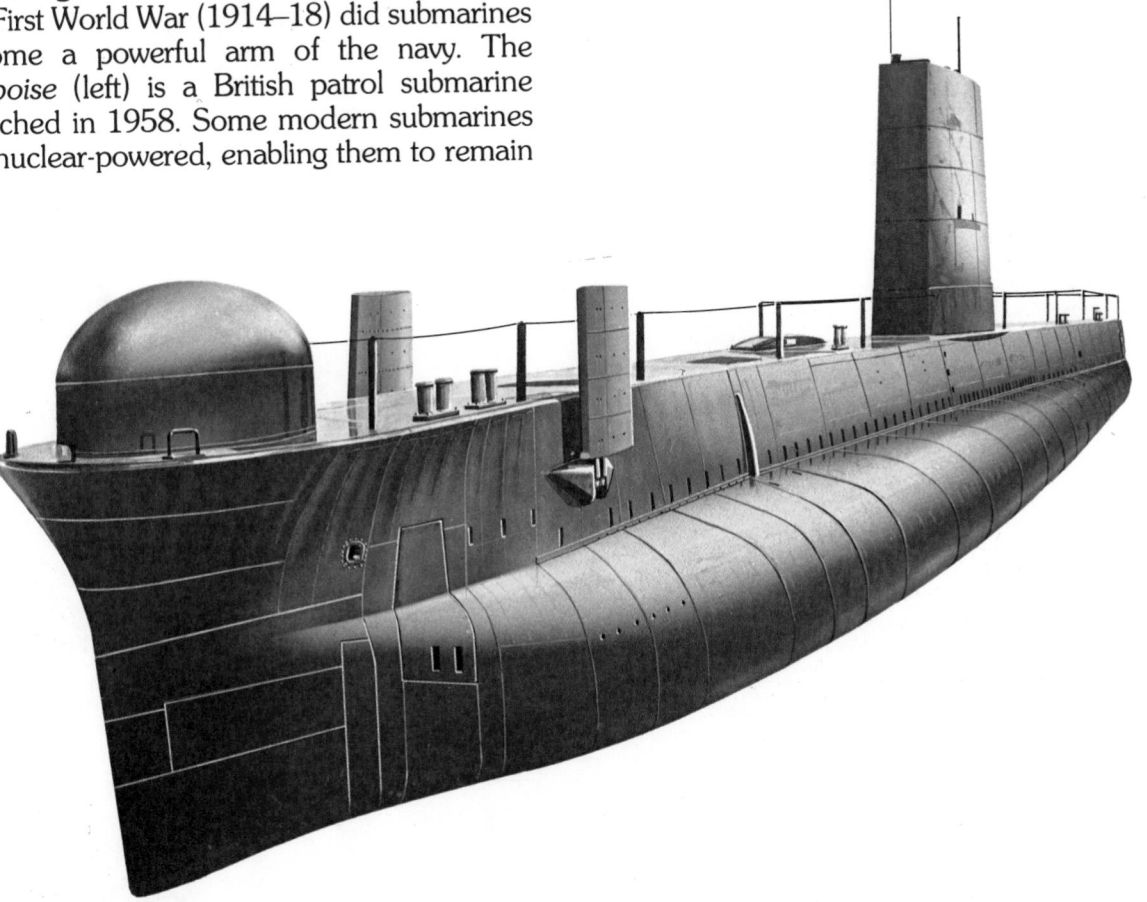

What lives in the sea?

When you stand on a cliff looking out to sea, you may not see many signs of life. You may see some birds, or a seal popping its head out of the water, but at a glance the sea might almost be empty.

Of course we know better! There are probably as many different kinds of animal in the sea as there are on land (no one has counted them!) and there are thousands of plants too. Even if we don't count the most typical of sea creatures – fish – we still have an enormous population of animals, ranging from the biggest animal in the world (the blue whale) to some of the smallest.

Not all sea creatures can be found in the same part of the oceans. Some live in cold regions, some like the water to be warm. Some live in the ocean depths, some live close to the shore. For example, although there are plants far out to sea, they are all tiny. The only large plants – seaweeds – grow in shallow water, usually near the shore.

You may – or may not – believe in the Loch Ness Monster, but there are almost certainly fish and perhaps other creatures living at great depths in the oceans which have not yet been discovered. In recent years we have learned

sea-lion

seals

dolphins

penguins

whale

porpoises

penguin

tropical fishes swimming through seaweed

shark

jellyfish

turtles

sea-anemones

more about life in those pitch-black depths, and some very strange animals have been found there. Whether there are really such creatures as giant squid, able to crush a ship, is less likely. But we cannot yet be certain that such monsters do not exist.

gannet

walrus

shag

puffins

turtle

plankton (greatly enlarged)

octopus

seahorse

crab

limpets

hermit crab

starfish

sea-urchins

mussels

brittle-star

Animals of the sea

Plankton

Sea water is full of tiny animals and plant organisms too small for the human eye to see. Named after a Greek word meaning 'drifting', plankton is carried around by ocean currents. It becomes very dense at certain places and is a vital food for many fish and whales. Plankton is the only food eaten by some whales, who gulp in millions of the tiny organisms with each mouthful.

Mammals

Seals are mammals, with fins instead of feet, which spend most of their lives in the water but come ashore to breed. Their skin is covered with coarse hair and under the skin they have a thick layer of fat which helps to keep them warm. The trained sealion you see in circuses is a type of seal from California.

Walruses look like large seals with tusks. The tusks are useful in fights, though normally walruses are not at all aggressive. They have no enemies except the polar bear and, of course, human beings, who have seriously reduced the size of the walrus herds.

Mammals lived in the sea before they learned to live on land, but millions of years ago whales went back to the sea from the land. There are nearly 100 species of whale divided into two main groups: toothed whales, like the killer whale which hunts seals, porpoises and even larger whales; and baleen (whalebone) whales, which have a kind of sieve in their mouths for catching the plankton on which they feed.

Porpoises and dolphins are actually small, toothed whales, and are well-known performers in zoos and 'dolphinariums'. They are highly intelligent and seem to like human beings. Wild dolphins have been known to give children rides on their backs.

shark

Fish

Sharks have a frightening reputation, but only about 12 species (out of over 200) are dangerous to human beings. Sharks are fish – the harmless whale shark, up to 15 m (60 ft) long, is the largest fish in the world – and developed to their present form many millions of years ago. Unlike most other fish, they have no bones, their skeleton being made up of cartilage. (Cartilage is strong but flexible – your nose and ears are supported by cartilage.)

In warm, coastal, tropical waters like those off Australia, live a large variety of small, brightly coloured and sometimes strangely shaped tropical fish. These attractive little creatures are often kept in aquariums.

The seahorse is an amazing creature, up to 30 cm (12 in) long, which looks like a tiny horse's head with a tail attached. Seahorses are fish, and one way in which they are unusual is that the male, not the female, looks after the eggs until they are hatched by carrying them in a special 'pocket'.

Turtles

Turtles are graceful creatures in the sea but look clumsy when they come on land, as they must do to lay their eggs. They are reptiles, and they have lived on the Earth far longer than human beings. Unfortunately, most species of turtle are rare today, mainly because their nests in the sand are so easily robbed of eggs, both by people and other animals.

squid

Octopuses, squid and shellfish

Octopuses and squid have eight 'arms' or tentacles, with suckers on them. Squids have two extra tentacles, longer and thinner, which dart out to seize their prey. The giant squid, the world's largest invertebrate (animal without a backbone), may grow to a length of 16 m (52 ft) including the tentacles. Squid can move through the water surprisingly fast, and the flying squid makes great leaps across the surface.

Mussels are shellfish which attach themselves

68

mussels

to rocks with little threads, and feed by sucking in sea water from which they filter out what is edible. They have two shells hinged together and are called bivalves. The mussels themselves are often eaten by human beings. They can be gathered by hand on many coasts.

The limpet is another shellfish and has given its name to anything which is attached very firmly to another object. Although they are so hard to pull off, limpets do move themselves. But they always return to exactly the same spot on the rock, anchoring themselves with their single, large foot.

Crabs

Crab shells are common on the beach. They do not mean that the crabs they belonged to have died. The shell cannot grow with the crab, and now and then the crab is forced to get rid of its entire outer shell, including the claws, and grow a new one. The hermit crab solves the problem by using shells cast off by other creatures.

Sea urchins and starfish

The round shells of sea urchins can often be found on the beach. When dried they make attractive decorations. The sea urchin's spines help in walking or burrowing – a sea urchin can bury itself in the sand with amazing speed – and in climbing steep, smooth surfaces.

Although they vary in shape and size (like the two on the previous page), starfish can usually be recognized by their five 'arms'. They have no head, and not a very large body, compared with the arms. They are carnivores (meat-eaters) which move on little tube-feet and hold their prey in their powerful arms.

Jellyfish and sea anemones

Jellyfish drift through the sea with the currents, trailing long, thin tentacles. One Atlantic jellyfish has tentacles up to 60 m (200 ft) long. Some jellyfish, which capture small fish with stinging tentacles, can give a very unpleasant sting to a human foot too.

There are some animals in the sea which look more like plants, and the sea anemone is a good example. They attach themselves to rocks and gently wave their colourful tentacles, which swiftly seize and sting any small fish that swim within reach. Small anemones are usually easy to find in rock pools.

Sea birds

Penguins live only in the southern hemisphere. Some, like the great Emperor penguin, which is over 1 m (3 ft) tall, breed in Antarctica. Although they are birds, penguins cannot fly: their wings are more like flippers. They do not walk very easily either, waddling comically along with frequent tumbles. The sea is their true home.

The 'home' of the puffin is a hole in a cliff, or perhaps an old rabbit burrow, but they are really birds of the open sea. In the breeding season, when the puffins return to their colonies, their bills become brilliantly coloured.

The shag is a diving bird, like its close relative, the cormorant (birdwatchers can seldom tell them apart). When it spots a fish, it dives sharply to seize it – or quite often, miss!

The gannet is another diver, which lives in large and noisy colonies on coastal cliffs and rocky islands. It has long pointed wings and looks quite distinctive in flight. It will dive for fish from a height of nearly 20 m (65 ft). An interesting feature of gannets is the air sacs under the skin which cushion the impact when they hit the water.

cormorant

Who invented tennis?

The indoor game of 'real' tennis was played in the Middle Ages. During the 19th century it overflowed on to the lawn, where players made up their own rules. In 1874 Major Walter Wingfield invented rules for lawn tennis. Even by 1890, however, 'real' tennis rackets were still being used, as below.

What reptiles run on two legs?

The frilled lizard of Australia (above) has a collar like the ruff of an Elizabethan gentleman. It is unusual because it sometimes runs upright on two legs. Certain other lizards also do this, like the Western collared lizard of California, USA.

What has eyes 1 m (3 ft 3 in) apart?

It is easy to see how the hammerhead shark (below) got its name. This strange hunter lives mainly in tropical seas and has been known to attack people. With one eye and one nostril on the end of each side of its head, it has a very good sense of smell.

What is a bayou?

There are a number of different stages in the development of a river valley. By the time a river is 'mature' it will have created a broad shallow valley, through which it meanders in a series of loops. Sometimes it will take a short cut between two loops. A whole loop is cut off and becomes an oxbow lake (above). Such lakes are common in the southern USA along the Mississippi, and are known there as bayous.

Who were the samurai?

The samurai were a class of warriors or knights in medieval Japan. They first became a force in Japanese society when the power of the emperors began to fail, about AD 1100. Bands of samurai were united by loyalty to their chief, fighting local wars against other chiefs, usually in order to win more land. They alone were privileged to bear arms, usually wearing two swords. Samurai (right) believed that life should be glorious even if it was short, like the cherry blossom.

The numbers and importance of the samurai began to decline when Japan became a more peaceful, united nation under the rule of the Tokugawa shoguns (military governors), which began in 1603. However, the tradition of the samurai, who had high principles of honour and devotion to duty, has remained strong in Japan to this day.

Quick Quiz

What do these creatures have in common?
(1) Great auk, (2) Dodo, (3) Sabre-toothed tiger, (4) Mastodon, (5) Passenger pigeon.

Answer: They are all extinct.

What do these have in common?
(1) Miller's thumb, (2) John Dory, (3) Guppy, (4) Ruffe, (5) Dace.

Answer: They are all fish.

Who lives in these places?
(1) Buckingham Palace, (2) the White House, (3) Never-Never Land, (4) Mount Olympus, (5) 10 Downing Street.

Answers: (1) the Queen of England, (2) the President of the USA, (3) Peter Pan, (4) the gods of ancient Greece, (5) the British Prime Minister.

Where is the world's largest waterfall?

Niagara Falls (right), between Canada and the USA, is only the fourth largest waterfall in the world, though probably the most famous. The largest fall is the Stanley Falls on the Zaire River; it is actually more a series of rapids than a waterfall. The highest single waterfall is probably the Angel Falls in Venezuela, which drops nearly 1000 m (3050 ft). Waterfalls occur when a river has to make a sharp descent, caused by reaching the edge of a plateau, or the hard rocky bed giving way to softer material which is worn away more quickly. Niagara, like other falls, is gradually moving upstream as chunks of rock are broken off.

Is this Concorde?

No, it's the TU-144 of the Soviet Union, which was the first supersonic airliner to fly (beating Concorde by a few weeks). The Soviet designers of a supersonic airliner produced an aircraft which looked very similar to Concorde (designed by British and French engineers).

Is it an antelope or a horse?

The okapi (right) is a most unusual animal. It is neither horse nor antelope. Its name is an African word meaning donkey, but it is actually a close relation of the giraffe. Another strange thing is that, except for the people who live in the tropical rain forests of Africa, nobody knew the okapi existed until this century. Although it is a large animal with striking colours and pattern, no European explorer or traveller had ever seen one before 1900. For the okapi is a very shy creature, living in the gloomy depths of the jungle and avoiding other animals – even other okapis.

Where is the Taj Mahal?

Many people think this is one of the most beautiful buildings in the world and it is regarded as the finest example of Islamic architecture. It was built on the Jumna River near Agra in India by Shah Jahan, emperor of India, between 1631 and 1653 as a tomb for his wife Mumtaz Mahal ('Jewel of the Palace'). The whole building is covered with white marble inlaid with coloured stones in abstract patterns. It stands on a rectangular platform 580 m (635 yds) by 304 m (333 yds) and the whole edifice is reflected in a pool lined with cypress trees. According to tradition, it is best to see it by moonlight.

Shah Jahan, who reigned from 1628 to 1666, belonged to the Mughal dynasty, and his court was famous for its artists, especially painters.

Who was Genghis Khan?

Nine centuries ago the Mongols were a fierce nomadic people, groups of whom constantly threatened the borders of China. In the late 12th century the warring Mongol tribes were united under one leader, Temujin. He gathered an enormous army of mounted archers which burst through the Great Wall to conquer north China. His conquests spread, and by the time of his death in 1227 Temujin had earned himself the splendid title Genghis Khan, 'universal ruler' (left). His empire stretched right across Asia into eastern Europe, and from the Arctic Circle almost to the Himalayas. People trembled at his name, for the Mongols encouraged tales of their cruelty in order to spread terror before them.

Who built a palace in Xanadu?

In a poem by the English poet Samuel Taylor Coleridge, Xanadu (a fictional place) was where Kublai Khan (above) ordered 'a stately pleasure dome'. Grandson of Genghis, Kublai Khan founded the Mongol dynasty of China, which he ruled as emperor until his death in 1294. As a conqueror he was generous to those he defeated.

Quick Quiz

What and where were the following mythical or legendary places?
(1) Hades, (2) Camelot, (3) El Dorado, (4) Atlantis, (5) Valhalla.

Answers: (1) the underworld home of departed spirits in Greek mythology, (2) the legendary palace of King Arthur in England, (3) a legendary city of treasure in South America sought by the early Spanish explorers, (4) a mythical island in the Atlantic Ocean, said to have sunk into the sea, (5) in Scandinavian mythology, the hall in which the souls of heroes slain in battle dwell.

Who built the Suez Canal?

A great French engineer (above), Ferdinand de Lesseps (1805–94), began building the canal between the Mediterranean and the Red Sea in 1860. Nearly 170 km (105 miles) long, it was finished in 1869 and cut 6500 km (4000 miles) off the sea route from Europe to Asia. The British acquired the shares in the canal in 1875, and subsequently took control of Egypt to protect it.

How can cars be driven with no driver?

When cars are moved from factory to showroom, it is easier for one driver to take them on a car transporter (below).

Quick Quiz

Where and what are the following?
(1) The Great Wall, (2) the Iron Curtain, (3) the Mason-Dixon Line, (4) a safety curtain; (5) Offa's Dyke.

Who are the Bulgars?

Bulgaria is one of the group of mountainous countries in south-east Europe known as the Balkans. The Bulgars are a Slavic people who belong by tradition to the Eastern Orthodox (Christian) Church. However, for about 500 years they were subjects of the Muslim empire of the Turks. They gained self-government in 1878 and full independence in 1908. After the Second World War, a Communist government took power and today Bulgaria is a loyal ally of the Soviet Union. About half of the population lives in towns, but traditional village life continues, and at times you can see people dressed in traditional costume, like the woman above who is from Lovech which is north of the Balkan mountains. They keep up the rural crafts of pottery, wood carving and weaving, and the rich tradition of folk music and dancing.

Answers: (1) The Great Wall of China, 2500 km (1550 miles) long, is a huge fortified wall begun in the 3rd century BC. Its purpose was to stop hostile tribes invading China. (2) The Iron Curtain is a name for the division between communist Eastern Europe and the West. (3) The Mason-Dixon Line is the boundary between Pennsylvania and Maryland in the USA and traditionally divides the North from the South. (4) A safety curtain is a fire-proof screen used on a theatre stage during each performance. (5) Offa's Dyke is an earth ditch and rampart on the border of England and Wales. It was built in the 8th century by Offa, the King of Mercia, to reduce raiding by the Welsh.

What use is a windmill?

Before the steam engine was invented in the 18th century, power was often provided by wind or water. The wind turned the sails of the windmill, and drove the great millstones which ground the corn. Windmills have been used for other purposes. In the Netherlands and East Anglia in England, they pumped water from low-lying areas. Some early windmills had canvas sails, but then slatted wooden sails like those on the windmill below were developed.

How do we get oil from the sea?

The diagram on the right shows a semi-submersible (half-sunk) oil rig in the North Sea. Oil and natural gas were formed millions of years ago from the remains of living animals and plants. As the Earth has changed, many of these deposits have been covered by the sea. A powerful drill penetrates the sea bed until the oil, trapped between layers of rock, is reached. Tankers or pipelines carry the oil ashore to be refined into petrol and other products.

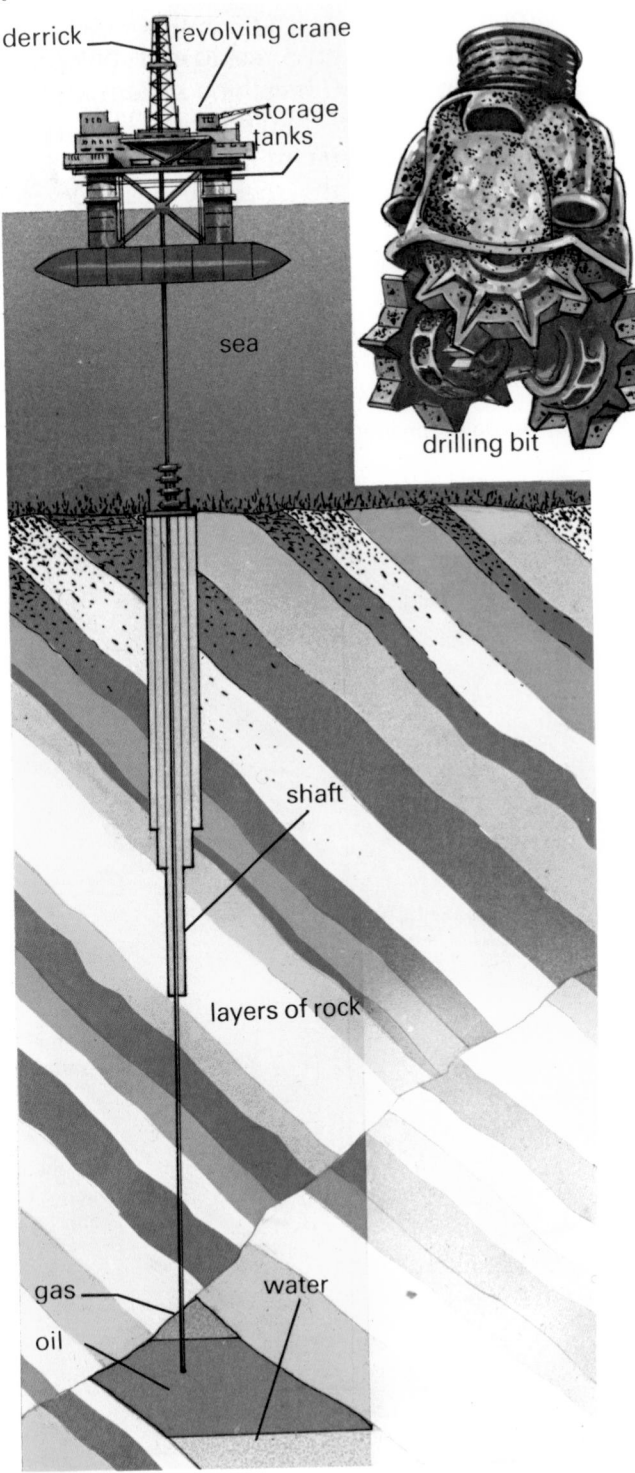

What would you wear for a walk on the Moon?

The space suit creates an environment for the astronaut which is as much as possible like the environment on Earth. It is pressurized (because the Moon has no atmosphere to exert pressure) and contains its own breathing system and its own cooling, or 'air-conditioning'. The space suit below was used by American astronauts on the Moon (with boots specially designed for Moon-walking). Heavy items like oxygen for breathing and the radio unit were carried in a backpack.

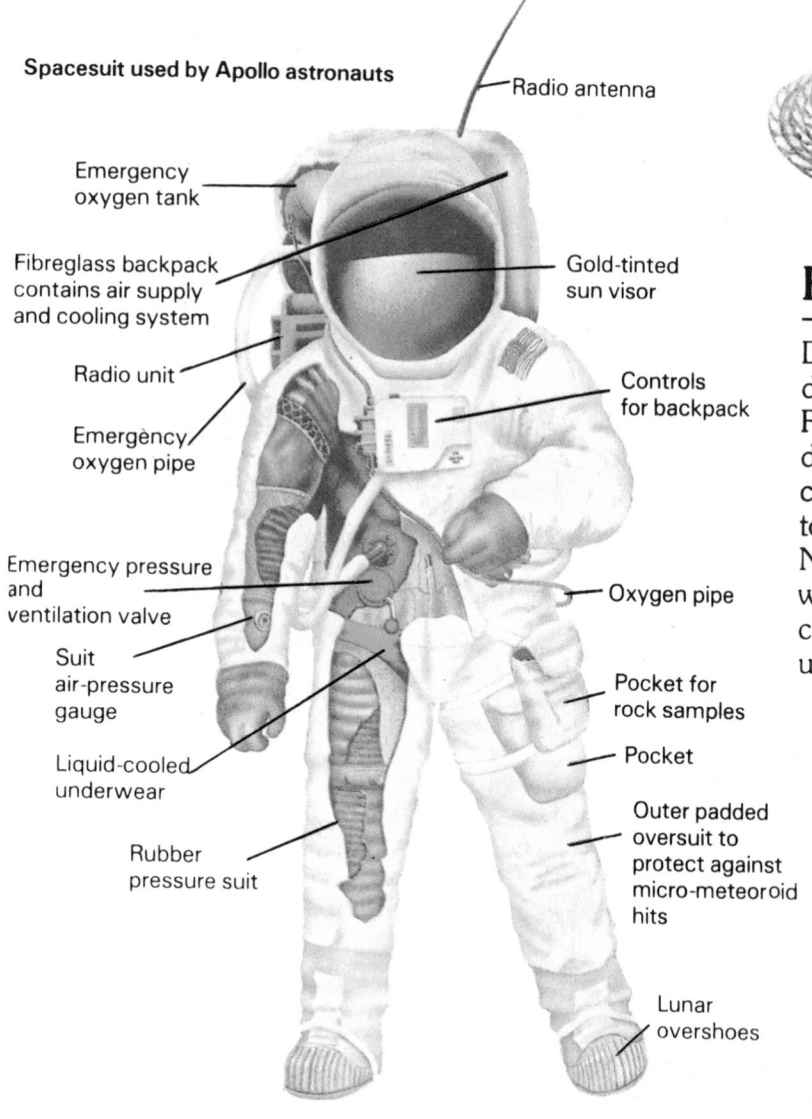

Spacesuit used by Apollo astronauts

- Radio antenna
- Emergency oxygen tank
- Gold-tinted sun visor
- Fibreglass backpack contains air supply and cooling system
- Radio unit
- Controls for backpack
- Emergency oxygen pipe
- Emergency pressure and ventilation valve
- Oxygen pipe
- Suit air-pressure gauge
- Pocket for rock samples
- Liquid-cooled underwear
- Pocket
- Outer padded oversuit to protect against micro-meteoroid hits
- Rubber pressure suit
- Lunar overshoes

How are dates grown?

Dates are the fruit of palm trees which grow in desert oases in North Africa and the Near East. Few other trees will grow in the desert, and the date palm is very useful to people. The leaves can be woven into mats or baskets, and the tough but pliant stems are used to make ropes. Nothing is wasted, even the trunks of old trees, which are burned as fuel. It has large flower clusters which produce the fruit and it can grow up to 30 m (100 ft) in height.

Who invented printing?

In ancient China, words were printed by cutting the symbols in blocks of wood (right). The Chinese later invented movable type, a process in which letters are made separately and assembled to form words. However, successful printing with movable metal type (letters) in Europe was not invented until the 15th century. The man usually called the inventor of printing was Johannes Gutenberg (c.1398–1468), a goldsmith from Mainz in Germany. Before that, all copies of a book had to be written by hand, often by monks (below). Printing made books far cheaper and easier to obtain because copies could be produced quickly.

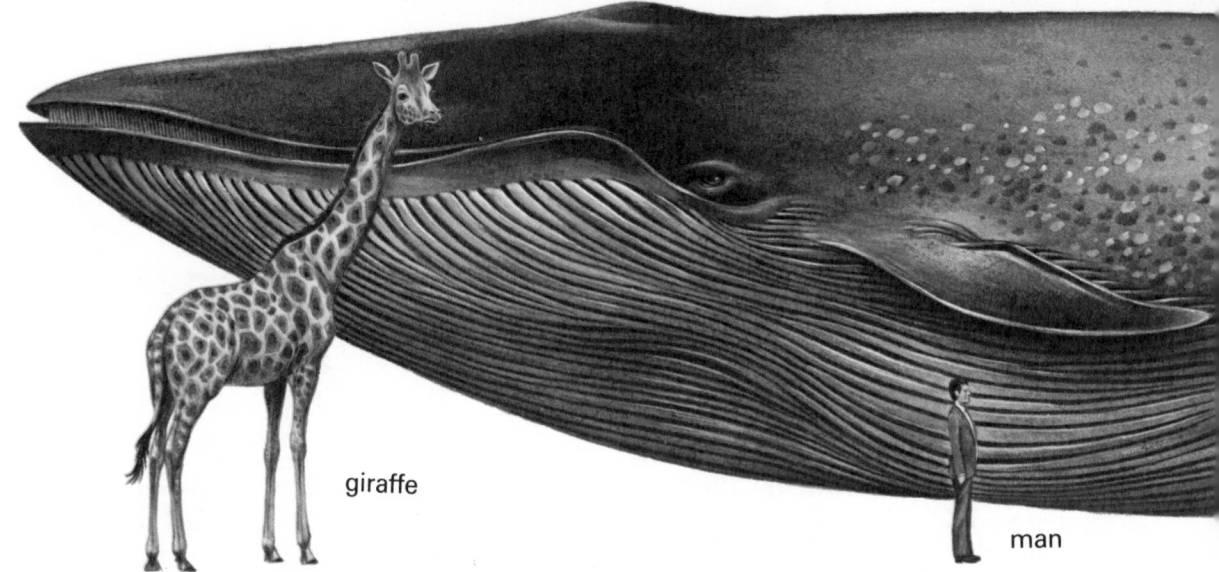

giraffe

man

How small is an elephant?

The African elephant is the biggest land animal. It can weigh over five tonnes. If you stand near an elephant at the zoo, you can easily believe this. By the side of an elephant, a human being looks – and feels – very small. Yet some animals are so small that a human eye cannot see them. Even among mammals, there are shrews and mice that weigh less than a human finger and are

Will it rain today?

A household barometer like the one above measures the pressure of the atmosphere. Low pressure means rain is likely; high pressure means fine weather may follow.

How old are Boy Scouts?

The Boy Scout movement was founded in 1908 by Sir Robert Baden-Powell, a British soldier (above). Its aim was to teach boys to be useful citizens and also the kind of crafts which were being forgotten as more things were made in factories and more people lived in towns. The movement soon spread to other countries, and in 1910 the Girl Guides were founded. The Scouts and Guides have changed with changing times, but the basic idea of good citizenship remains the same. There are about nine million scouts in the world today.

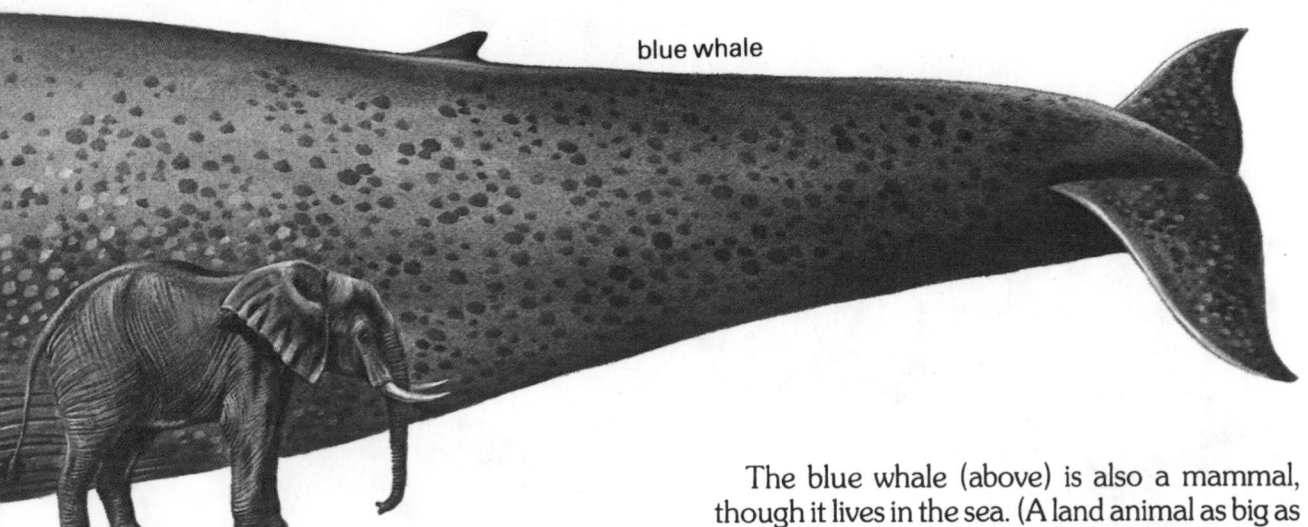

blue whale

african elephant

The blue whale (above) is also a mammal, though it lives in the sea. (A land animal as big as a blue whale would be impossible: its bones would not bear its weight.) If you put an elephant next to a blue whale, it does not look large any more. From a whale's view, an elephant is smaller than a man is from an elephant's view. The size of anything depends on your point of view!

much smaller than the elephant's smallest toe. A human being is an enormous creature next to a pygmy shrew, but the largest person in the world is small beside an elephant or a giraffe, which is the tallest mammal, about 6 m (20 ft) tall.

How does hair grow?

When you comb your hair, a few hairs may come out in the comb. Hairs grow in follicles (below) which are embedded, along with sweat glands, in the inner, dermis layer of the skin (the epidermis is the hard outer layer). Hairs are continually shed and replaced by new hairs forming in the old follicles. Hair 'standing on end' and 'goose bumps' are caused by a tightening of the muscles attached to the hair follicles, which pulls the hair upright.

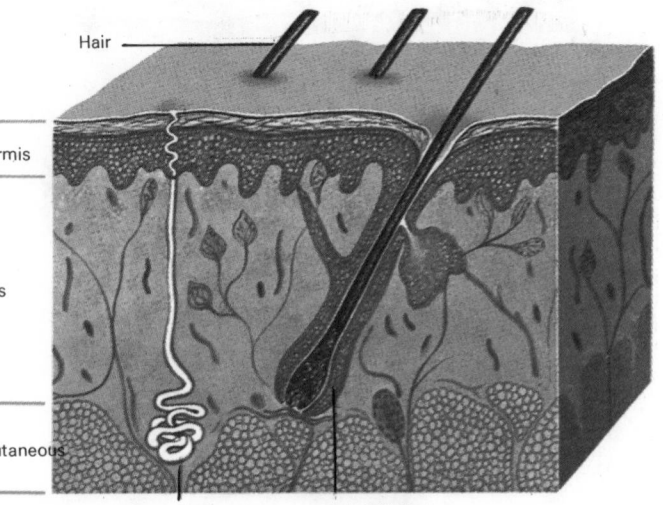

Hair

dermis

mis

cutaneous

Sweat gland   Hair follicle

How is coal mined?

In most coal mines, vertical shafts are made down to the layers of coal, with tunnels branching off them (above). Miners usually go up and down by lift, and the coal is taken out by mechanical means – moving belts, railways, derricks, etc. An open-cast mine is simply a big hole, from which shallow coal deposits are dug.

Virginia opossum with babies

Kangaroo with 'joey'

Sugar glider

Koala and baby

Where do marsupials live?

Marsupials are a group – 'order' is the correct scientific word – of mammals. The word marsupial means a creature with a pouch, and all female marsupials have a kind of pocket in their skin where their babies spend the first few weeks of life after birth. The marsupials are thought to have appeared early in the evolution of the mammals. In general, however, they were replaced by later, non-marsupial mammals, which were more efficient at the business of life (eating, reproducing and surviving).

However, there is one region where a great variety of marsupials survive – Australia. Because Australia was cut off by sea from the rest of the world, it developed its own, distinctive plant and animal life. The Australian marsupials were not challenged by other, more 'efficient' mammals, and they prospered – at least until Europeans settled there in the 19th century. Two special favourites are the kangaroo and the koala. Some of the most unusual marsupials are the gliders. They make giant leaps from tree to tree using their gliding membrane, a web of loose skin between the front and hind legs.

The only type of marsupial outside Australia is the opossum, or 'possum for short, of which the best-known is the Virginia opossum of North America. The mother 'possum carries her babies which have left the pouch clinging to her fur.

The opossum sometimes saves itself from its enemies by pretending to be dead (below left). This habit gives us the expression 'playing possum' which means pretending to be ill or dead.

What is a hurdy-gurdy?

A hurdy-gurdy is a guitar-shaped musical instrument. Turning a handle in the end causes a wooden wheel to sound the strings. It was important in medieval music, but is now mainly used by folk musicians. The 16th-century *Geigenwerk* above combined the principle of the hurdy-gurdy with a keyboard.

What was the wisdom of Confucius?

China has the oldest civilization in the world. Perhaps the greatest person in the foundation of Chinese culture was Confucius, who lived 500 years before Christ (c.551–479 BC). He was a teacher, who hoped to reform Chinese society. Although he failed in his lifetime, his thoughts had enormous influence for over 2000 years, becoming a kind of state religion. Confucius taught that people should try to achieve 'perfect virtue', in themselves and as the servants of society.

Where does the ibex live?

The ibex is a type of wild goat. There are many different species, but, like the one on the right, they all have powerful horns and a rugged appearance. They live in mountainous areas, and are much more agile than they look, finding their way swiftly and surely among rocky crags and cliffs. Ibex are generally rather rare. The Alpine ibex, the only European species, is carefully protected.

Who was 'the Enlightened One'?

Buddhism is not a religion so much as a way of life, as it has no god and no prayer. Buddha, which means 'the enlightened one', was Gautama Siddhartha who founded the religion about 528 BC. He came from an aristocratic family in northern India. Having decided that worldly success meant nothing, he had a vision one night, as he sat under a Bo tree, which became the foundation of his teaching. The aim of Buddhism is to gain *nirvana*, a state of enlightenment gained through the extinction of all desires. Buddhists believe in reincarnation and that acts in this life affect future lives. It is still a powerful religion, and has influenced many people who are not Buddhists.

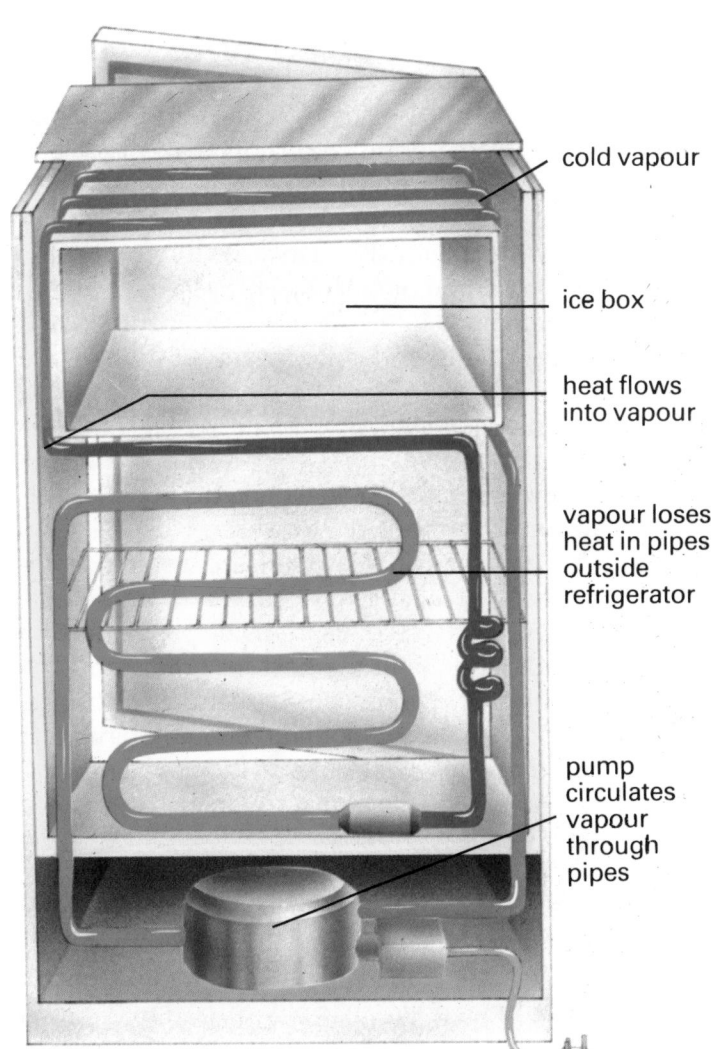

cold vapour

ice box

heat flows into vapour

vapour loses heat in pipes outside refrigerator

pump circulates vapour through pipes

What's in the fridge?

Apart from ice-cream and other foods, refrigerators contain the machinery that makes them cold (above). To cool the inside of a fridge you have to extract the heat. This is done by using a liquid which has a low boiling point. Releasing it into low pressure pipes inside the fridge causes it to evaporate, absorbing heat from the fridge to do so. The same effect is produced if you wet your finger and let it dry. Your finger will feel cold because the evaporating liquid takes heat from it. Finally the vapour is pumped into pipes outside the back of the fridge and compressed, causing it to become liquid again and give off heat. The pipes feel warm if you touch them. In this way the vapour (called the refrigerant) carries heat from inside the fridge to the outside.

Who was Marco Polo?

In 1271, when he was 17 years old, Marco Polo set out from Venice on one of the most exciting journeys anyone could take. With his father and uncle, who were merchants, he crossed almost the whole length of Asia to reach the court of the Mongol emperor of China, Kublai Khan (right). He remained in the Far East, visiting India and other countries, for 20 years, and when he returned he described his adventures in a book called *The Description of the World*.

Unfortunately, most people simply did not believe Marco Polo. In writing his book he was helped by a popular storyteller, Rustichello of Pisa, who put in some fanciful, invented incidents. But really Marco Polo was a very reliable witness and his book remained a source of information about the East for 600 years. The trouble was that his subject seemed so strange; Europeans knew nothing about China and could not believe (for example) that Hangchow was so great a city it made Venice seem like 'a dirty village'!

The 'hero' of the book is Kublai Khan himself, (see page 75), whom Polo admired. He gave a marvellous description of the emperor hunting, with his pet leopard sharing his saddle, and at home in his great white palace, 6.5 km (4 miles) around.

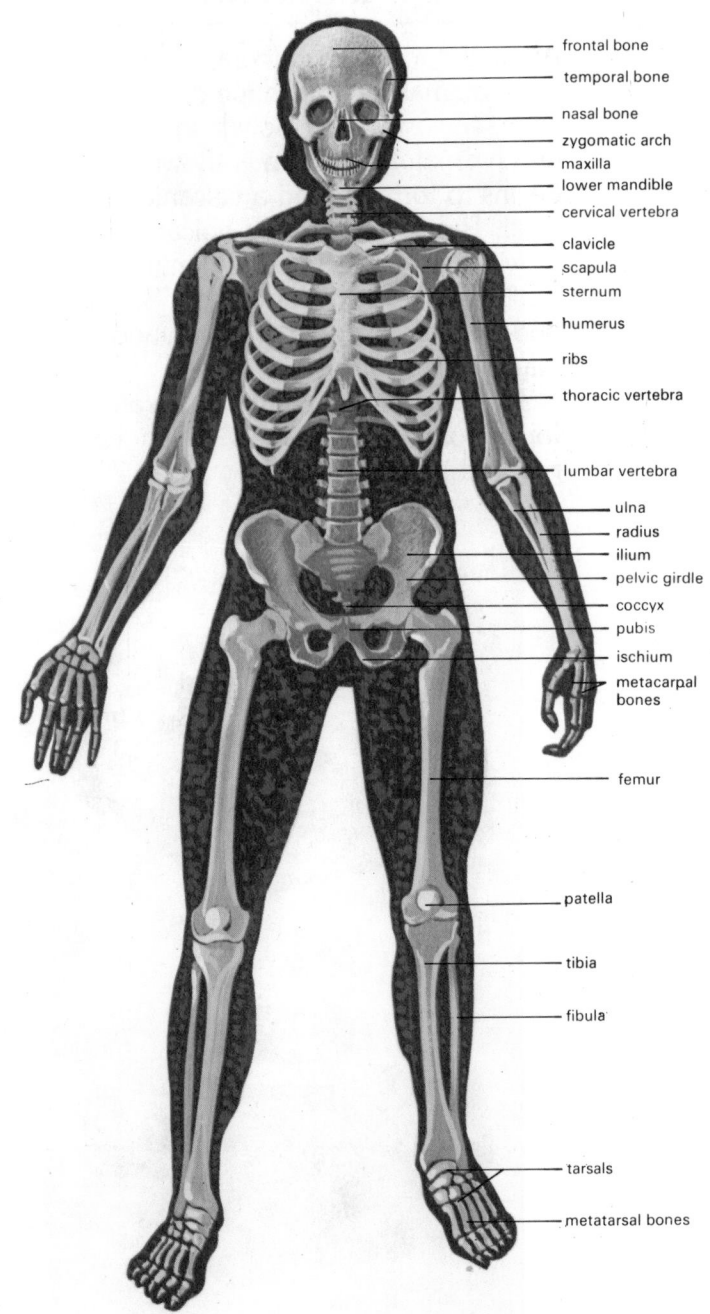

frontal bone
temporal bone
nasal bone
zygomatic arch
maxilla
lower mandible
cervical vertebra
clavicle
scapula
sternum
humerus
ribs
thoracic vertebra
lumbar vertebra
ulna
radius
ilium
pelvic girdle
coccyx
pubis
ischium
metacarpal bones
femur
patella
tibia
fibula
tarsals
metatarsal bones

How many bones are in a human body?

The human skeleton (above) is the framework upon which the rest of the body is built and can be divided into skull, body (or 'trunk') and limbs. If the skull is counted as just one, the total number of bones is about 180.

How are atolls formed?

An atoll is a coral reef (coral is the skeletons of small animals) in the shape of a ring or horse-shoe, enclosing a shallow lagoon. One way in which an atoll can form is shown below. Coral begins to form around a volcanic island (most small Pacific islands are volcanic). The land slowly sinks and the coral continues to grow, until the coral ring alone is left. Scraps of shell and sand are piled up by waves, and eventually plants take root.

As coral grows underwater, an atoll can also form from volcanic reefs which have never reached the surface.

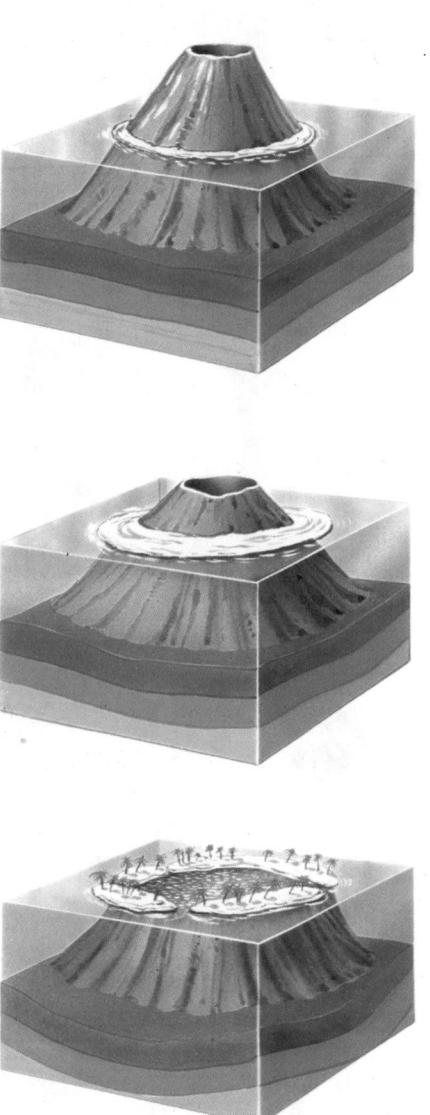

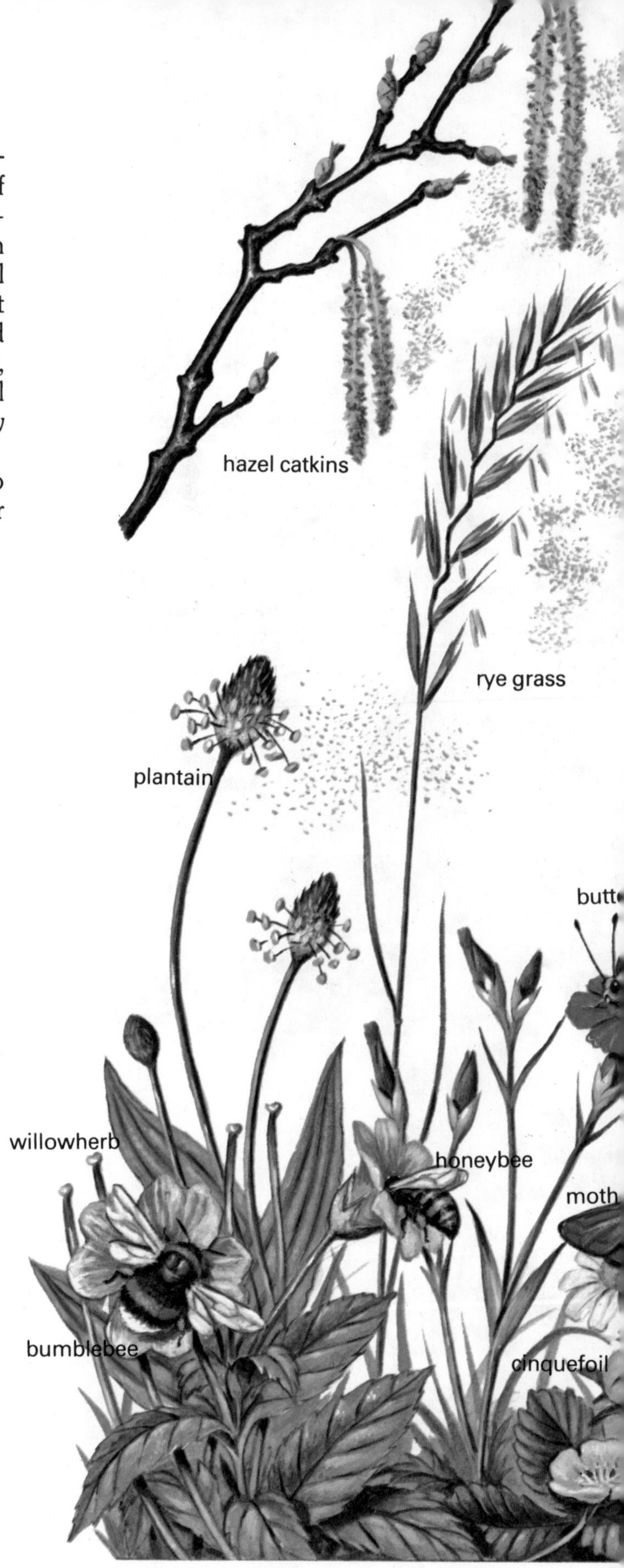

hazel catkins

rye grass

plantain

butt

willowherb

honeybee

moth

bumblebee

cinquefoil

88

How do wild flowers grow?

If you want to grow flowers in your garden, you plant seeds or bulbs. Wild flowers do not have gardeners to do this job for them, but they have other helpers, like the wind and birds to carry their seeds (below and left).

But before seeds form, the flowers must be fertilized by pollen. Sometimes the same flower provides both pollen and – later – seeds. But often the pollen must come from another flower of the same species. The wind does the job for hazel catkins or rye grass. The bright colours and scents of many flowers are designed especially to attract bees and other insects, which carry the pollen on their legs. When the insect lands on another flower, the pollen brushes off on to the ovary. Pollen and ovary produce seeds.

figwort

wasp

gnat

n

mile

knapweed

beetle

Where were cats sacred?

Archaeologists in Egypt have found many mummified cats. For the ancient Egyptians the cat was a sacred creature, linked with a goddess, Bast, who was often pictured as a cat-headed woman. The mummy above was perhaps a temple cat and may have been considered an incarnation of the goddess herself. The Egyptians normally mummified, that is treated with preservatives, the bodies of people before burial.

Who signed the Queen of Scots' death warrant?

In 1587 Mary Queen of Scots was beheaded (left) at Fotheringhay Castle in England. She had been driven from her Scottish kingdom nearly 20 years before and sought asylum in England. Her subjects had been converted to the Protestant faith by John Knox and objected to her being a devout Catholic. In the England of Elizabeth I (above), her cousin, she was a very unwelcome visitor. For Elizabeth was the Protestant queen of a Protestant country, and the Catholic Mary was next in line for the throne. Mary foolishly joined in Catholic plots against Elizabeth. Discovered, she was condemned as a traitor. Elizabeth hesitated before she signed the warrant, for not only was Mary her cousin, she was also a queen – like Elizabeth herself!

What is a field gun?

Artillery is the general name for large guns, as distinct from small arms like rifles which are carried by infantry. Big guns which can be moved fairly easily, and can thus be used on a battlefield, are known as 'field' or mobile artillery. Below is a German field gun of the First World War. It had a calibre (barrel diameter) of 77 mm (3 in) and fired a high-explosive shell up to 8 km (5 miles). Such guns were usually pulled into position by horses. Besides firing high-explosive shells, shrapnel, poison gas and white phosphorus smoke shells were also used.

What lived on Earth before human beings?

Our remote ancestors appeared on Earth over three million years ago, modern man about 100 000 years ago (see page 184). That seems a long time to us, but it is a very short time in the life of the Earth. The Pre-Cambrian Period, at the top of the chart on the right, ended about 500 million years ago. Life had begun much earlier, but was still at a very simple stage. Fishes were the dominant animals in the Devonian Period, about 350 million years ago. Reptiles appeared in the Permian Period. Dinosaurs, the dominant reptiles, survived until the Cretaceous but were replaced by mammals in the Tertiary. Finally, in the Quaternary, early man shared the Earth with creatures like the sabre-toothed tiger and woolly mammoth.

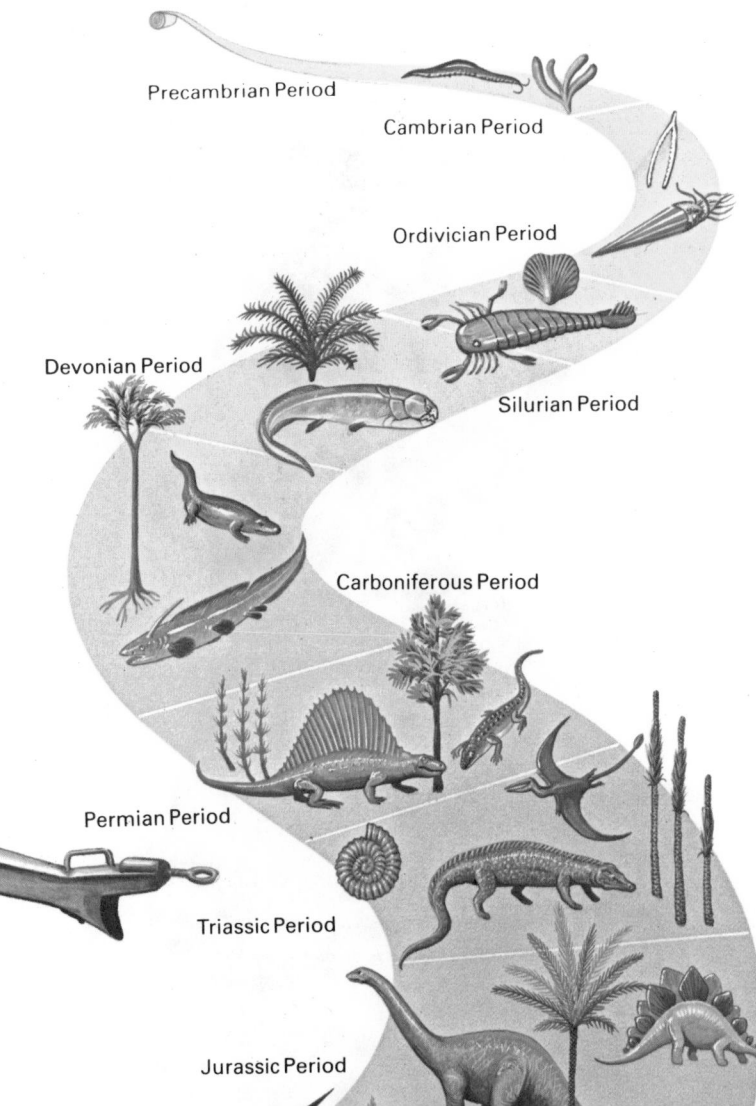

Precambrian Period

Cambrian Period

Ordivician Period

Silurian Period

Devonian Period

Carboniferous Period

Permian Period

Triassic Period

Jurassic Period

Cretaceous Period

Tertiary Period

Quaternary Period

Who lives in Australia and New Zealand?

Most Australians and New Zealanders are descended from European, especially British, settlers. But when the Europeans first arrived, the Maori had already been living in New Zealand for perhaps 600 years. The Maori girl (left above) wears traditional dress, though today she probably more often wears jeans.

The Aborigines had been living in Australia much longer – over 25 000 years. Because they wore few clothes and grew no crops, Europeans wrongly thought they were a simple race. The number of Aborigines like the old man (left below) who live in the old ways is now small.

Is it a duck, is it a mole . . .?

When the first skin of a duck-billed platypus was sent from Australia in the late 18th century, European zoologists thought it was a hoax. A furry animal with a duck's beak, a beaver's tail and a poisonous claw in its hind feet – preposterous!

The platypus (below), which spends much of its time in the water, is a monotreme – a primitive type of mammal which has many of the features of a reptile. For example, the platypus lays eggs, like reptiles, but feeds its babies on its own milk, like mammals.

Who invented the six-shooter?

Below is the Colt Single Action Army revolver of 1873. It fires six shots before reloading. The first pistol with a revolving chamber was invented in England in 1661, but this model, developed from Samuel Colt's first revolver of 1836, is probably the most famous. Variously known as the Peacemaker or the Frontier, it was immortalized in Western movies.

What came before the piano?

The first piano was probably made in Florence in 1709. The spinet below is an earlier keyboard instrument in which, like a harpsichord, the strings are plucked. The piano's strings are struck by hammers operated by the keys.

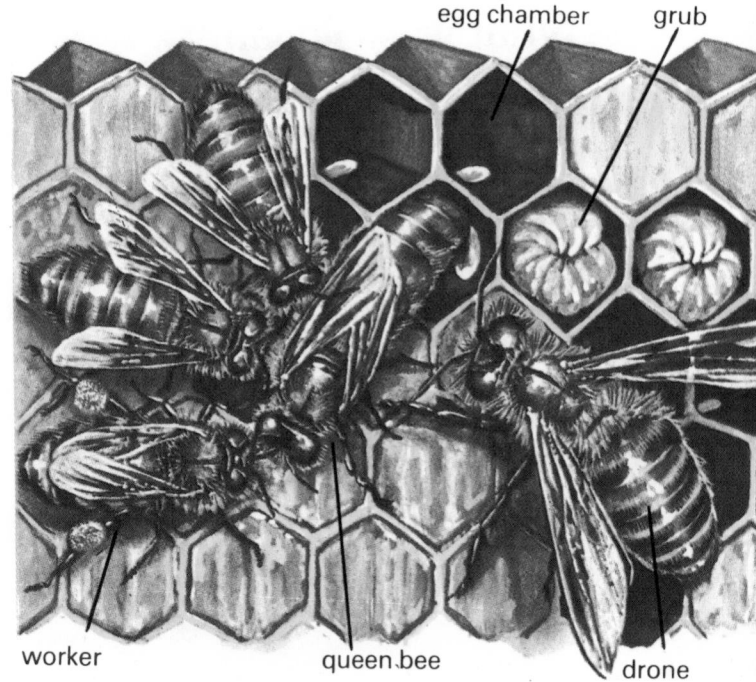

egg chamber   grub

worker   queen bee   drone

What happens inside a beehive?

In a honeybee colony, life is complicated. The large and solitary queen lays the eggs in little cells: she can lay 3000 eggs a day. The eggs are fertilized by male drones and hatch into larvae. All the work – making the cells and collecting nectar and pollen from plants to feed the larvae – is done by the worker bees. They are females which cannot breed. Workers are hatched from fertilized eggs, and drones from unfertilized eggs. Honey is made by the workers from the nectar they gather. They also make beeswax, from which they build the honeycomb.

Quick Quiz

What are the following musical instruments?
(1) Sackbut, (2) rebec, (3) sitar, (4) zither.

Answers: (1) a trombone-like instrument used in the Middle Ages, (2) a medieval instrument with three strings played with a bow, (3) an Indian instrument with a long neck and usually seven strings plucked like a guitar, (4) an Austrian folk instrument with many strings stretched over a flat box.

93

What was Skylab?

The early spacecraft which took people into orbit were very small and cramped. An astronaut could hardly sneeze without bumping into something. The American Skylab (below), launched in 1973, was entirely different. Made from an unwanted Saturn-rocket body, it measured 26 m (85 ft) in length and weighed over 80 tonnes. It was much the largest craft launched by the Americans at that time. It even had a dining-room table and a lavatory which flushed! More importantly, it was equipped, like any other laboratory, for scientific experiments. It could generate most of its own power supply through four panels, looking like the sails of a windmill, which drew energy from the Sun.

Three teams of astronauts used Skylab over a period of 10 months. They reached it in an Apollo spacecraft, shown here docked at the rear of the airlock module. One crew spent 84 days in orbit.

The Soviet Union also had an orbiting laboratory, known as Salyut, in which Soviet cosmonauts stayed in space for even longer periods.

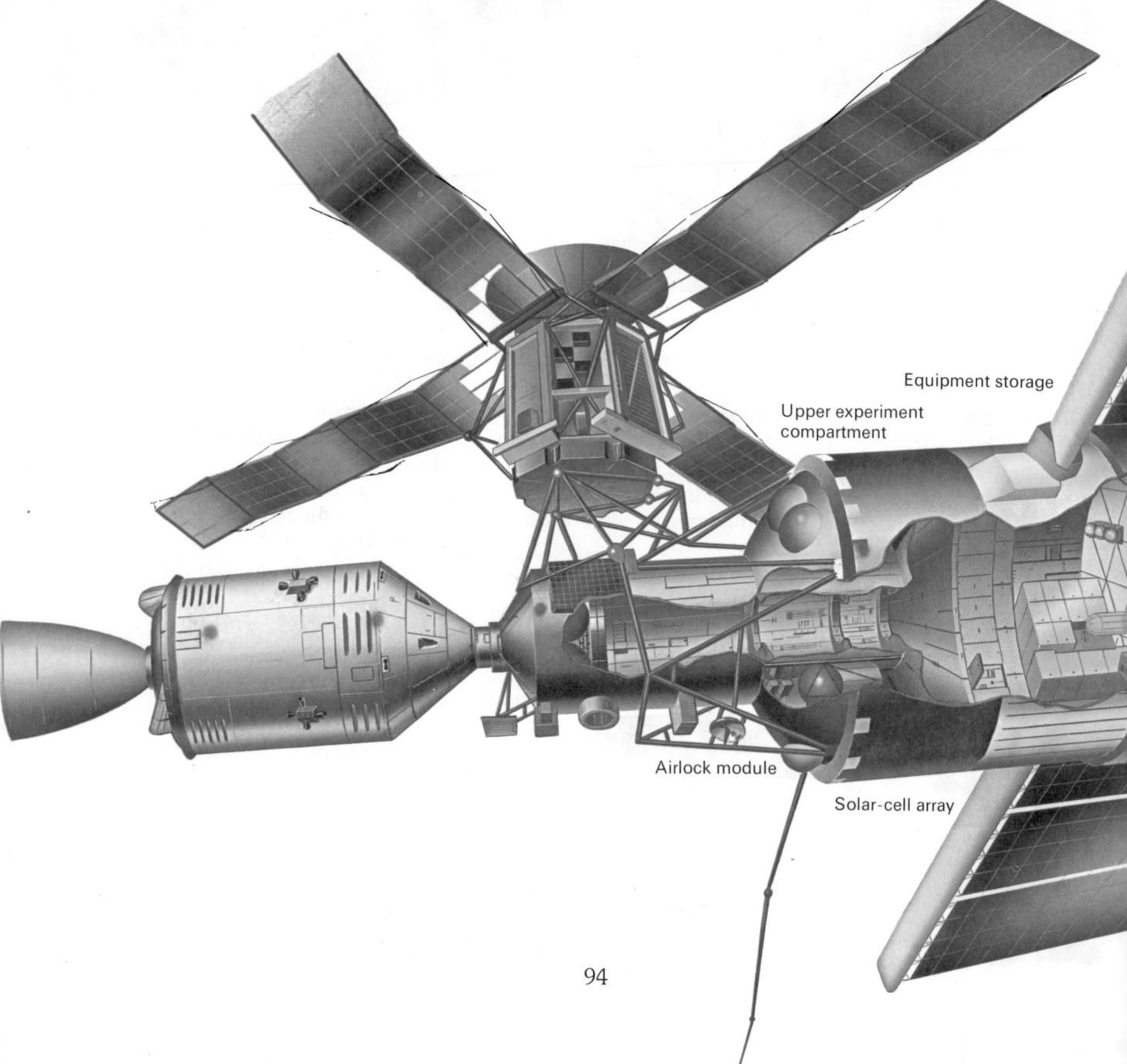

Equipment storage

Upper experiment compartment

Airlock module

Solar-cell array

94

Where is the Kariba dam?

Many African countries are poor because they lack industries, and one of the chief reasons why it is so difficult to make them more prosperous is the cost of energy. The Kariba hydro-electric scheme provides energy for Zambia and Zimbabwe by using the power of the mighty Zambezi River. The dam (right) rises over 100 m (1000 ft) from the bed of the river in the Kariba gorge, and is over 500 m (5000 ft) long. Behind it a lake has been created which is about 200 km (155 miles) long. The scheme can provide roughly three-quarters of all Zimbabwe's electricity.

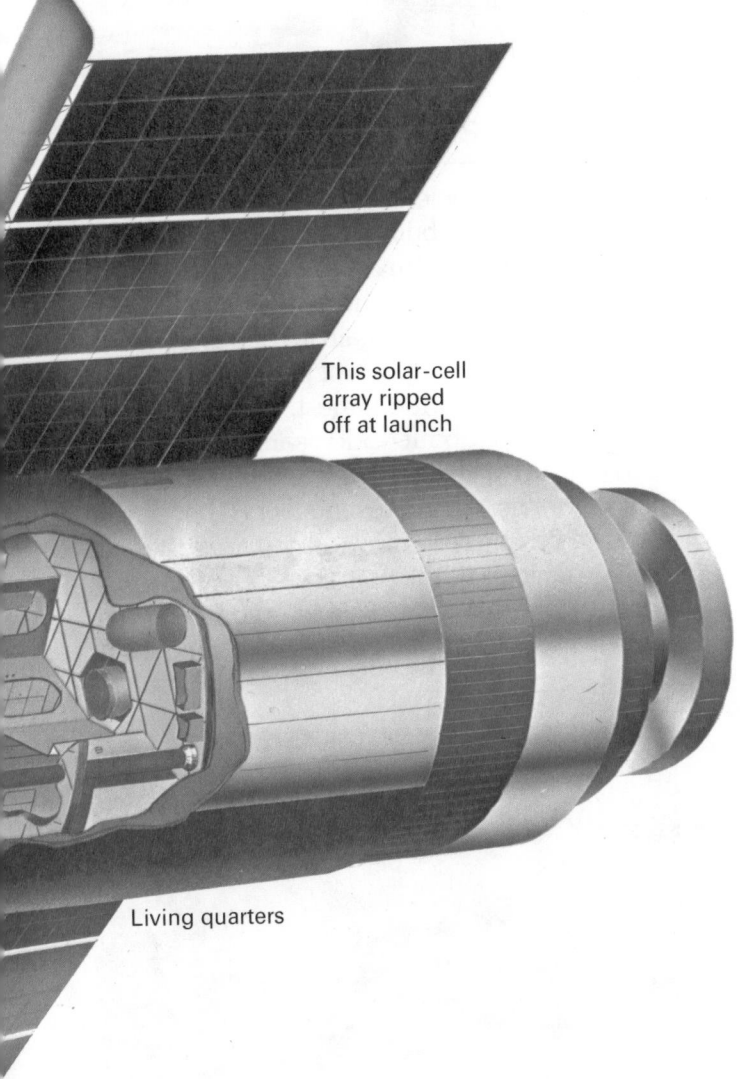

This solar-cell array ripped off at launch

Living quarters

What birds dig burrows?

Puffins (above) are seabirds of the Northern Hemisphere. They are small, parrot-like diving birds of the auk family and have beaks which are brightly coloured in the breeding season, but less so at other times. They nest in large colonies on cliff tops. Their single eggs are laid in burrows, either abandoned by rabbits or dug by the birds themselves, about 1 to 2 m (3 to 6 ft) deep. It finds its food, mostly fish, entirely underwater, catching small or slow-moving varieties for itself or its chick.

What is a sampan?

In parts of China, including the British colony of Hong Kong, many families live not in houses but in boats. The sampan (above) is probably one of the oldest types of boat in the world. They do not seem very suitable as houseboats. They are light, fast – but broad-bottomed – skiffs, which are moved with a single scull (oar) over the stern. The centre of the boat is covered by an awning of bamboo matting.

Quick Quiz

What are the following?
(1) Galley, (2) Caravel, (3) Junk, (4) Curragh, (5) Dhow.

Answer: They are all ships or boats.

Where would you find the following?
(1) The Sphinx, (2) The Empire State Building, (3) The Eiffel Tower, (4) The Colosseum, (5) Nelson's Column.

Answers: (1) Egypt, (2) New York, (3) Paris, (4) Rome, (5) London.

Where are the Pyramids?

A number of ancient peoples, including the people of Mexico, built pyramids, but the most famous are the pyramids of Egypt. They were tombs, built to protect the bodies, which were expected to be needed again in a life after death, of kings and other important people. The Great Pyramid at Giza is the largest, built for a ruler named Cheops about 4500 years ago. It is over 150 m (490 ft) high and weighs about five million tonnes. An interesting fact is that one of its main passages is directed towards the star Thuban which was the pole star 4500 years ago. Because Earth's axis wobbles, completing a circle every 26 000 years, Polaris is the pole star today.

How many moons has Mars?

The planet Mars was named after the Roman god of war because it appears to be the colour of blood. As it is more like Earth than other planets, people have often wondered whether it supports any form of life. Now that American and Soviet spacecraft have investigated Mars closely, that seems unlikely. The photograph below, taken by an American Mariner spacecraft, clearly shows the two tiny moons of Mars, Phobos (to the left) and Deimos. They were first discovered in 1877 and are less than 20 km (12 miles) in diameter. The photograph also shows the predominantly red colouring of the planet and the dark patches, originally thought to be seas by early astronomers.

Which widow is deadly?

Although it is unusual for a person to die after being poisoned by an animal, some creatures do produce very dangerous poisons. Usually, the poison is for self-defence; sometimes to kill prey. But the large box jellyfish of the Pacific can kill a human being in minutes if the sting is a bad one. The sea snake is also armed with powerful venom, stronger than any viper or rattlesnake. The little arrow-poison frog provided the paralysing poison which was smeared on arrows by hunters in South America. A number of spiders, like the American black widow, can give a very painful, occasionally deadly, bite.

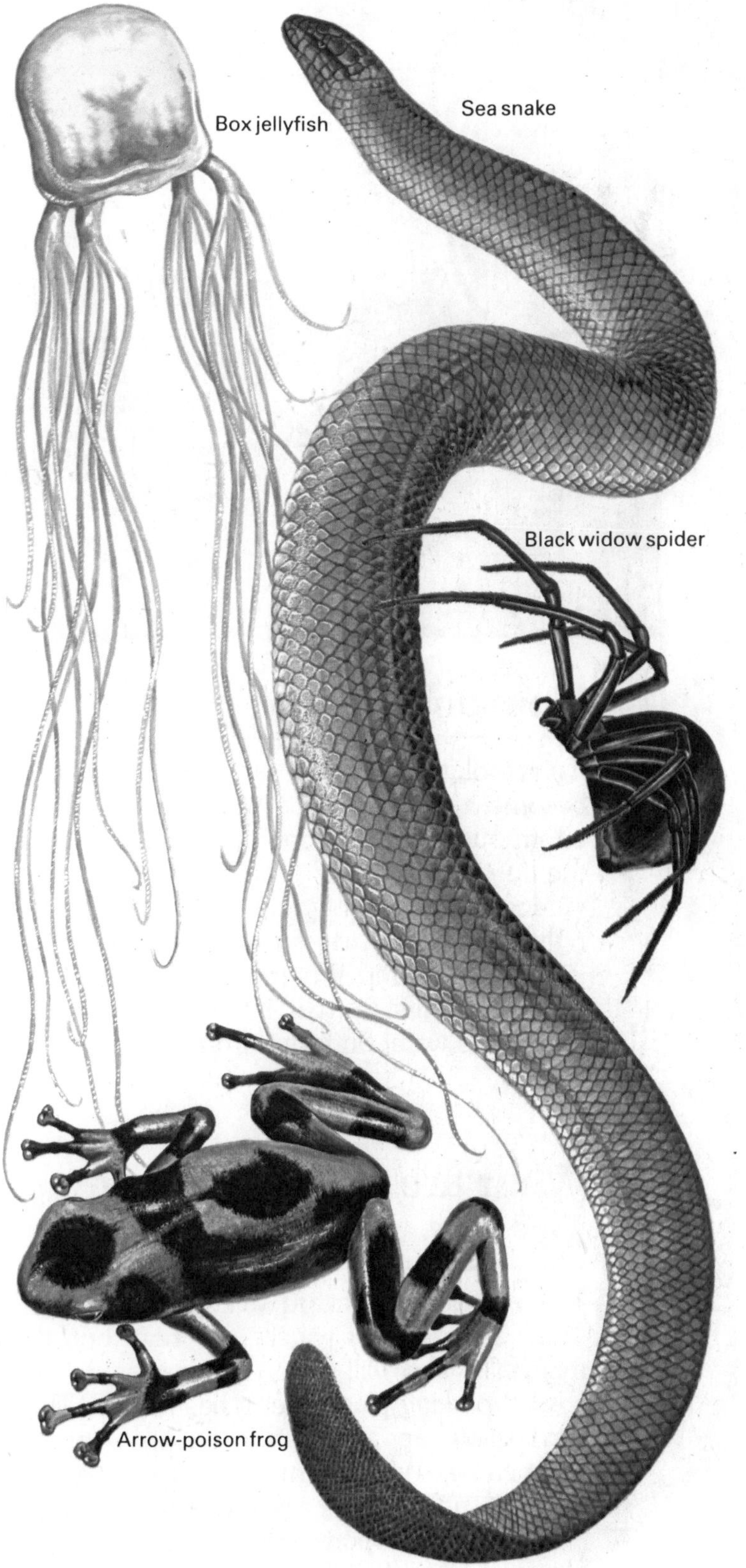

Box jellyfish

Sea snake

Black widow spider

Arrow-poison frog

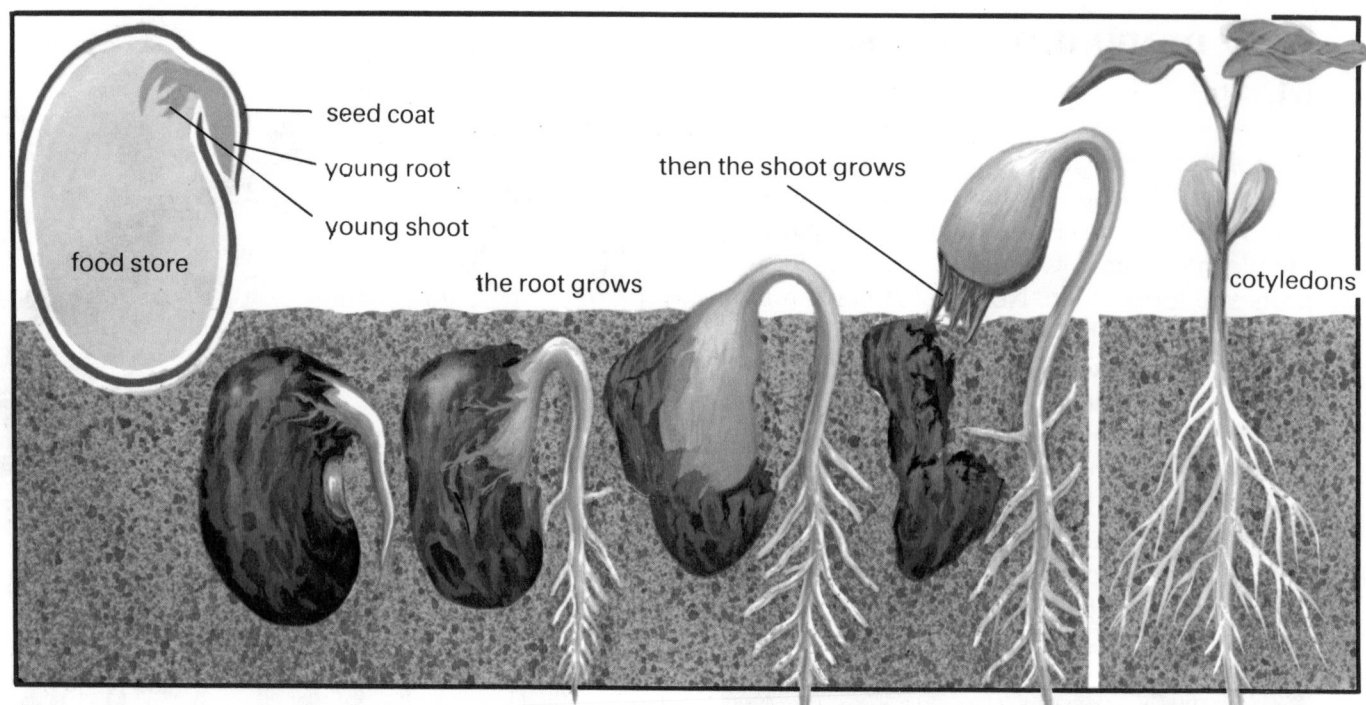

seed coat
young root
young shoot
food store
then the shoot grows
the root grows
cotyledons

How does a seed grow?

If you look at a seed and think of the plant it will become, it seems almost a miracle. How does an enormous tree grow from a seed no larger than the tip of your finger?

Most seeds will not grow until they are in the right place to do it, which usually means soil that is warm and damp. When you plant a seed, the root sprouts first (above). It holds the plant firm and draws water and food from the soil, while the green shoot grows upward, producing leaves, flowers and, in time, more seeds.

Most garden plants are dicotyledons, which means that their seeds, like the one above, have two cotyledons or seed leaves. These store food for the embryo plant until it grows normal leaves to produce its food. Some plants have only one seed leaf and are called monocotyledons.

What are these men waiting for?

The men on the right are waiting for an airliner! They are not passengers or crew, but the marshalls who will guide the aircraft to the correct parking place after it has landed. They wear yellow caps and coats so that pilots can see them easily, and the earmuffs protect their ears from the noise of the aircrafts' engines.

A modern airport is a complicated, busy place, and if a pilot takes a wrong turning on the ground, the result may be disastrous.

What did this dinosaur have for breakfast?

This 'overgrown lizard' is that most frightening of extinct animals, *Tyrannosaurus rex*. There were some dinosaurs even larger than *Tyrannosaurus*, but they were harmless, placid, grazing animals. *Tyrannnosaurus* was a carnivore – a meat-eater – and its breakfast was probably another, less powerful dinosaur.

Thanks to fossil remains, we have a good idea of what this monster looked like. It stood nearly 7 m (23 ft) high to the top of its horny head, and its great jaws were lined with curved teeth up to 15 cm (6 in) in length. It walked upright (as some lizards do now) and probably moved quite fast, rocking from side to side as it pounded along on its claw-like feet. The tail helped it to keep its balance.

Is a vintage car a veteran?

Officially, a 'veteran' car is one built before 1918, while a 'vintage' car is one built between 1918 and 1930. Cars like the two illustrated on the right are seldom seen outside museums today. Splendid machines they certainly are, but few people could afford to drive them today because their big engines used a great deal of petrol. The vintage 4½-litre Bentley (above), first made in 1928, had a maximum speed of close to 160 km/h (100 mph) – just the thing for touring if someone else pays for the petrol! The veteran Rolls Royce Silver Ghost of 1907 (below) had a 7-litre engine and a top speed of 130 km/h (80 mph). You could have the seats covered in ostrich hide with ivory buttons of you wanted.

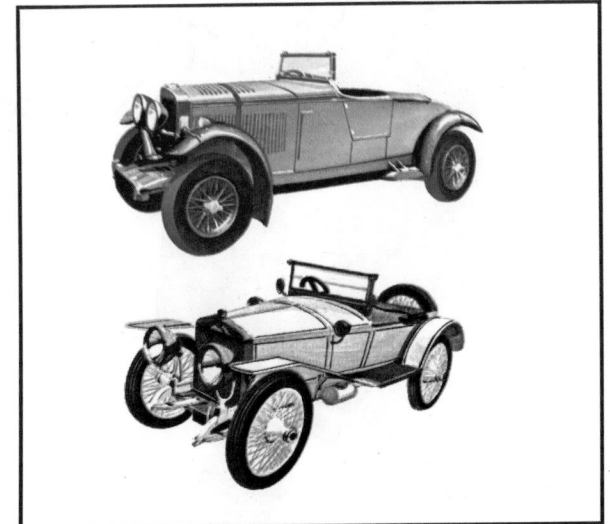

Where do these people come from?

China has a quarter of the world's population, and yet we know relatively little about life there. The government is attempting to keep the population from growing, and Chinese parents are discouraged from having more than one child.

The man at the bottom is from Hong Kong (see map opposite), a British colony which will become part of China in 1997. He is using the pole to push a sampan. The old man at the top is a peasant. The vast majority of Chinese live in rural areas and produce agricultural goods. The man in the middle is from the cold and remote country of Mongolia, between China and the Soviet Union.

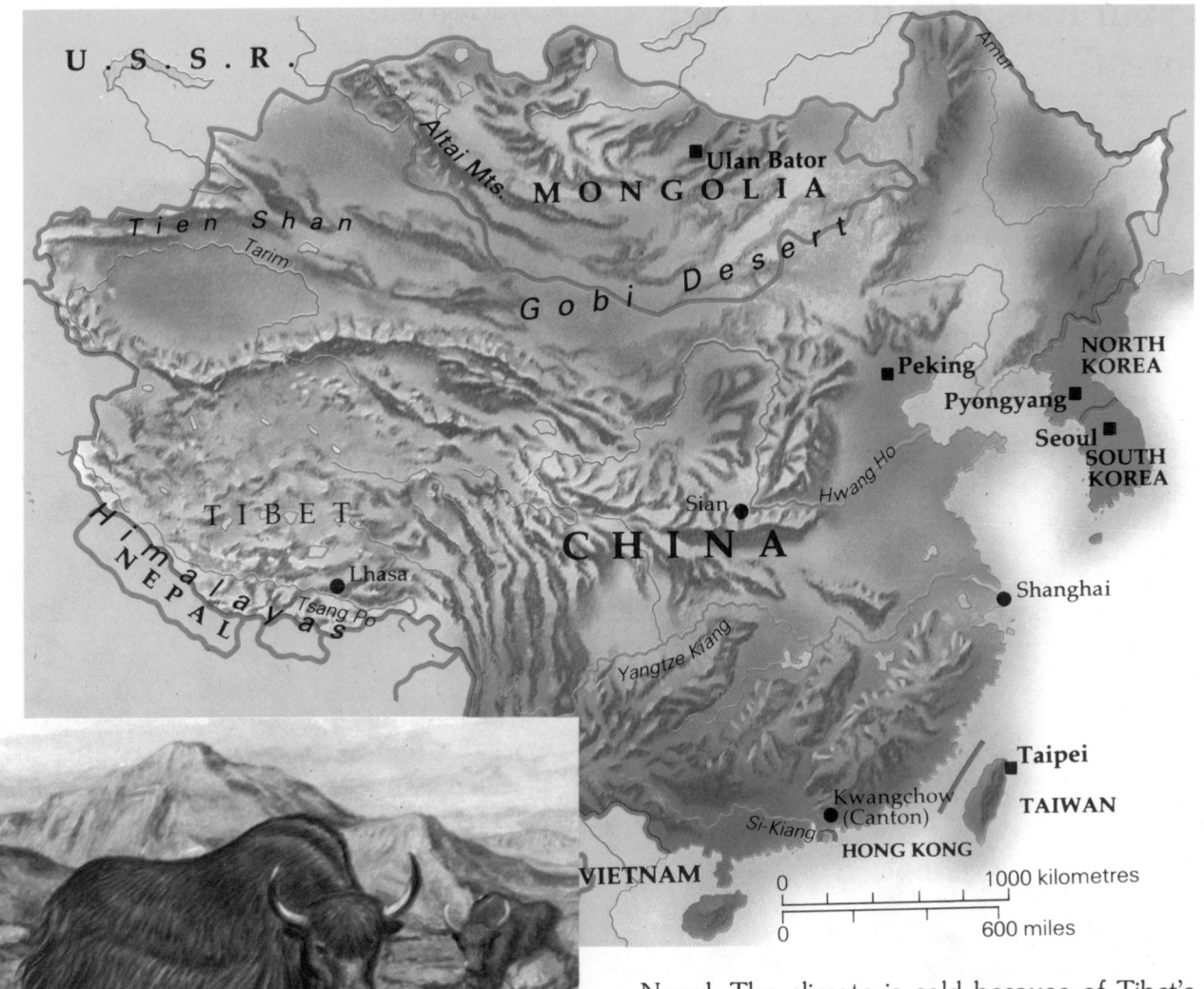

Where is Tibet?

Tibet is now part of the Chinese People's Republic (*see* map at top). Until the Chinese invasion of 1950, Tibet was an independent country under the rule of a Buddhist religious leader, the Dalai Lama. However, in earlier periods the country had been dominated more often than not by the Chinese.

Tibet is a remote country, cut off from India and the south by the Himalaya Mountains. Mount Everest, the highest mountain in the world, stands on the border between Tibet and Nepal. The climate is cold because of Tibet's height above sea level, and winds and rainstorms are violent. Asia's largest rivers, including the Yangtze, Mekong, Indus and Brahmaputra all rise in Tibet. The Chinese have tried to improve communications and industry, but it is still mainly a country of isolated groups of nomadic herdsmen.

The yak (above left) is the most important animal for the Tibetans. An ox-like creature, it lives wild on the bleak plateaux, but is also kept in domestic herds. Its heavy fur protects it against the cold weather, and in the wild it usually lives near the snow line. The domestic yak is used as a beast of burden, but it also gives rich milk, from which butter and other products are made. Its flesh provides meat; its fringe of long hair is made into rope; its fur into cloth; and its skin into leather.

What lives in a tropical rain forest?

Tropical rain forest is a more respectable name for what we often call a jungle. This is a region where the climate is hot and wet and trees grow

leopard

gibbon

spider monkey

hornbill

python

spoonbill

ibis

capybara

tapir

butterfly

chimpanzee

frog

toad

butterfly

very thickly. Another name for it is equatorial forest, for these regions are only found near the equator. There is no dry season, and not much change between summer and winter.

Many of the trees grow to great heights, and lianas (creepers) swing from the branches. Rain forests also contain valuable hardwood trees, like mahogany and ebony.

If you fly over a rain forest in a helicopter, it looks like a great green sea, stirred by the wind. On the ground it is a very gloomy place, as hardly any sunlight gets through the thick roof of leaves. There are few flowers therefore, and as they do not have to flower in a particular season you never see many flowering at the same time.

toucan

boa

squirrel monkey

gorilla

elephant

tiger

tree frog

chameleon

crocodile

iguana

mudskipper

Some of them are plants called epiphytes, which grow on other plants (or trees) but get their food not from the host plant, as parasitic plants like mistletoe do, but from the air. Some rare orchids are flowers of this kind.

The world's largest rain forests are in the immense Amazon basin of South America, in West Africa and the Zaire River basin, and in Malaysia and Indonesia (South-east Asia). Read on to find out more about forest animals and the world they live in.

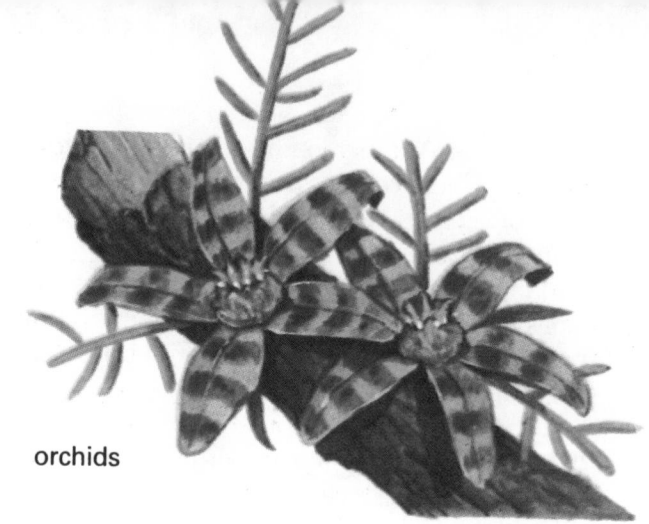

orchids

Animals of the rain forest

There are many animals in a rain forest, but they are not easily seen. It is easy to stay hidden, and forest animals are shy. Even such a large and showy animal as the okapi (see page 61) was completely unknown to zoologists until 1901.

Although all the animals pictured in the scene on the previous two pages are jungle dwellers, you would not, of course, find them all in the same forest.

The rain forest is not a single environment. Different animals live in different parts: some where the trees grow thickest, some where they can find more space and sunlight, and some where they are close to water.

Apart from a few deer, there are not many grazing animals because there is very little grass or small-plant life. Environments also change vertically: life at ground level is quite different from life among the tree tops, and different types of animals live at each level.

Birds

The creatures with the greatest freedom are, as always, the birds. Many species of birds live in these regions. You can often hear them, but trying to see them through the leaves is much harder. People who try to study birds of the rain forests in the wild need the patience of a saint.

At least the brilliant red plumage of the scarlet ibis makes it unmistakeable. It is in fact easy to spot if you are in the right part of tropical America, for it is a wading bird and lives in large colonies.

The ibis is closely related to the spoonbill, and their habits are similar, though they have bills of

a quite different shape. Instead of the long, downward-curving bill of the ibis, the bill of the spoonbill is broad and – as you would expect – spoon-like. It wades through shallow water moving its head from side to side while sieving food from the water.

Stranger still are the prominent bills of the hornbill and toucan. They are tree-dwelling birds. The hornbill (there are 45 different species) lives in the tropical forests of Africa and Asia. Toucans look rather like hornbills but they are American birds, related to the woodpeckers. They often take over woodpeckers' holes for their own nests (perhaps thinking, if one can use it, toucan). In some species the huge bills are brightly coloured. No one knows why the toucan should have developed this vast – but not particularly strong – bill.

Mammals

Other creatures which spend most of their time in the trees are the monkeys and apes. The gibbon, with its musical chatter, swings through the branches of the rain forests of South-east Asia with the grace and athleticism of an Olympic gymnast. The gibbon is so quick and

monkey

agile it can catch young birds by hand. Its larger brother-ape, the orang-utan, whose name means 'old man of the forest', moves at a more dignified pace.

In Central and South American forests, monkeys like the spider monkey have the advantage of a tail which can grip a branch, as well as hands and feet. The squirrel monkey lives in the Amazon forests, moving about in large family groups, often close to water and following well-established paths through the trees.

The larger apes of Africa may spend more time on the ground. The loveable chimpanzees often sleep in trees but spend most of their waking time on the ground. Experiments with chimps have shown beyond doubt that these animals are capable of reason: they can find an answer to a simple problem by thinking it out. The gorilla, largest of the apes, used to be completely misunderstood. It was unknown to science until the mid 19th century, but there were stories and rumours of its terrible ferocity. In fact, the gorilla is one of the most shy and gentle of animals.

The gorilla's only enemy, apart from man, is the leopard, a big cat which hunts its prey in the trees. The leopard ranges over large areas of Africa and Asia, while its part in the tropical forests of the Americas is played by the jaguar, which looks very similar. Another great cat of the forest is the tiger, found only in Asia and now very rare in the wild. Possibly the only tigers left by the year 2000 will be in zoos.

The big African elephant is an animal of the plains, but the Indian elephant prefers the shade of the forest, where it spends most of its time gathering leaves to eat. Indian (but not African) elephants are easily tamed, and they have been used as working animals for centuries, hauling timber from the forest.

Varieties of the tapir, which is related to the rhinoceros, are found in South-east Asia and tropical American forests. They have poor eyesight but excellent hearing and sense of smell. Capybara, the largest rodents in the world today, are not true jungle creatures. These aloof-looking guinea-pigs have partly webbed feet and are water animals, living on the banks of rivers in tropical America.

Reptiles, amphibians and fish

The jungle harbours some awesome snakes, like the boas and pythons which squeeze their prey to death. The python of Asia and Africa grows to 10 m (33 ft) in length and can swallow a gazelle whole. The American anaconda may grow even larger.

A great number of frogs and toads live in equatorial forests. There may be some species still undiscovered. Some of the most interesting are the tree frogs, which live their entire lives in the trees, even breeding there.

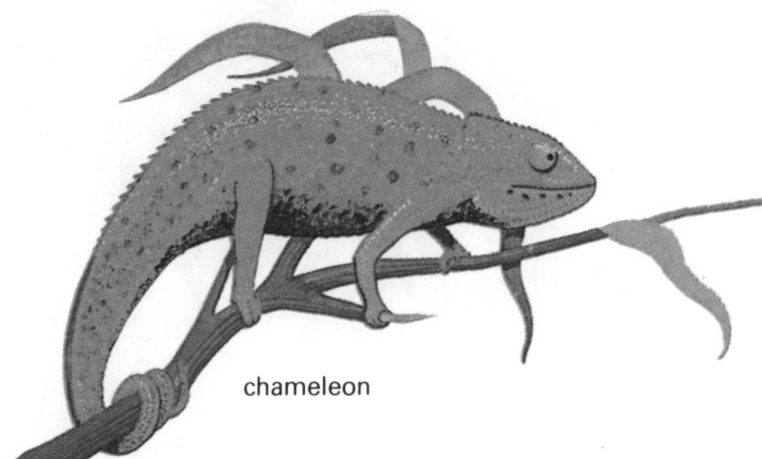

chameleon

Iguanas and chameleons are lizards. The chameleon in particular is a true tree creature, with feet specially made for gripping twigs and branches. Crocodiles and alligators are also lizards of a sort – giant-sized ones – which live in and near the water in nearly all tropical regions.

The mudskipper is a strange creature which inhabits the mangrove swamps, between land and sea, in parts of South-east Asia. It is a fish which lives as much out of the water as in it. With its flippers and fins it 'skips' nimbly across the mud between tides. When awash, its periscopic eyes enable it to see above the surface of the water. One species even climbs trees.

Insects

Finally, the tropical rain forest is the home of more insects than can be counted. Among them are grasshoppers coloured like jewels, and several large and splendid butterflies (especially in South America). Many insects are so little known that they don't have common names, only Latin names.

What happened to the Bastille in 1789?

In 1789 the ordinary people of Paris were ready to rebel against the royal government. Trouble had been brewing for years, and the rise in food prices and the lack of jobs had brought things to a crisis. The government plainly could not solve the country's economic problems. In May the King called a meeting of the Third Estate, representatives of the people, which had not met since 1614. The representatives soon discovered they would not be allowed any real power in government, so they decided to form a National Assembly and work out a new, fairer constitution for France.

On 14 July Paris burst into open revolt. The people needed weapons, so a band of them went to the great government fortress of the Bastille (above) and demanded them. The governor of the Bastille refused, and as the people moved forward, ordered the guards to open fire. Several people were killed. News of this outrage ran swiftly through the city, and hundreds more people came running to the Bastille, shouting their fury. Among them were soldiers with cannon. The governor was forced to surrender, and the people of Paris captured the Bastille.

This was the first important act of violence in the French Revolution, which sent the King to the guillotine and turned France into a republic. It was also to change the whole history of Europe.

What is a mink coat?

Mink coats are made from the fur of this small, fish-eating animal. The minks are now raised on special farms, so people buying mink coats (they need to be rich!) cannot be accused of helping to make an animal extinct (unlike those who buy leopard skin).

106

Can you name the fruits of these wild shrubs?

The dog rose is the wild rose which is so common in English hedgerows. It can grow up to 3 m (10 ft) in height, and has a very delicate pink flower. The fruit, called hips, are hard and shiny, and are well worth picking to make rose-hip syrup.

Sloes are the fruit of the blackthorn bush. They look like small blue plums. Though not pleasant to taste, they are sometimes added to gin, giving it a fruity taste.

The elder is really a small tree rather than a shrub, and it can grow up to 10 m (33 ft) high. Elderberries are small, black and juicy (but bitter). Many people make elderberry wine.

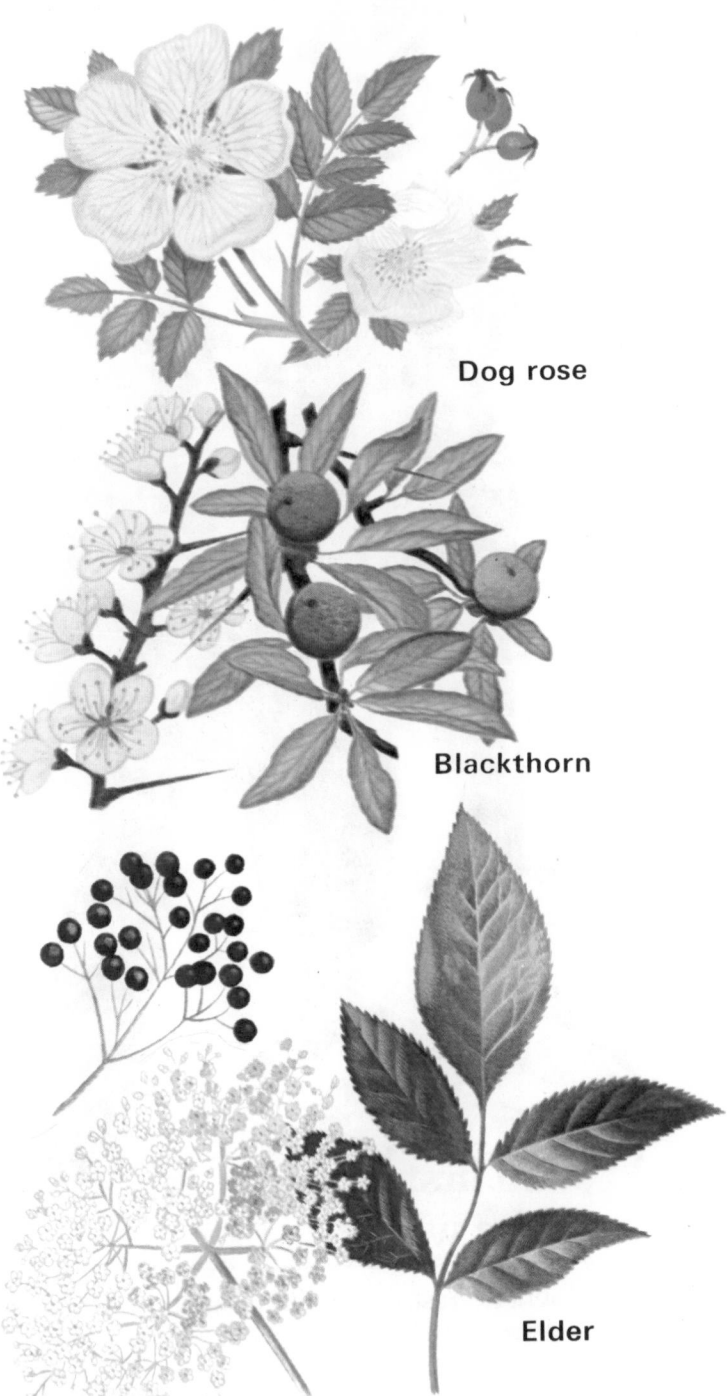

Dog rose

Blackthorn

Elder

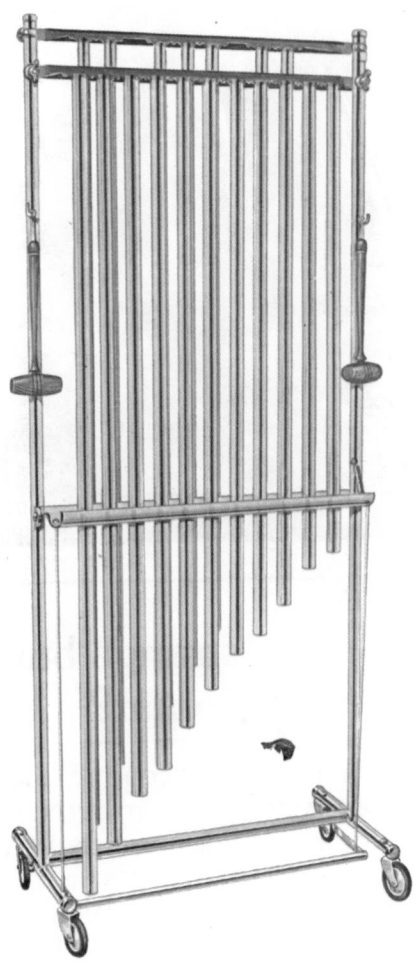

What sound does this instrument make?

Some pieces of music – Beethoven's 'Emperor' concerto for example – call for the sound of bells. The tubular bells (left) are the ones in the orchestra which do the job. The metal tubes are struck with the hammers hanging at the sides.

Who first stood on the 'roof of the world'?

Mount Everest, the highest mountain on Earth – 8848 m (29 028 ft) – which stands on the borders of Nepal and Tibet, was first climbed in 1953 by a British expedition led by Sir John Hunt. The two men who reached the top were Tensing Norkey, a Sherpa guide (the Sherpas of Nepal specialize in guiding mountaineers in the Himalayas) and the New Zealander, Sir Edmund Hillary. Hillary took a photograph of Tensing on the peak, with flags of the United Nations, Britain, India and Nepal tied to his icepick (above). News of the successful climb reached London a few hours before the coronation of Queen Elizabeth II.

What is the strange building on Mount Palomar?

The giant reflector telescope in the Mount Palomar observatory, California (above), has a reflector (the mirror, which does the job of a lens in a refracting telescope) 508 cm (200 in) in diameter. It was completed in 1948 and with it many stars became visible for the first time.

When did the balloon go up?

The brothers Joseph and Etienne Montgolfier, who lived at Annonay in France, were convinced that flight was possible in a balloon filled with hot air. In 1783 the Montgolfier balloon (above), which was made of linen lined with paper, drifted triumphantly over the roofs of Paris with two men riding in the basket underneath. It was the maiden flight of the first successful hot-air balloon. Those men, however, were not the Montgolfier brothers. Excellent inventors though they were, they were quite willing to allow the honour of being the first airborne men to be earned by others.

Not long afterwards, another Frenchman made a balloon filled with hydrogen, which was more reliable than hot air.

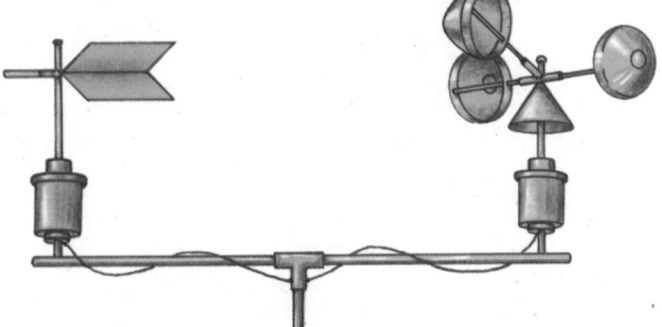

How can you measure the wind?

A weather vane (on the left of the apparatus above) tells which direction the wind is blowing. On the right is an anemometer, which also measures the speed of the wind. The wind spins the cups around, and the rate at which they turn is measured electrically.

How big were the dinosaurs?

That strange race of extinct monsters, the dinosaurs (below), included the largest animals that have ever lived on the land surface of the Earth. The biggest of the dinosaurs was *Brachiosaurus*, which belonged to a group called the sauropods. It could be as much as 16 m (53 ft) high and 80 tonnes in weight. Among its giant cousins were *Diplodocus* and *Apatosaurus* (or *Brontosaurus*). These giants were all plant eaters, with small heads and weak teeth, possibly feeding mainly on water plants. In spite of their great size, the sauropods had dangerous enemies, like *Allosaurus*, a fiercer, more agile animal which was one of the meat-eating carnosaurs.

There were even flying dinosaurs like *Rhamphorhynchus*, which lived on fish.

How were Indian canoes made?

Modern canoes are made of canvas stretched over a frame, or moulded from fibre-glass. This North American Indian (above) is making a birch-bark canoe. They were highly developed craft, with a thin lining of planks held against the inside of the birch bark by a tight framework of wooden ribs. In the wooded and mountainous areas of North America, canoes were an essential means of transport.

rhamphorhynchus

diplodocus

brontosaurus

brachiosaurus

allosaurus

Who sat on this throne?

On 4 November 1922 a British archaeologist named Howard Carter, who was working in the Valley of the Kings among the pyramids of Egypt, discovered a flight of steps which led to a royal tomb. When the tomb was opened, amazing treasures were revealed. This was the tomb of Tutankhamun, a young pharaoh or king of ancient Egypt who had died at the age of 18 in about 1346 BC. His tomb had been entered once soon after his death, and after that it had not been disturbed for over 3000 years.

The throne below, decorated with gold, stood in the first room of the tomb, along with chariots, weapons and other furniture. Beyond a closed door was another room, the burial chamber, where the body lay. It was inside four coffins, the first made of stone and the last made of solid gold. Two further chambers contained still more treasures and objects, including a model bakery and brewery to be used to make bread and beer for the pharaoh in the next world. Although not an important king, his tomb was enriched by the priests because he had ended the religious reforms of his predecessor Amenhotep IV.

Who were the Fascists?

After the First World War Italy was crippled by war losses, unemployment, inflation, strikes and violence. This led to conservative fears of a socialist revolution. Benito Mussolini (above) formed the Fascist Party in 1919 to combat left-wing groups. He became premier in 1922, and eventually dictator of Italy.

Mussolini, known as *Il Duce* by his followers, the blackshirts, terrorized and disposed of his opponents; he controlled the press, the courts and the unions. Fascism was anti-democratic and saw military strength as the basis of national pride. Hitler's Germany and Franco's Spain were also fascist states.

Mussolini was the natural ally of Hitler, and Italy entered the Second World War in 1940 with Germany. However, Mussolini fell from power after the Allied invason of Italy in 1943, and was eventually executed in 1945 by Italian resistance fighters.

When does the Sun stop shining?

All life on Earth depends on heat and light from the Sun, and if the Sun stopped shining the Earth would become a dead planet in a matter of days, if not hours. Today scientists are able to study the Sun in great detail. Several space satellites, especially those known as orbiting solar observatories, keep a close watch on our parent star, though they have not yet solved all the Sun's mysteries.

Among other things, the orbiting observatories can study the outer regions of the Sun's 'atmosphere', including the corona, a thin but faintly luminous layer of gas. The corona cannot be seen from the Earth's surface except when the Sun is totally eclipsed, as in the photograph below. An eclipse occurs when the Moon passes in front of the Sun and only lasts for a short time. A total eclipse is seen from an area covering only a small part of the Earth because the Moon's shadow projected on the Earth is no more than 300 km (185 miles) across.

What does a snowflake look like?

It is rather difficult to examine a snowflake, but they are extraordinary and beautiful things. They are made of crystals of ice stuck together. The crystals come in an endless variety of patterns, but snowflakes usually form in the shape of a six-pointed star.

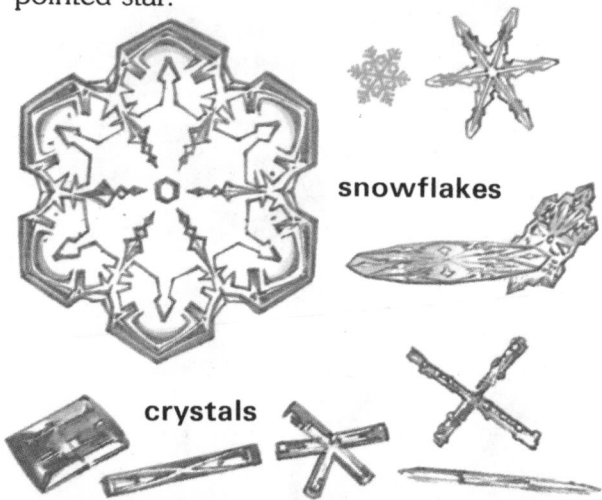

snowflakes

crystals

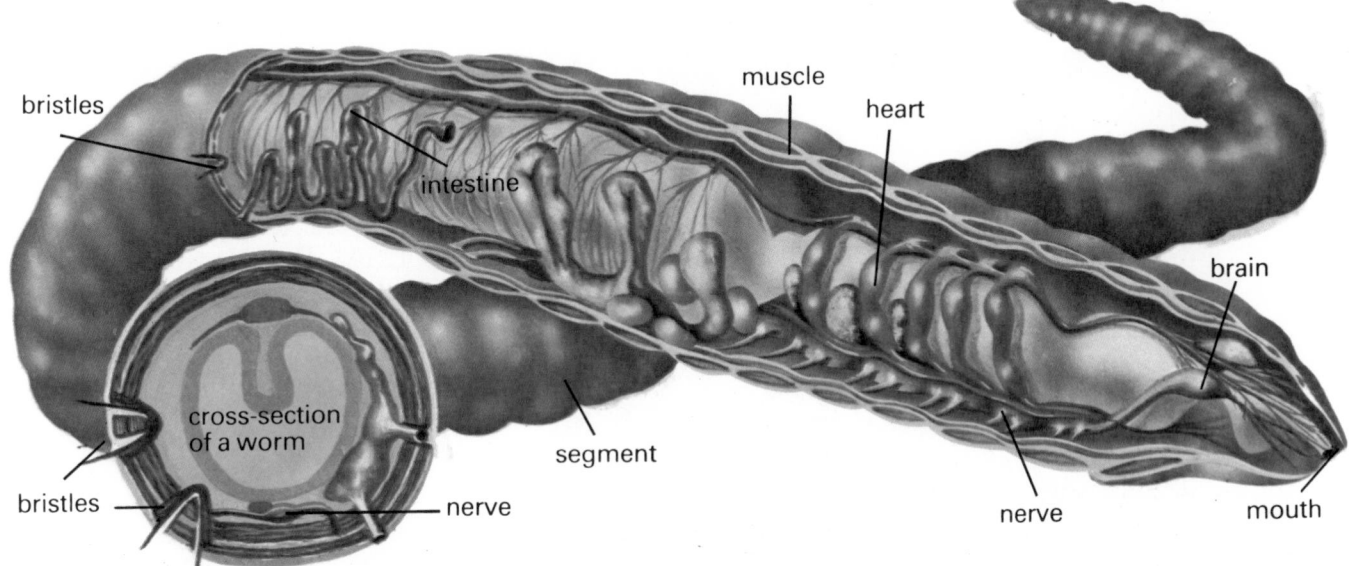

bristles
muscle
heart
intestine
brain
cross-section of a worm
bristles
nerve
segment
nerve
mouth

How do worms live?

The picture above shows the insides of an earthworm, much enlarged. (Below is a picture of the whole worm, about life size.) This is the type of worm you find when digging the garden. Earthworms have long, soft bodies which are divided into segments, or sections. They can stretch and contract, and that is how they move along. Tiny bristles stop them slipping backwards as they move through the soil.

Worms pass soil through their bodies working like little underground ploughs, and as there are a huge number – six or seven million in 1 ha (2½ acres) – they play an important part in keeping

the soil drained, aired and healthy. Worms are the food of many other creatures, such as moles and, of course, birds.

Worms come to the surface at night, and though they get some of their food from the soil, they also eat leaves. They spread digestive juices over the leaves to soften them and then suck them up.

The ragworm (bottom left) and the lugworm (bottom right) are bristle worms that live in sand or mud by the sea. The hairy ragworm is a favourite bait of fishermen. Unlike the earthworm it has powerful jaws, and eyes.

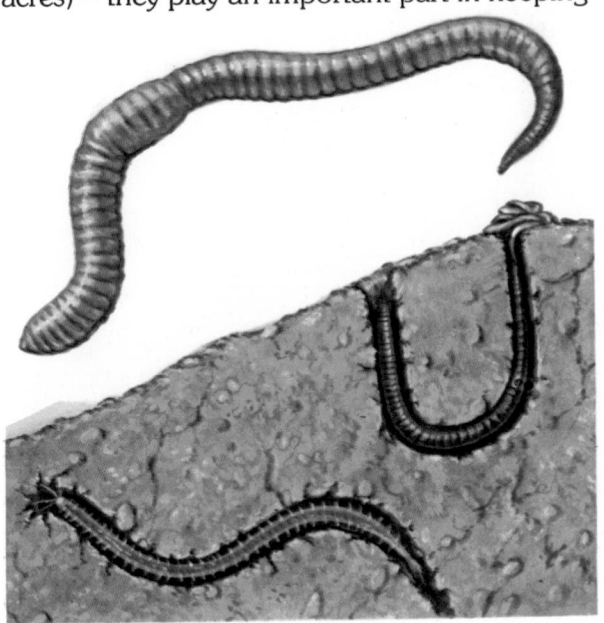

Quick Quiz

In what way are the following alike?
(1) Laika, (2) Yuri Gagarin, (3) John Glenn, (4) Neil Armstrong.

Answer: They all travelled in spacecraft (Laika was a Russian dog).

In what way are the following alike?
(1) Moles, (2) Rabbits, (3) Worms, (4) Badgers.

Answer: They all live partly underground.

What caused the American Civil War?

During the early 19th century strong rivalry developed between the Northern and Southern states of the USA. The North was largely industrial, while the South was entirely agricultural. Many Northerners were against slavery, but Southerners believed their way of life depended on it.

In 1860 the Republican Party chose Abraham Lincoln as its candidate for president. The Republicans were a new, Northern party and were against slavery. When Lincoln was elected, seven Southern states seceded, that is, they declared they were leaving the union of states which had been founded in 1776. President Lincoln (opposite, watching troop manoeuvres) would not permit the country to be split in two. When he attempted to maintain a garrison of Federal (Union) troops in Fort Sumter, South Carolina, one of the seceding states, soldiers of the South attacked the fort, thus starting the war.

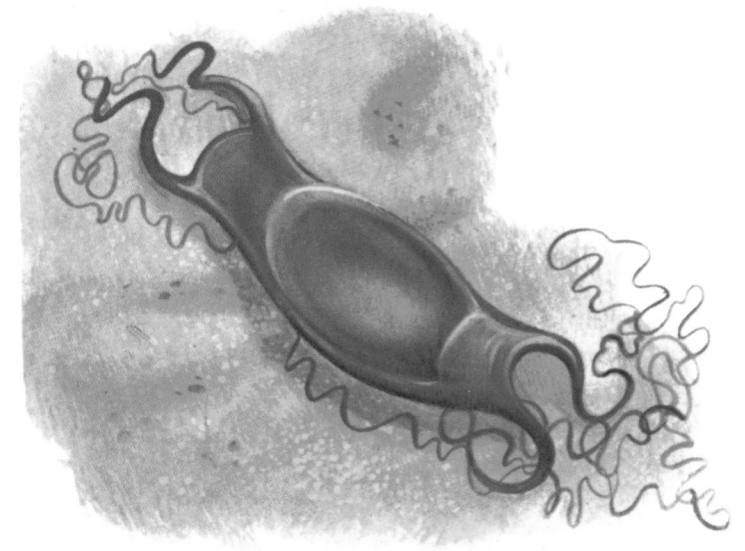

When was slavery ended?

As shown above, slaves in the American South were generally sold by auction. By the 19th century slavery was widely disliked – except by slave-owners – and it was one of the causes of the Civil War which began in 1861. On 1 January 1863 President Lincoln issued the Emancipation Proclamation, which ended slavery as a legal institution in the USA.

Where does a mermaid keep her cash?

The black, horny object above, with a spike or a long tendril at each corner, is common on the beach. It is called a mermaid's purse, and is actually the empty egg-case of a fish – a ray or a shark. The case grows around the egg inside the mother fish. After it leaves her body a tiny fish grows in the egg until, after about eight months, it is ready to break out.

What is a pipistrelle?

The pipistrelle above is the smallest bat found in Europe, with a body length up to 50 mm (2 in). It can be seen flying around at dusk, turning and twisting all the time as it chases the insects it catches in flight.

What is a Chinese junk?

The junk (below) is probably the oldest type of sailing vessel still in use today (you can see them in Hong Kong harbour). It has a flat bottom and a high stern. The sails are sometimes made of matting.

How do you blow up a boat?

All ships should carry lifeboats of some kind. This one above is an inflatable rubber liferaft, which can be stowed away in a small space until needed. It has a cover like a tent to protect its occupants from exposure to the weather.

Do hamsters have pockets?

The golden hamster (below) has roomy pouches in its cheeks, in which it carries the food or material for its nest. These animals were discovered in Syria only in this century. They are now very popular pets, despite their short tempers and sharp teeth!

Is it a plant, or is it an animal?

The creatures above are called sea cucumbers, but they are actually animals, not plants, and are related to starfish and sea urchins. Around their mouths are long tube-feet-like feelers.

Are there paddy fields in Ireland?

'Paddy' in this sense means rice (it has nothing to do with an Irishman called Patrick!). In mountainous countries of South-east Asia, the slopes are terraced (below) to enable rice to be grown on them.

What was the first jet?

Jet-propelled aircraft were foreseen by an RAF engineer, Frank Whittle, in the 1920s, and he designed the engine that powered the first British jet fighter in 1941. But the first jet plane to take to the air was the German Heinkel HE 178, in 1939. However, jet fighters were not used until 1944 and did not play an important part in the Second World War.

How did a knight fight?

Above is a full suit of armour as worn in the 15th century by an Italian *condottiere* (captain of a band of mercenaries, soldiers who fought for anyone who paid them). It was very uncomfortable and very sweaty. Think of fighting a battle under the Italian sun while covered in steel plates! Armoured knights fought on horseback, bashing away with such weapons as swords, lances, maces (spiked clubs), war hammers and daggers. Soldiers suffered from aching joints and pains in the back, caused by falls from their horses. Guns were soon to put an end to this type of fighting.

117

Why does a mole live in a hole?

Moles are perfectly adapted to life underground (below). Their velvety fur lets them slip easily through the tunnels they dig with their powerful forepaws. Earth shoveled out forms mole-hills. The mole has ear-holes instead of external ear flaps, which would get in the way. It doesn't need to see much and has tiny eyes. It builds a nest, called a fortress, for its young and its chief food is earthworms, which it eats in colossal numbers.

mole-hill

nest

tunnel

What do we get from trees?

In spite of plastics and other artificial materials, wood is still best for making many things, from furniture to matchsticks. Paper too is usually made from wood (below). The wood is first made into pulp. It is mixed with various other ingredients and lots of water. The mixture passes in a layer over a wire mesh, which drains off the water. Then it is pressed, heated and rolled until it emerges as a long sheet of paper.

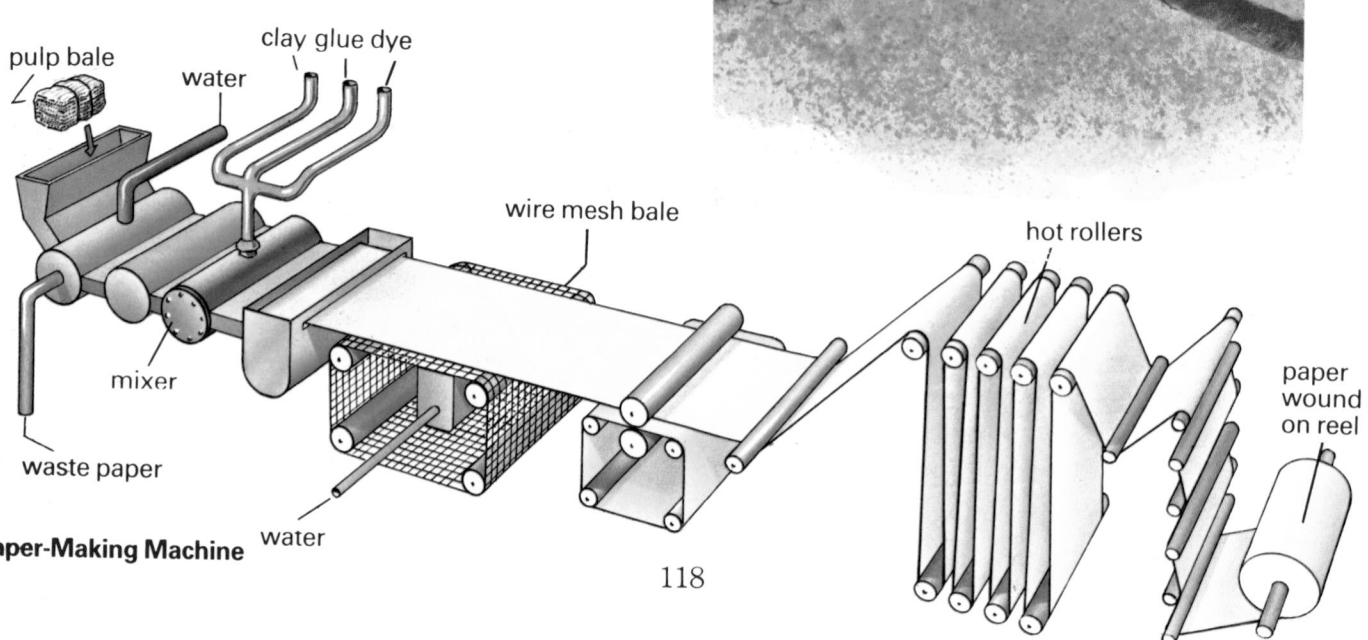

pulp bale

clay glue dye

water

waste paper

mixer

wire mesh bale

hot rollers

paper wound on reel

Paper-Making Machine

water

118

Why do plants have green leaves and flowers?

This wild rose (below) is a good example of the huge number of flowering plants which are so important to our planet. They provide food and shelter for an enormous variety of animals. Most plants are green because they contain a chemical called chlorophyll. Chlorophyll traps energy from sunlight and enables the plant to convert carbon dioxide from the air and water from the soil into sugar, which is food for the plant.

Flowers are the breeding organs of plants, and pollen from one flower needs to be transferred to another flower in order to produce fruit and seeds. The petals and scent of flowers attract insects, which carry the pollen on their legs (see page 122). Fruit, with the seeds inside, grow from fertlized flowers and may be eaten by animals.

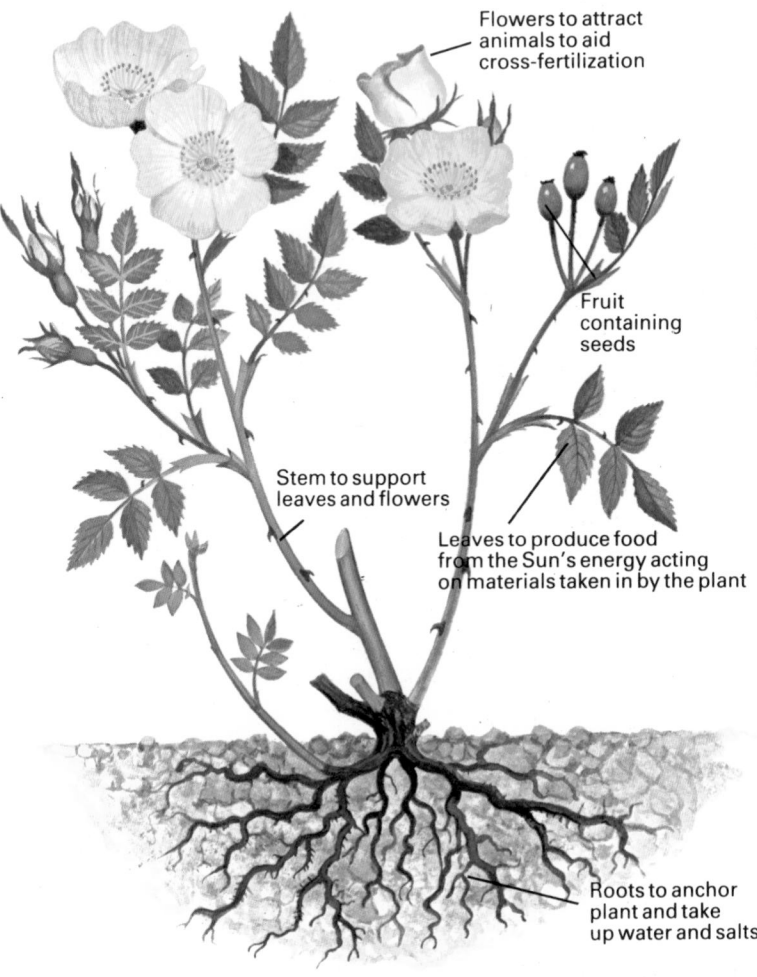

Flowers to attract animals to aid cross-fertilization

Fruit containing seeds

Stem to support leaves and flowers

Leaves to produce food from the Sun's energy acting on materials taken in by the plant

Roots to anchor plant and take up water and salts

How was this rock formed?

Beside the gate of the old town of Le Puy in the Auvergne (southern France), the church (above) stands perched high on an isolated rock. Built nearly a thousand years ago, it is reached by a staircase of 271 steps. This is a region of volcanic mountains, and the rocky pillar on which the church stands is the 'plug' or 'neck' of an ancient volcano. Once there was a cone-shaped hill here, but the slopes were worn away by time and weather, leaving only the hard core of solidified lava which had filled up the central vent of the volcano.

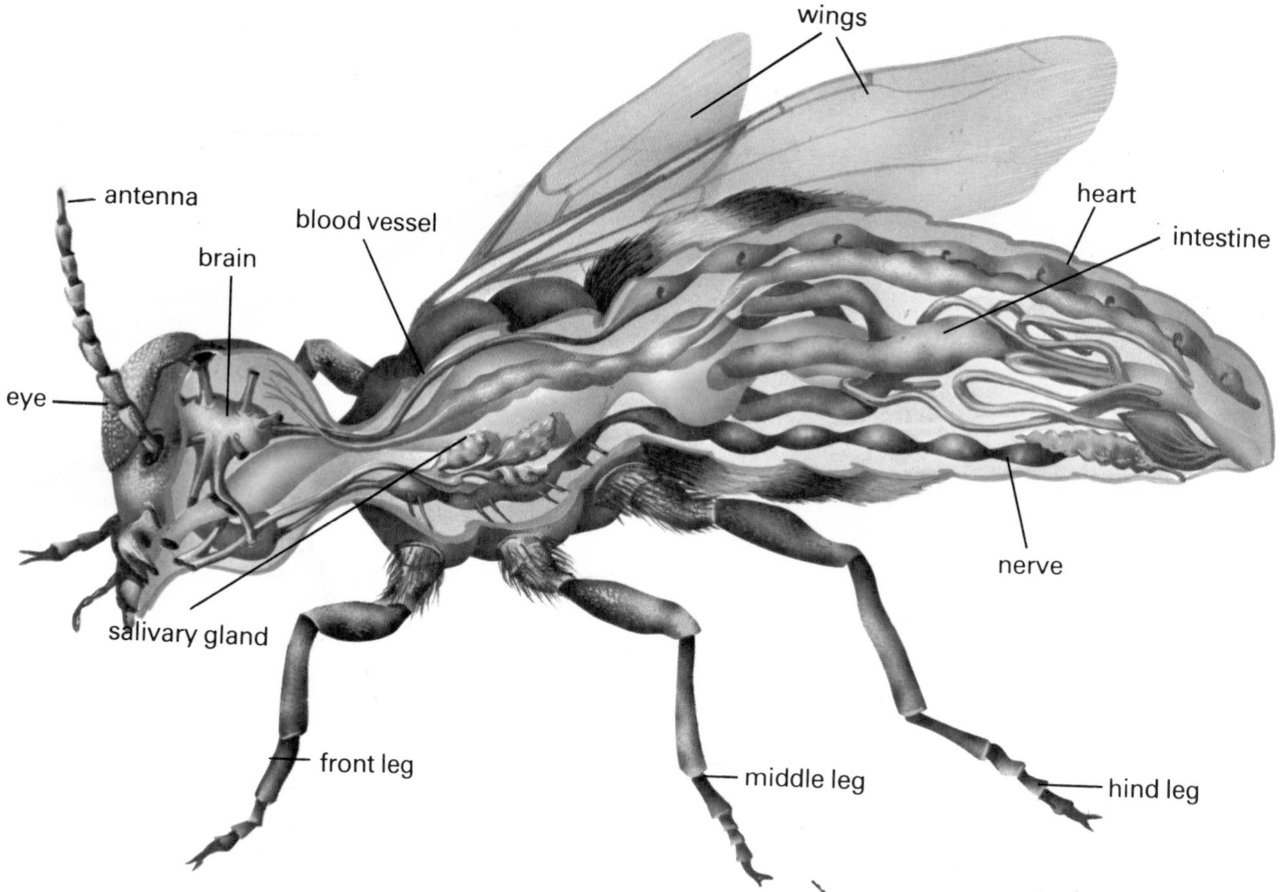

Diagram labels (clockwise from top):

wings

heart

intestine

antenna

blood vessel

brain

eye

nerve

salivary gland

front leg

middle leg

hind leg

What is an insect?

Insects belong to a class of animal which has a body in three sections (head, thorax or chest, and abdomen or stomach) and three pairs of legs. Most have a single pair of antennae, or 'feelers', and many have one or two pairs of wings. The drawing above shows the sturcture of a typical winged insect.

Insects are the most successful form of life on Earth. Over three-quarters of all known types of animal are insects; in fact there are more different kinds of insects than all other living things put together, including plants. Nearly one million species are known, although the true figure is probably twice that.

Not only are there a lot of types, there are a lot of individual insects of each type. As many as 24 000 aphids have been found on one tomato plant and over half a million ants in a single colony.

On the right are three insects you may have seen around the house: earwig (top), clothes moth (middle) and silverfish (bottom).

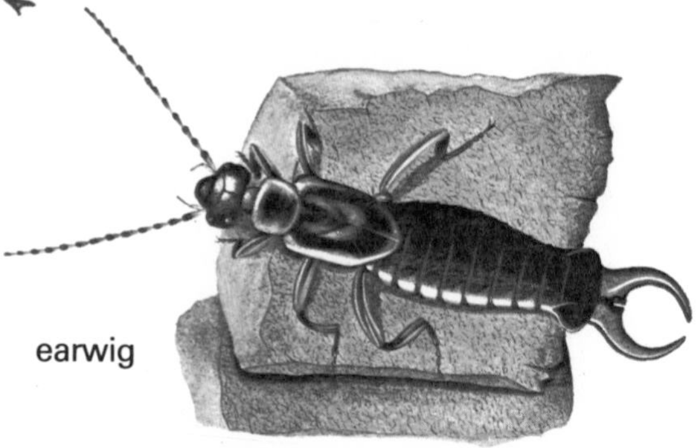

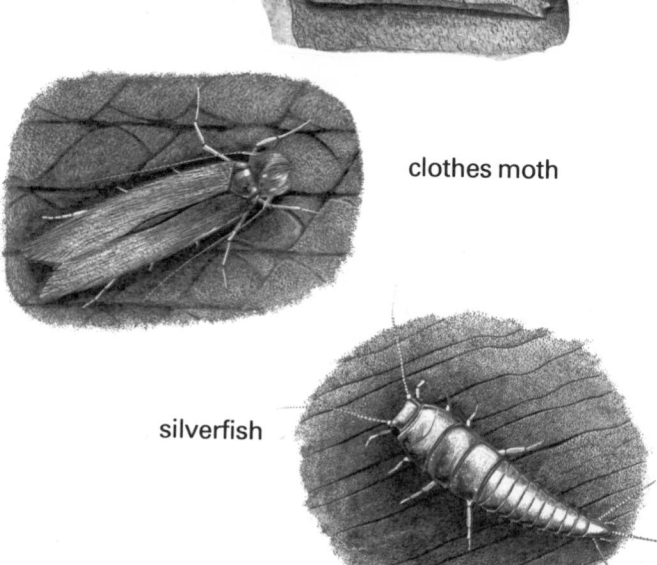

earwig

clothes moth

silverfish

What was buried at Sutton Hoo?

Sutton Hoo, near the Suffolk coast of England, is the site of an Anglo-Saxon ship-burial which took place about the middle of the 7th century. The ship (below), which was probably made specially for this ceremony, contained great treasures, including a helmet, a clasp and the lid of a purse in gold and ivory (far right, top to bottom). Ship-burials are known in other places, and the Sutton Hoo burial was probably a

memorial for a king who had died elsewhere, perhaps at sea.

The Sutton Hoo treasure was discovered in 1939 and is the most valuable archaeological discovery made in Britain. Historians were astounded at the evidence it contained of international trade (one plate came from Byzantium, now Istanbul in Turkey; the helmet is Swedish) and of the fine native craftsmanship at so early a period in English history. The ship itself had rotted away, but the nails were held in position by the sand, and it was possible to reconstruct the shape of the vessel.

Quick Quiz

Who were the original inhabitants of the following countries?
(1) New Zealand, (2) North America, (3) Peru, (4) Australia.

Answers: (1) the Maoris, who arrived from Hawaii and Tahiti about AD 1300, (2) the North American Indians, descended from people who migrated from Asia, (3) the Incas, a highly civilized race of South American Indians, (4) the Aborigines, an ancient race of stone-age people.

What is a meteorite?

Meteors and meteorites are chunks of rock flying through space. Occasionally, a very large meteorite hits the Earth (smaller objects burn up in the atmosphere). The crater below, in Arizona, was made by a meteorite in prehistoric times. No traces remain except the hole 1 km (0.6 miles) across, but it must have weighed about 50 000 tonnes.

Why are flowers pretty?

Flowering plants produce blossoms which usually look beautiful and often smell nice as well. When the flower is still a bud, it is protected by small hard leaves called sepals. The most important parts of the flower (see below) are the stamens, which are little 'boxes' of pollen on stalks, and the ovary, which is a collection of ovules, often in their own little containers. From the ovules the seeds will grow. But before seeds can develop, the ovules must be fertilized by pollen. Sometimes this can be done by pollen from the same flower, but often the pollen must come from another plant.

Pollen is often carried from one flower to another by insects like bees or butterflies. When an insect is attracted to the flower by its colour and smell, and by the nectar on which it feeds, pollen sticks to it. When the insect flies to another flower, pollen is, with luck, brushed off on to the ovary. Then a very small tube grows from each pollen grain through the ovary wall. Fertilization is completed when the pollen grain is united with an ovule.

stamen

petal

sepal

all these make the ovary

How many elephants?

There are two types of elephant: the Indian or Asiatic and the African or bush elephant (below). The African is larger, has bigger ears and tusks, and has two 'fingers' instead of one at the end of its trunk.

However, there are two different subspecies of the African elephant: the bush elephant and the much smaller forest elephant.

Indian elephant

African elephant

lives in hot, dry plains

lives in shady forests   smaller ears

large ears which are fanned to keep it cool

tip of trunk has two fingers

tip of trunk has one finger

Where does this warrior come from?

The man on the right is a tribesman from New Guinea, where Europeans are recent arrivals and in some ways life has not changed much for centuries. At one time, the tribes of New Guinea were at war with each other almost all the time, and some fighting between different groups probably still goes on in remote parts. There are still villages where all the men sleep in one building, and the women and pigs in another. New Guinea is a large island north of Australia covered by high mountain ranges and dense jungle, making some areas very difficult to reach.

123

Who said that?

Of all 'talking' birds, the mynah (above) is the most talented. It is a member of the starling family; the variety usually kept as a pet is the Indian hill mynah. A bird that 'talks' is of course just imitating sounds it hears; it does not understand speech.

What was the Spirit of St Louis?

This was the aircraft in which the American pilot Charles Lindbergh made the first solo flight across the Atlantic. He left New York at 7.52 am on 20 May 1927 and landed at Le Bourget airport near Paris 33 hours and 39 minutes later.

Who drives a Chieftain?

Below is the modern equivalent of a knight in armour, the British Army's Chieftain tank. It weighs 51 tonnes and has a top speed of 40 km/h (25 mph). Its 120-mm gun fires shells that can penetrate practically anything. To find the range, the gunner fires a machine gun which is linked to the main gun, and when the target is found the gun is automatically ranged. A stabilizing system keeps the gun trained on the target even when the tank is moving over rough country. The tank has a crew of four: commander, gunner, loader-operator and driver. If necessary, they can seal themselves inside their armoured vehicle and continue operating it for two or three days. There is even room for two of the crew to lie down and rest.

There are tanks larger than the Chieftain, but a tank which weighed over 70 tonnes would be of little use. It would sink in soft ground and crash through most bridges.

Does a Surveyor have three legs?

In the 1960s the Americans planned to put an astronaut on the Moon with their Apollo space programme. In preparation for this they set up two unmanned Moon-probe programmes to investigate the surface of the Moon specifically for the Apollo landings. One was the series of five Lunar Orbiter probes which mapped in detail the entire surface of the Moon, aiding the choice of landing sites for the astronauts. The other programme comprised the Surveyor lunar landers (below).

The Surveyors had the same type of landing system, using rockets to reduce the rate of fall, as the piloted Mooncraft used later, and they stood on the surface on three legs. Seven Surveyors were sent to the Moon in all, though two failed. They had television cameras and a mechanical scoop, for taking samples of the soil, besides other instruments, which showed that the surface of the Moon was safe for human beings.

Who was Churchill?

Winston Churchill (above) was British Prime Minister during the Second World War. Many people would say he was the greatest leader the British ever had. He was already 66 years old when he became Prime Minister in 1940, and had been in politics nearly 40 years. But his energy and determination during the next five years were colossal. He was not always right about military matters, but his powerful personality brought Britain through the war.

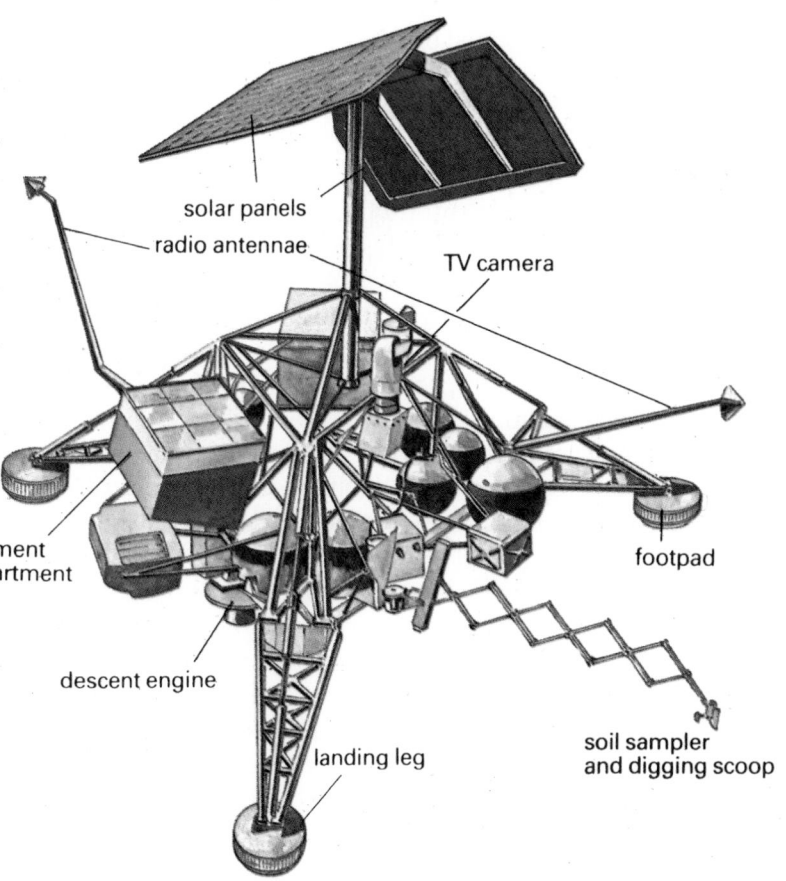

solar panels
radio antennae
TV camera
instrument compartment
footpad
descent engine
soil sampler and digging scoop
landing leg

125

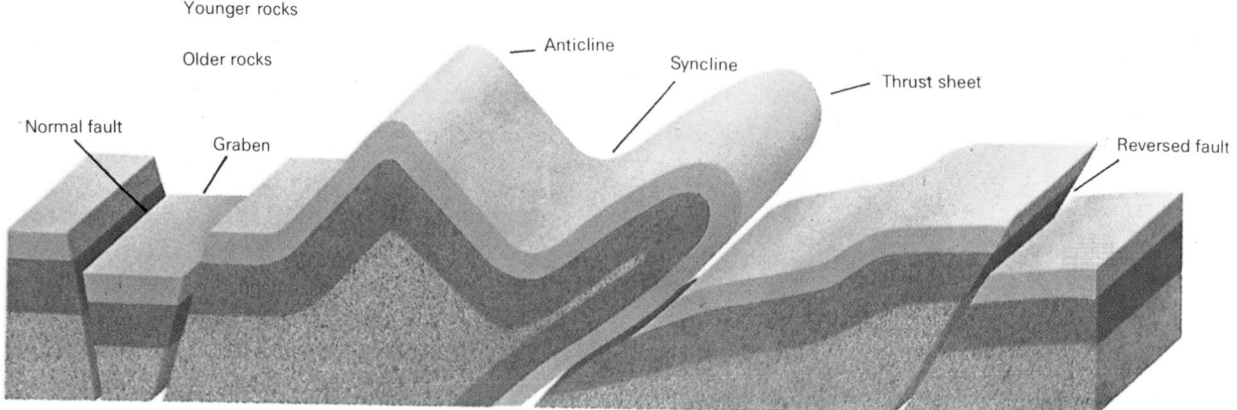

Younger rocks

Older rocks

Anticline

Syncline

Thrust sheet

Normal fault

Graben

Reversed fault

What causes mountains and valleys?

The Earth is roughly the shape of a ball, but, unlike the surface of a ball, its surface is not smooth. The bumps and dents, including high mountain ranges and deep ocean trenches, are caused by the powerful forces inside the Earth, which can bend and break the comparatively thin layer of rocks which form the Earth's crust.

Formations which are caused by the surface rocks bending under strain are called folds. When an actual break occurs, it is called a fault. These folds and faults are of several different types (above). A simple upward fold which makes a ridge is an anticline. A downward fold which makes a trough is a syncline. Beds of rock can be transported great distances by folding, producing enormous mountain ranges. If the rock layers of the Alps were flattened out, Italy would be 100 km (60 miles) longer. A 'normal' fault is caused by tension. A 'reversed' fault is caused by compression; the slope of a reversed fault is usually less steep than that of a normal fault. Where a whole section of rock sinks between two parallel faults it is called a rift valley or a 'graben'. The Great Rift Valley in East Africa is a famous example.

As a rule these folds and faults take place over a long period of time. In fact they are going on at present all over the planet, so slowly that we do not notice them. Sometimes a fault occurs very quickly, in a matter of seconds or minutes, when rocks under strain suddenly snap. This produces an earthquake. In the past, whole cities have been destroyed by earthquakes.

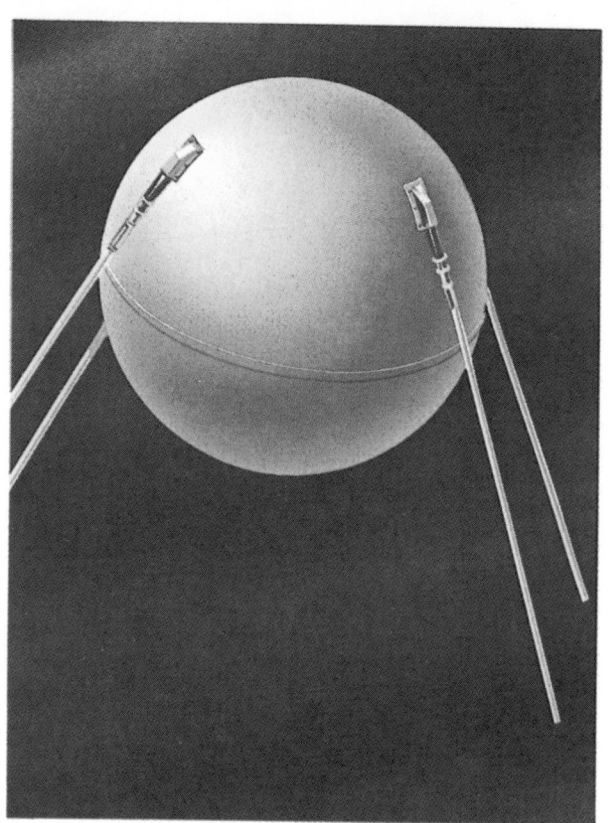

When did the Space Age begin?

If the Space Age can be said to have started on one particular day, that day was 4 October 1957, when the first man-made satellite was placed in orbit around the Earth. Weighing only a few kilogrammes, it was the Soviet Union's Sputnik I (above). Even though it did not perform any other function, it showed that it was possible to put craft into space.

126

Who signed Magna Carta?

Magna Carta, the 'Great Charter', was a royal charter signed – unwillingly – by King John of England (who reigned from 1199 to 1216) in 1215 at Runnymede, near Windsor (below). It marked a defeat of the monarchy by the barons – the great landowning families who at that time were the only class of people with political power. The opposition to the monarchy had been growing for some time. John distrusted everyone except a small number of courtiers, many of them foreigners, and the barons wanted more influence. The crisis was brought to a head by John's failures in war, his high taxes and his unreliable behaviour.

Some of the questions the charter dealt with were unimportant, such as the right to put fish traps in the River Thames. In general, the charter tried to control the King's power to demand money or seize property more or less as he liked. In this and other ways, it attempted to make the monarchy subject to law.

The barons were only concerned with their own welfare. Neither they nor the King spared a thought for the mass of the people, who had no power. All the same, Magna Carta can be seen as an early attempt to establish the rights of the king's subjects according to fundamental law. This idea of the charter was strongly held by American colonists 500 years later and influenced the constitution of the USA.

Do you love *all* animals?

The tsetse fly (below) is a blood-sucking fly that looks very like its relation, the common housefly. It lives in Africa south of the Sahara and is the carrier of an unpleasant, sometimes fatal, disease called sleeping sickness, which affects people and animals. One result is that in the 'Tsetse Belt' (a large region) it is impossible to raise cattle or other livestock.

Tapeworms (bottom) are parasites which live in the bowels of people and animals. They attach their head to the wall of the stomach with hooks and suckers. Some tapeworms have been known to reach a length of 3 m (10 ft). Sections of the ribbon-like body often break off, but if the head survives, so does the tapeworm. Parasites in general are very unpleasant – those associated with people include fleas, lice and leeches.

How did the English lose an empire to a woman?

Medieval kings of England also claimed the French throne, a cause of constant warfare. The greatest leader in the later stages of the Hundred Years' War was a French peasant girl, Joan of Arc (Jeanne d'Arc, 1412–31). Joan (above) had visions of saints who told her she must rescue France from its suffering, and in 1429 she persuaded the Dauphin Charles to give her command of troops to help the besieged city of Orléans. She roused the spirits of the citizens and drove off the English. More victories followed, enabling the Dauphin to be crowned Charles VII, before she was captured and handed over to the English who accused her of being a witch. After a famous trial, Joan was condemned and burned at the stake.

But she had fired the French with patriotism: by 1453 the English had lost all their French territory except for Calais.

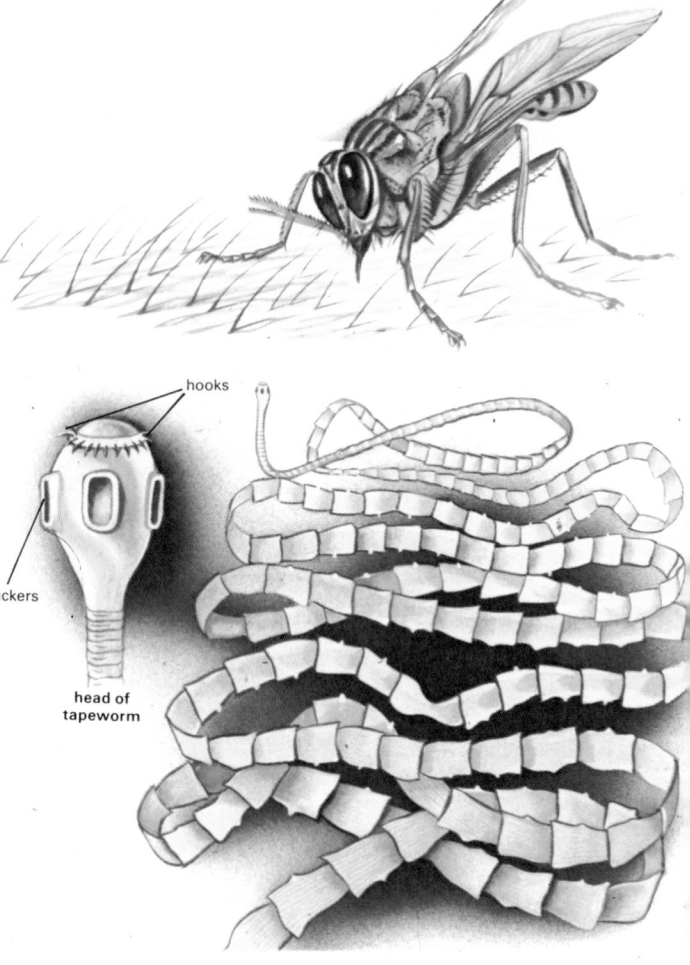

hooks

suckers

head of tapeworm

Who invented writing?

The Sumerians (below) were people who lived in the Middle East between four and six thousand years ago. They began to use a picture form of writing in about 3800 BC. A thousand years later they developed a written script, using symbols (left). They also made pottery, and invented the potter's wheel, on which clay vessels such as bowls could be turned to a regular shape. They were also skilful farmers and built great cities.

Why has this aeroplane got a swollen nose?

The strange protuberance on the nose of the aircraft on the right contains radar equipment which can track the movements of other aircraft. 'Radar' is short for 'radio detection and range finding'. It can locate objects much farther away than the eye can see by means of radio 'echoes'. Radio waves are transmitted by the radar, and can be reflected back by large objects, especially metal ones. These 'echoes' can be seen as light signals on a screen.

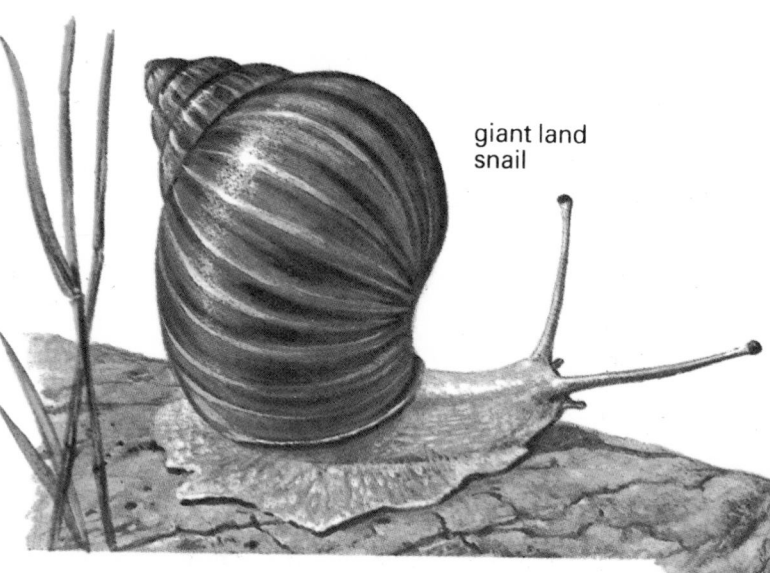

giant land snail

three-toothed snail

black slug

garden snail

white or sandhill snail

Can you find molluscs in a garden?

Molluscs are animals with soft bodies and hard shells, and we expect to find plenty of them at the seaside. They include, of course, all the shellfish, and even such animals as the squid and octopus which have 'internal' shells. But there are molluscs on land too, like the snail and slug (a shell-less snail), though some snails live in the sea or in freshwater. Snails have coiled shells into which they pull their whole body. Their tongues have rows of tiny teeth and they eat by using it to rasp away at soft plants. This makes them very unpopular with gardeners!

Rye

Barley

Maize

Wheat

What can tractors do?

The tractor below is ploughing a field, which is probably its most important work. But tractors have hundreds of uses, not only on the farm but also in road-building, hauling timber, and many other industrial jobs.

The first tractors were built about 100 years ago: they were heavy, steam-driven machines that were often used simply as stationary sources of power for machines such as threshers and pumps. Some modern tractors have large rear wheels and small front wheels close together (almost a tricycle) to make it easier to cultivate crops sown in rows. Large tractors today run on diesel fuel; smaller ones often have petrol engines.

Are cereals good for you?

The cereals are plants. Breakfast cereals are just one of the foods made from them. There are six cereal plants: rice (grown mainly in tropical countries), wheat, maize (or sweetcorn), barley, rye and oats. As far as human beings are concerned, these plants – members of the grass family – are the most important. Their dried fruits, which we call grain, provide most of our food. Even animals raised to provide meat are often fed on cereals.

Wheat is probably the oldest crop; it was being grown over 5000 years ago. Maize is American in origin and was unknown in Europe or Asia until about 1500. Rice, the chief food of southern Asia, is the third main cereal crop. Barley, rye and oats are minor cereals which will grow in cooler climates and poorer soils.

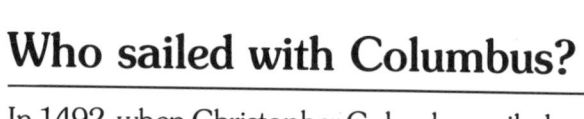

Who sailed with Columbus?

In 1492, when Christopher Columbus sailed on the voyage which ended with the discovery of America, people were very religious. They believed that everything happened according to God's will, and God was always present in their words and thoughts. Sailors, whose life was so dangerous, were perhaps more religious than most. On Columbus's ships (above) the day started with a boy singing:

> *Blessed be the light of day*
> *And the Holy Cross, we say.*

After that he said the Lord's Prayer and the *Ave Maria*. Every hour was marked by another religious chant, and each day after sunset the whole crew attended evening prayers.

Who was Adolphe Sax?

In the 19th century the French army wanted a new brass instrument for military bands. So in 1841 Adolphe Sax, a well-known instrument maker, invented the saxophone. They come in various sizes (above) and are used mostly in jazz and dance bands, seldom in symphony orchestras.

Illustration captions:

axe head, encrusted
with silver wire

axe head

damascened spearhead

How did the Vikings fight?

The main weapons of the Danes and Norsemen
(above) who invaded Britain and Europe in the
9th century were iron swords, axes and spears.
They wore helmets but little armour, though the
man with the plaited beard has a coat of mail
(iron links sewn together). Axe- and spearheads
were sometimes damascened – inlaid with silver
wire. The Vikings also sometimes carried a long
knife called a *seax*, and a round shield.

With their magnificent longships, the Vikings
were able to attack places all over Europe, and to
reach Iceland and Newfoundland. Driven by
oars and sail, Viking ships had a keel which
made them stable in rough seas.

Is this the first trumpet?

Known as a *lur*, the ancient horn below was
blown in Scandinavia about 2500 years ago.
Made of bronze, it was discovered at the bottom
of a Danish bog. Such instruments were probably used in some kind of religious ceremony.
One possible explanation of its strange shape is
that its ancestors were made from the tusks of
mammoths. We know that, much later, horns
were made from elephant tusks.

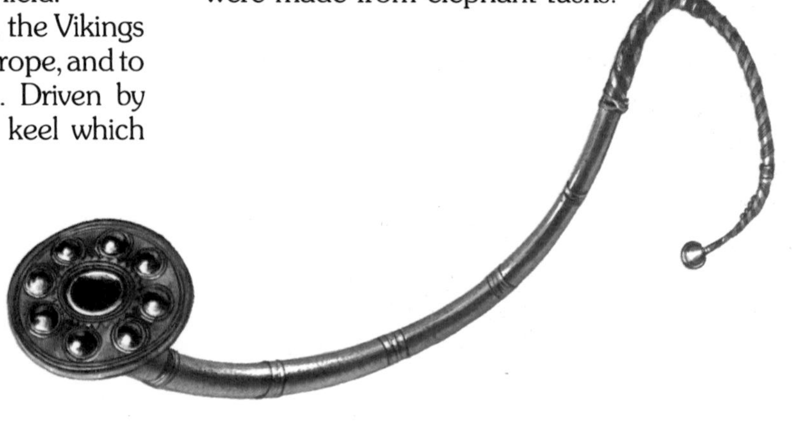

Who lives in these buildings?

The simple thatched house on stilts above is the home of a fisherman's family in Thailand. A wooden 'box' (often of bamboo which is cheap and easy to work) with a thatched roof was a typical dwelling in many parts of South-east Asia. The walls were either lashed together or held with wooden battens. The people inside sometimes slept on shelves. Below is a village in Botswana, with the small, round houses which were at one time found in many southern African countries. The large forked sticks support the smaller sticks of the roof, which was often thatched.

In complete contrast to these simple dwellings is the 'skyscraper' office block, made of glass on a steel frame, in a North American city. Such modern buildings are dependent on other modern inventions such as lifts, central heating and air conditioning, besides the materials from which they are made.

Where could you see these machines?

The machines below and right are all farm machines, but the only one you would see on a farm today is the combine harvester on the right. This machine cuts the ripe crop and threshes it, separating the grain from the straw. Some combine harvesters not only sort the grain into a bin but also tie the straw up in neat bales.

You would have to travel back in time a century or so to see the other two machines at work. The top one is a horse-drawn plough. A horse or pair of horses (or oxen) did the heavy work of pulling, while a man walked behind, holding the two handles and guiding the blade

of the plough to cut a single furrow. The plough had been in existence for thousands of years, but in the 18th century it was improved by the addition of the metal blade and wheels at the back.

Below the plough is a seed drill for sowing seed in rows. Before this machine was invented, seed was scattered by hand. That wasted a lot of seed – birds ate a great deal of it – and it was impossible to cultivate the growing plants by weeding between the rows. The seed drill made furrows with an iron share and the seed dropped from the bins, called hoppers, into the furrows. A

rake at the back covered the seeds with soil – no more free bird food – as the drill moved on. The seed drill was invented by Jethro Tull and first used in 1701. It was one of many improvements in agriculture which allowed a much greater amount of food to be grown in Britain in the 18th century.

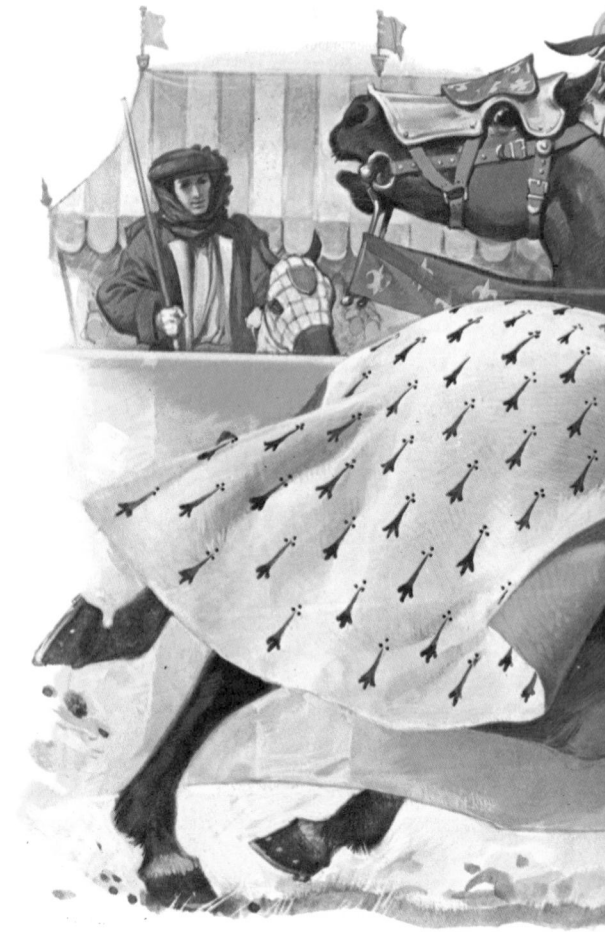

136

Was a joust just a joke?

The tournaments of the Middle Ages were competitions which were partly practice for battle and partly an aristocratic sport. When they started in the 12th century, they were mainly military – a chance for knights to show what brave and skilful warriors they were. Men could be killed or badly injured. Tournaments were condemned by the Church, and King Henry II of England also banned them, perhaps fearing that so many armed knights and barons gathered in one place might use it as an opportunity to rebel. Some knights travelled from country to country, challenging anyone to fight.

As time went by, jousting (as the form of duelling illustrated below was called) became more of an entertainment. Music and dancing were part of the tournament. Weapons were adapted to prevent serious injury (though some still happened). The jousters were separated by a 'tilt', a wooden barrier covered with cloth, and the point of the lance was replaced by a coronall (a crown-shaped tip). The idea was to knock your opponent off his horse, not injure him.

Jousting was taken up by the lower classes too. Young Londoners arranged team combats at Smithfield on Sundays during Lent.

What lives in temperate forests?

Temperate means 'moderate', neither too hot nor too cold. Most of Western Europe has a temperate climate, as does much of Canada and the USA, Japan and eastern China, New Zealand, and parts of Australia and South America. In temperate woods and forests, most of the trees are deciduous, losing their leaves in autumn. Common trees of this kind are oaks (the owl on the far right is perching in an oak tree), beeches, maples (especially in North America) and silver birches, with their silvery-white trunks. The trees are less dense than in a tropical rain forest (see page 102), and below them grow shrubs and smaller plants, including many wild flowers.

In a temperate climate there are four distinct

seasons – spring, summer, autumn and winter. The picture below shows a wood in the different seasons. In winter the woods look dead; the trees are bare, there are no flowers blooming and you will see fewer animals.

When spring comes and the weather becomes warmer, buds on the trees and shrubs start to sprout, and flowers begin to grow. Most animals have their young about this time. Summer is the time when plants grow most quickly and produce their fruit. Most animals busy themselves raising their young.

In autumn the leaves of the trees begin to turn brown, red and yellow, and eventually fall to the ground.

For more facts about the animals of temperate forests, see the next two pages.

Animals of temperate forests

You might see nearly all the animals in the picture on the previous two pages in the same wood, although you would have to be both very observant and very lucky. Most of them are quite common in north-western Europe.

Deer

The biggest British wild animal is the red deer. The male is easily recognized by his fine antlers, which are shed and regrown each year. Red deer are common enough in private estates, but in the wild they live on treeless moors. There are two other deer which, like the red deer, are more common in parks than in wild forests. The fallow deer has a reddish-brown coat with white patches (actually, they vary a great deal, some being almost black, some white). The male has wide, flat antlers. Roe deer are the smallest and shyest deer. They are reddish-brown with a white patch around the tail. The male has rather small, spiked antlers.

red fox

Weasels, foxes and badgers

Though you may easily see a weasel or a stoat in a European wood, you are less likely to see another member of this family, the polecat, which is less common. Polecats are really wild ferrets, though ferrets have been bred so long in captivity that they have become a different animal. Another member of the weasel family is the marten, a brilliant tree-climber which hunts squirrels and other animals, leaping acrobatically from branch to branch.

The largest hunter of the woodlands is the red fox. The fox has few enemies except man; it is, of course, the quarry of hunters. Fox hunters sometimes defend themselves by saying that if it were not for their interest in this animal, the fox would become extinct in the English countryside. However, the fox has shown that it can look after itself by taking up residence in towns as well as woods and fields. Foxes are now more often seen in the suburbs than they are in the country!

The badger is a hunter of a different kind. It is a shy animal, and in daylight hardly ever emerges from its set – the system of tunnels in which it lives. Its quiet habits have helped it survive in quite large numbers in Europe, despite the horrid (and illegal) 'sport' of sending terriers into their sets to kill them, or the government policy of poisoning them with gas in places where, it is said, they infect cattle with disease. Badgers have another advantage in their fight for survival: they will eat a great variety of things, fruit and berries as well as small animals, worms and even insects.

Small mammals

Rabbits and squirrels are perhaps the best-known inhabitants of the woodlands. Some

fallow deer

years ago, wild rabbits came near to extinction in parts of Europe as a result of a disease called myxomatosis, but they are now as common as they ever were. The disease spread quickly because of the way rabbits live – in a system of burrows called a warren. Since the epidemic, some rabbits have taken to living above ground. A female rabbit, or doe, can have up to 12 babies at a time and often has two or more litters a year. So the population soon builds up!

The most common types of squirrel in temperate woods are the red squirrel of Europe and Asia, and the grey squirrel of North America. For some reason grey and red squirrels will not share the same environment, and in much of England, where the grey squirrel was introduced, the red squirrel has disappeared. In Europe, the grey is almost unknown – at present!

Although they may not be easily seen except by a very careful and silent observer, the woods contain a very large number of small rodents. The common shrew is only about 70 mm (2¾ in) long, including its long, pointed snout but not its tail. It is dark brown and furry, lighter – almost white in fact – underneath, and it has a shrill, squeaking voice when excited about something. There are no shrews in Ireland, but they are common throughout most of the rest of Europe.

The vole is larger than the shrew and also fairly dark in colour, though this varies. It looks more like a mouse, but has a rounder, blunter head and a shorter tail.

Among several kinds of mice, perhaps the best known is the dormouse. The dormouse hibernates during winter, as its name suggests (in French *dormir* means to sleep), making itself a comfortable nest of dry grass and leaves.

Frogs and toads

Among the cold-blooded creatures of the woods, the commonest are probably frogs and toads. They live somewhere not too far from water, as they are amphibians – creatures which live partly on land and partly in water. Toads are better adapted to life on land than are frogs, but both must return to the water to breed. Neither are very quick-moving animals but they have long, sticky tongues which flick out fast enough to catch insects in flight.

purple emperor butterfly

Insects

Of the thousands of different insects which live in the woods, the most beautiful are surely the butterflies. The tortoiseshell, reddish-orange with black markings, is one of the easiest to recognize, being equally common in private gardens. You would be lucky to see the splendid purple emperor or the bright yellow brimstone butterfly.

Birds

The woods at dawn on a spring morning are, in the words of the song, 'alive with music' – the music of dozens of species of birds. Among them are such favourites as the blackbird and the robin; the robin's bright appearance and reasonably friendly nature make it a welcome creature on cold winter days. Wrens are tiny but very active, and are easily identified by their cocked tails. They forage in the undergrowth for food.

Where there are trees you would expect to find woodpeckers, although the greater spotted woodpecker is less common than the green. Sometimes you will hear it drumming on a tree but without seeing it among the leaves.

Like the woodpeckers, owls are more often heard than seen. They tend to be most active in twilight and at night, their highly sensitive ears and eyes and silent flight making them deadly hunters. Most owls are dark coloured, but the barn owl is almost white and looks quite ghostly when seen at night.

barn owl

What is a conifer?

A coniferous tree is a tree that bears cones, which contain seeds or pollen. Most of them are evergreen, keeping their leaves all through the year. The leaves are narrow spines, often called needles. There are about 520 different species of conifer. The great coniferous forests of pine, fir and spruce grow in fairly cold regions, but conifers also grow in warm lands and some, like the cedar or the cypress, prefer warm conditions.

Some well-known conifers are pictured here. The Douglas fir is a North American tree, also called the Oregon pine, among other names. The Norway spruce is the usual Christmas tree and the sitka spruce, another American, is often planted in Scotland. The cedars of Lebanon are famous from the Bible (there are still some left). and the European larch is unusual among conifers because it loses its leaves in autumn.

Conifers are often called softwoods because they produce timber which is soft by comparison with that of trees such as maple, oak, mahogany and cherry (the hardwoods). Because conifers grow quickly, they provide 80 per cent of the world's timber and are often planted on open heathland which can't be used for farming.

Common toad

Midwife toad

What's wrong with toads?

If someone calls you a toad, you feel insulted. But if someone called you a frog, you would probably just feel surprised. Toads may have got their bad name because in former times people believed they were poisonous. Also, they have a rough, warty skin which makes them less attractive than frogs. The midwife toad gained its name because the male carries the eggs on his back until they hatch.

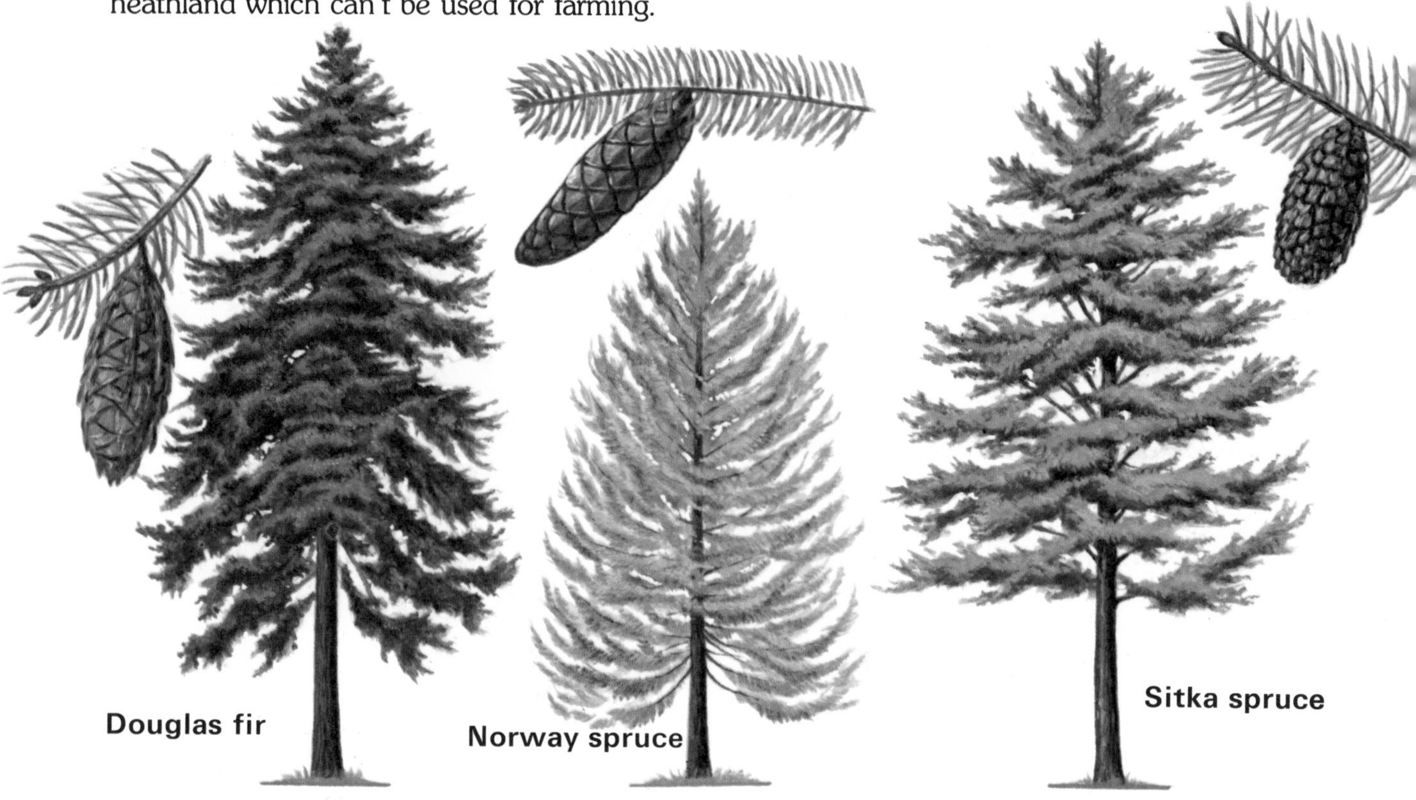

Douglas fir

Norway spruce

Sitka spruce

What happened to the trams?

For many years the most common public transport in cities was the tram (below right). A cross between a bus and a train, it ran on tracks in the street. Early motor cars, like this Rolls Royce (below left), gave London trams a wide berth. A collision with a tram was no joke.

Trams have disappeared almost completely, but city transport authorities are now beginning to adopt the light rapid transit vehicle (or LRTV). This looks like a tram but runs on its own rail system, like an underground train. It has the advantage of being much cheaper to build and run than a conventional railway. An LRTV system was opened in the early 1980s in Newcastle upon Tyne in England and has proved very efficient.

Cedar of Lebanon

European larch

143

What is the solar system?

The solar system is made up of the Sun and the nine planets which circle around it. The Earth seems a very large place to us, but it is only one of the Sun's satellites, and far from the largest. Compared with a giant like Jupiter or Saturn, the Earth is quite small. The Sun itself, which is much larger than any of its satellites, is just one of many millions of stars in the galaxy, and the galaxy is just one of many millions of galaxies in the universe.

A star like the Sun gives heat and light, because it is burning. Planets generally do not; without the Sun, the Earth would be cold and lifeless. The Earth is unique because conditions have developed in which plants and animals live. It is unlikely that life exists on any other planet.

The solar system is held together by the gravitational pull of the Sun, which keeps the planets circling around it, just as the gravitational pull of the Earth keeps the Moon in place. The time taken by a planet to make a complete circle around the Sun varies according to its distance from the Sun. The Earth takes one year (actually $365\frac{1}{4}$ days), but Mercury, the nearest planet to the Sun, takes only 88 days. On Pluto, the planet farthest from the Sun, the 'year' lasts almost two and a half centuries of Earth time.

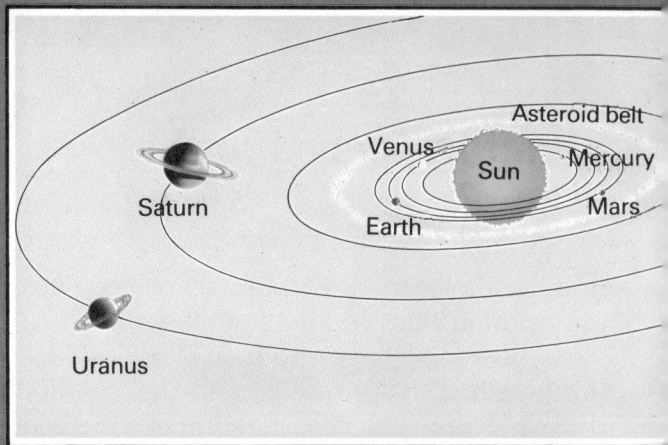

Saturn
Venus
Asteroid belt
Sun
Mercury
Earth
Mars
Uranus

Earth's Moon

Earth

One of Neptune's moons

Saturn

Venus

Neptune

Mars

Mercury

Pluto

Uranus

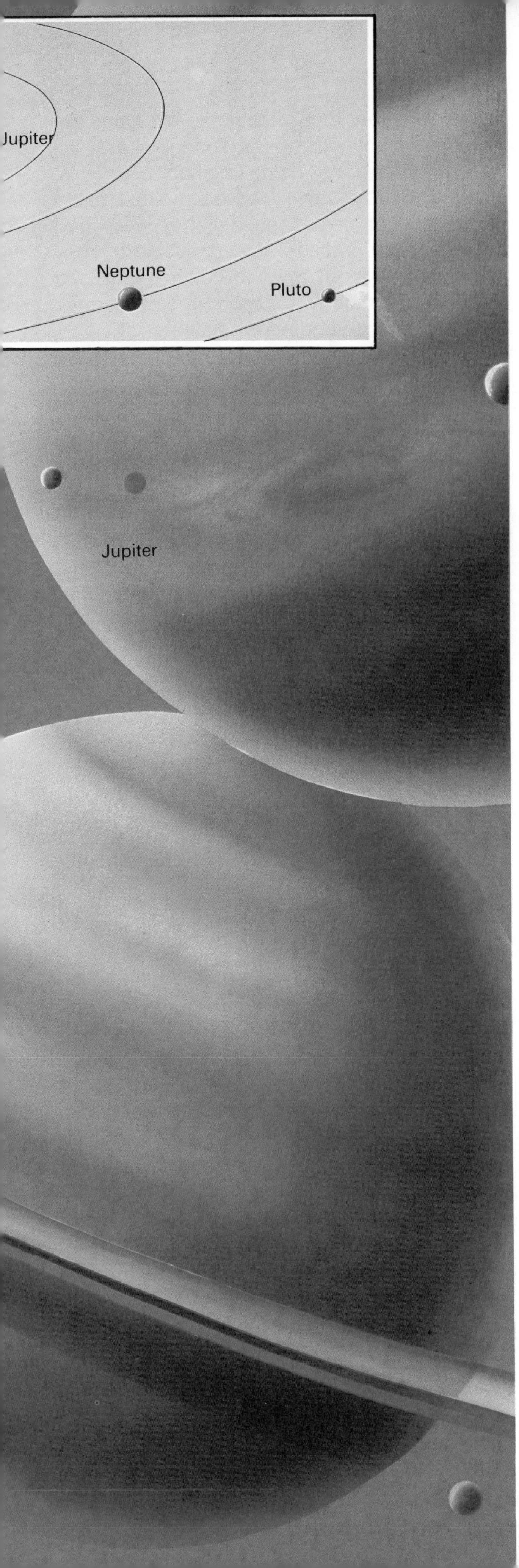
Jupiter
Neptune
Pluto
Jupiter

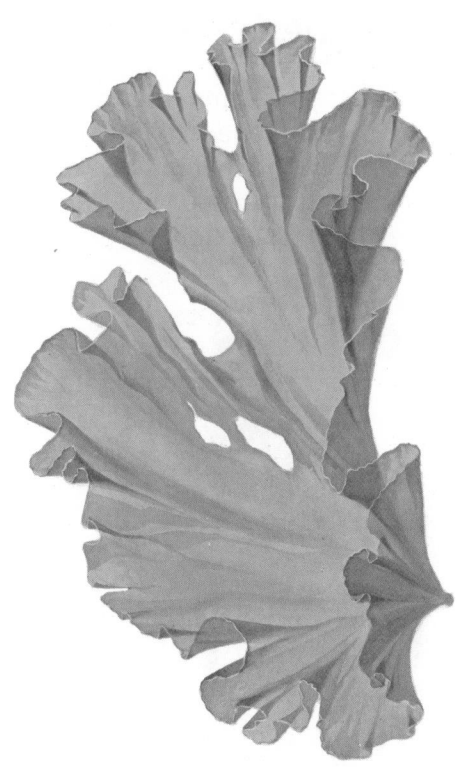

Is this a plant?

This is a leaf of the sea lettuce, a fairly common seaweed which is a beautiful pale green when young, though it grows darker with age. It often grows where a stream trickles down to the sea.

COLES
ARUP
ARUP

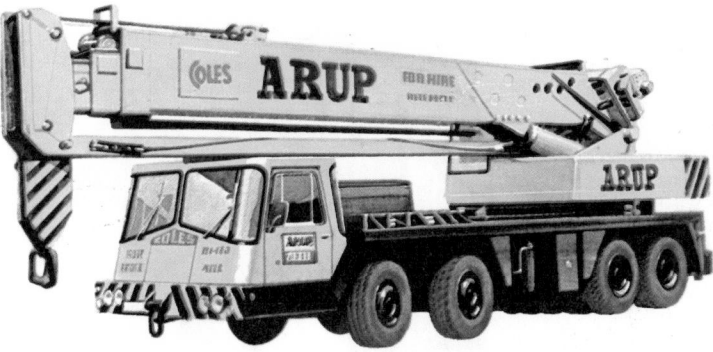

Would this vehicle give you a lift?

Not the right sort of lift! It is a 30-ton mobile crane – no good to hitchhikers.

How are Americans Indians?

This man is wearing the ceremonial dress of an American Indian chief. When Columbus discovered America in 1492 he thought he was in the East Indies (South-east Asia) and called the people he met 'Indians'. Although he could not have been more wrong, the name stuck, and the original inhabitants of the Americas are still called Indians. They came originally from Asia, crossing what is now the Bering Strait many thousands of years ago, when Alaska and Siberia were probably joined by land. They spread throughout the two continents of the Americas, forming a huge number of quite separate and quite different nations.

Scree

Arête

Cirque

Hanging valley

Fan

Rock step

How can ice shape the Earth?

Above is a valley which was formed by a glacier – a slowly moving mass of ice – during the Ice Age. The Ice Age started one million years ago and ended about 12 000 years ago. As the ice moved it widened, deepened, and straightened valleys, converting old V-shaped river valleys into U-shaped glacial valleys. Old tributary valleys were often left at a higher level, as a result of the deepening of the main valley, forming hanging valleys. At the head of the glacial valley there is a cirque or corrie, which was once the source of the glacier. A narrow, knife-edged ridge separating two corries is called an arête, and if a mountain has been eroded by several corries, a pyramidal peak or horn will result.

What happened at the Winter Palace?

In 1917 the Tsar (emperor) of Russia was forced to abdicate. A provisional republican government was formed, but it was badly organized and inefficient. The best-organized revolutionary group in Russia was the Bolsheviks (Communists), under the leadership of Nikolai Lenin (right) who returned from exile after the overthrow of the Tsar. The Bolsheviks, whose ideas were based on the writings of Karl Marx (see page 57), opposed the moderate republican government. In November Lenin ordered his Red Guards to attack the Winter Palace, a grand building in St Petersburg (now Leningrad) which was the home of the provisional government. This was the vital event of what is called the 'October Revolution' (the Russians used a different calendar then: the actual date was 6 November). It brought Lenin to power as leader of the Union of Soviet Socialist Repub-

lics. When he died in 1924 he was succeeded by Joseph Stalin, who is seen behind his left arm.

Who died at Culloden?

In 1745 Prince Charles Edward, grandson of James II, landed in Scotland with the aim of overthrowing the Hanoverian King George II and restoring the crowns of England and Scotland to the exiled Stuarts. 'Bonnie Prince Charlie' gained great support in the Highlands and invaded England. He reached Derby, only 225 km (140 miles) from London, before he was forced to retreat. The following spring an English army under the Duke of Cumberland, George II's son, marched into the Highlands and on a bleak moor at Culloden near Inverness slaughtered Charles' army. Charles escaped to France, never to return. The battle of Culloden destroyed the Highland clans, and many Highlanders left the country.

How many flowers has a flower?

The word 'flower' describes a single bloom. Some plants produce single flowers, each on its own stalk, like the yellow one below left. Other plants produce flowers which grow in groups or sprays. Such flowers are called inflorescences, and the rest of the flowers below show the different forms they can take. The scientific name for all flowering plants is angiosperm.

Who fought the American Revolution?

In 1776 the 13 British colonies on the Atlantic coast of North America declared their independence, although the war had started the year before. By 1783 they had defeated the British and established the United States of America. The American recruit (above left), fresh from the frontier in deerskin coat with musket and powder horn, was fighting for his country's freedom. The British soldiers, like the one above right, included German mercenaries, as well as men who had been forced or tricked into joining the army. In spite of better training and equipment, the British armies, fighting far from home and poorly led, were defeated by men defending their own homes.

What was a 'boneshaker'?

The first true bicycles, such as this machine (top right) made by Kirkpatrick Macmillan in 1839 (and often described as the earliest), had solid wheels and gave a very bumpy ride. They were hardly fit for ordinary roads, then made of gravel, and the name 'boneshaker' was all too accurate. (Other vehicles, such as an old, worn-out horse-drawn carriage were probably called boneshakers first.) Note how the shape of the saddle, the wooden wheels – made like carriage wheels – and the horse's head echo the age of the horse and carriage.

Pneumatic (inflated) tyres made bicycles more comfortable, and the modern sports bicycle (bottom right) is a very different machine from the old 'boneshaker'.

Where is the Giant's Causeway?

This extraordinary, natural rock formation (above) is on the coast of County Antrim, Northern Ireland. According to legend, it was built by a race of giants as part of a roadway to the island of Staffa, where there is a similar formation. Some later explanations were just as strange. One was that the columns were the remains of a petrified bamboo forest. Actually they are basalt, like those in the Auvergne (see page 40).

Quick Quiz

In what way are the following alike?
(1) Rudge, (2) Vélocipède, (3) Raleigh,
(4) Penny-farthing, (5) Moulton.

Answer: They are all makes or types of bicycle.

With what sport are the following associated?
(1) Calcutta Cup, (2) Tour de France, (3)
Monte Carlo Rally, (4) Wimbledon.

Answers: (1) Rugby football, awarded to the winner of the match between England and Scotland, (2) Cycling, a three-week race ending in Paris, (3) Motor racing, a European event which converges on Monaco, (4) Tennis, the world's foremost championship on grass.

Where does the bladderwort grow?

The bladderwort (below) is one of the most common types of seaweed to be found on the seashore. It gets its name from the tough little air bubbles or 'bladders' in its fronds. The fronds may grow up to about 1 m (3 ft 3 in) in length. Bladderwort is usually a brownish colour.

151

How does a cassette tape recorder work?

The microphone of a tape recorder picks up sounds and turns them into electric signals, which produce a magnetic field. The changes in the electric signal are reproduced as a magnetic pattern on tape. When it is played back, the magnetic pattern causes an electromagnet and pick up coil to produce electric signals which pass through an amplifier and loudspeaker, reproducing the sound recorded.

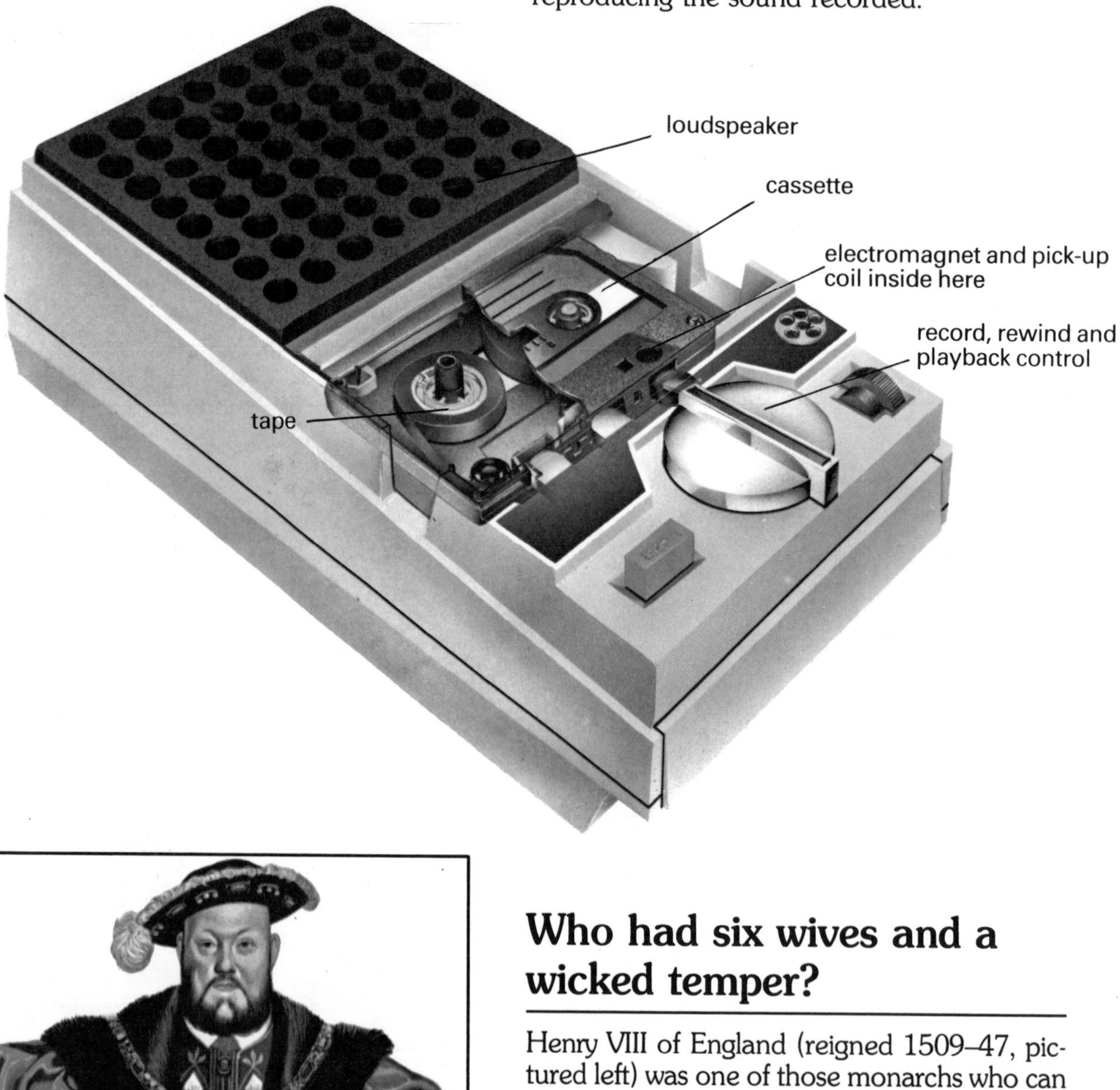

loudspeaker

cassette

electromagnet and pick-up coil inside here

record, rewind and playback control

tape

Who had six wives and a wicked temper?

Henry VIII of England (reigned 1509–47, pictured left) was one of those monarchs who can be admired as well as disliked. He was pleasant enough as a young man but grew imperious and cruel when he was old. He certainly helped make England a great country. Although six wives ('divorced, beheaded, died; divorced, beheaded, survived') seems gross, he would probably never have divorced Catherine of Aragon, his first wife, if she had borne a son.

Who flew Jason?

Amy Johnson (1903–41), an English airwoman, was a tomboy, and thought being a secretary was boring. A pleasure flight she took with a friend gave her the ambition to fly. People 50 years ago thought it odd for a woman to fly an aeroplane, and by all accounts she was not, at first, a very good pilot. But she persevered. With borrowed money she bought a Gipsy Moth aircraft (above), which she painted green (her lucky colour) and named Jason, after the ancient Greek traveller. It was equipped with extra fuel tanks for long-distance flying, and she was determined to beat the record for a flight from England to Australia – 16 days, set in 1928. She made the flight in 1930 with 15 stops and many mishaps, including two near-fatal accidents. Because of the delays caused by the damage to the aircraft (two propellers, three undercarriages and a wing were replaced during the flight), she did not break the record, taking 20 days. However, her efforts to overcome the problems she faced attracted the attention of newspapers all over the world, and she became a celebrity.

She made many more long-distance flights, alone and with her husband, and then after her marriage had broken up, alone again. She set a record for the London to Cape Town flight and survived more than one crash. When the Second World War broke out in 1939 she joined the Air Transport Auxiliary (the RAF did not take women pilots), and in January 1941 her aircraft crashed into the Thames estuary. Her body was never recovered.

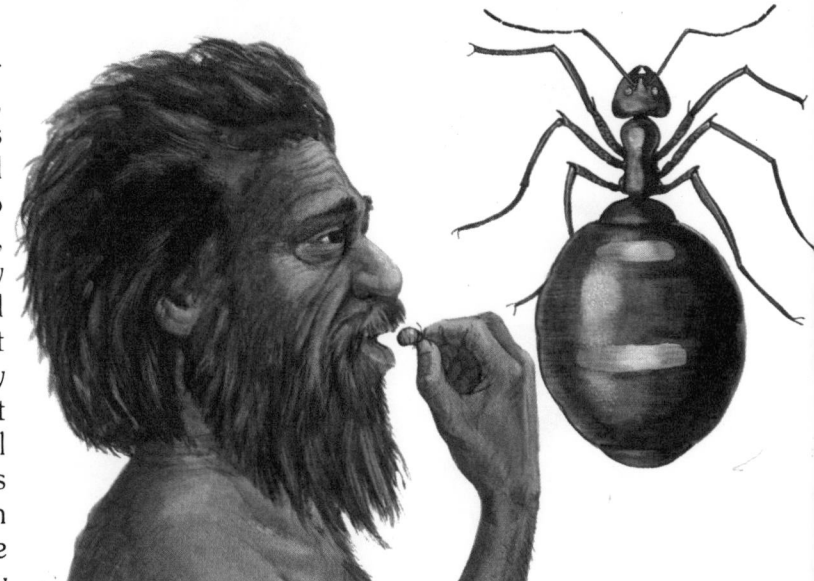

What kind of honeypot has six legs?

Australia has many strange and wonderful animals, but few of them are stranger than the honeypot ant (above). Most ants like honey, and honeypot ants have a most peculiar way of storing it. They collect nectar from flowers and honey-like fluids from other insects and stuff it into certain individual honeypot ants until the abdomen (stomach) is so stretched that light passes through it. These ants stay in the nest, acting as larders for their more active relations. They were considered a great delicacy by the Aborigines, who used to dig out their nests to capture the 'honeypots'.

Would you care to dance?

Many birds and other animals perform very strange – to us, often comic – rituals as part of their courting behaviour (when they are looking for a mate). One of the strangest of all is the 'penguin dance' of the great crested grebe (above), a large water bird which is now much less common that it once was. In this display the courting birds dive for a piece of weed – the material they use for making a nest – and then rise high in the water, breast to breast. They may also bow to each other and scurry across the water as if they were running on the surface. These elaborate courtship rituals serve to establish rapport between the male and female, so that they can co-operate in nest-building and feeding young.

What is a delta?

When a river reaches the sea it spreads out into many channels, forming a roughly triangular area called a delta (the Greek capital D, one sign for which is a triangle). Deltas are caused when the river carries down more silt and solids than the tide can wash away. As the material builds up, the river makes new branches on either side. The picture shows part of the Amazon delta in Brazil. The Amazon carries more water than any other river in the world.

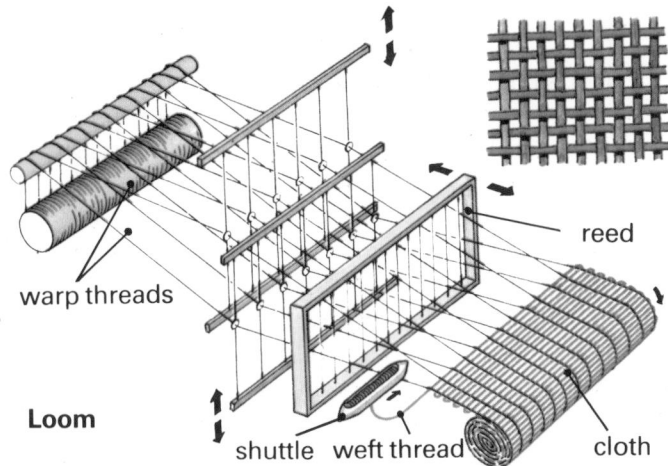

warp threads

Loom

reed

shuttle weft thread cloth

What is the difference between warp and weft?

Thread is woven into cloth on a loom, shown above. All that happens is that the weft threads (going across) are passed under and over each thread of the warp. The shuttle carries the weft threads and the reed tightens them. After each pass of the shuttle, the warp threads that are raised, are lowered, and vice-versa.

Who wrote Handel's Water Music?

Yes, of course it's a silly question! George Frideric Handel (1685–1759) was a German composer who settled in England and became very successful. His *Water Music* was written in 1717 for King George I, who had earlier been Handel's employer in Hanover, and who paid him an official pension of £600 a year – a lot in those days. No one is sure how or why the *Water Music* was composed. According to one story it was specially written for a royal party on the River Thames (below), and Handel was later to write his famous *Fireworks Music* for a royal fireworks party on the river (little could be heard at its first performance because of the accompanying bangs and whizzes). Probably Handel's most famous work is the oratorio *The Messiah*. King George II was so impressed that he stood up during the 'Hallelujah' chorus. Audiences have done the same ever since.

Anyone for the shuttle?

When the first manned satellites went into space in the early 1960s, many people felt that the wildest dreams of science-fiction writers were coming true. It was only about 50 years earlier that the first aeroplanes had flown. What amazing progress had been made in half a century!

But in the next 20 years events moved still faster. In the USA two special achievements marked the progress of space exploration. First was the landing of men on the Moon in 1969; second was the first flight of *Columbia* in 1981. The Moon landing was a more sensational event, but *Columbia* was probably more important for the future of space exploration. For *Columbia* was the first reusable space vehicle – the first in a shuttle service between the Earth and space.

She looks like a fast, stubby aeroplane, and

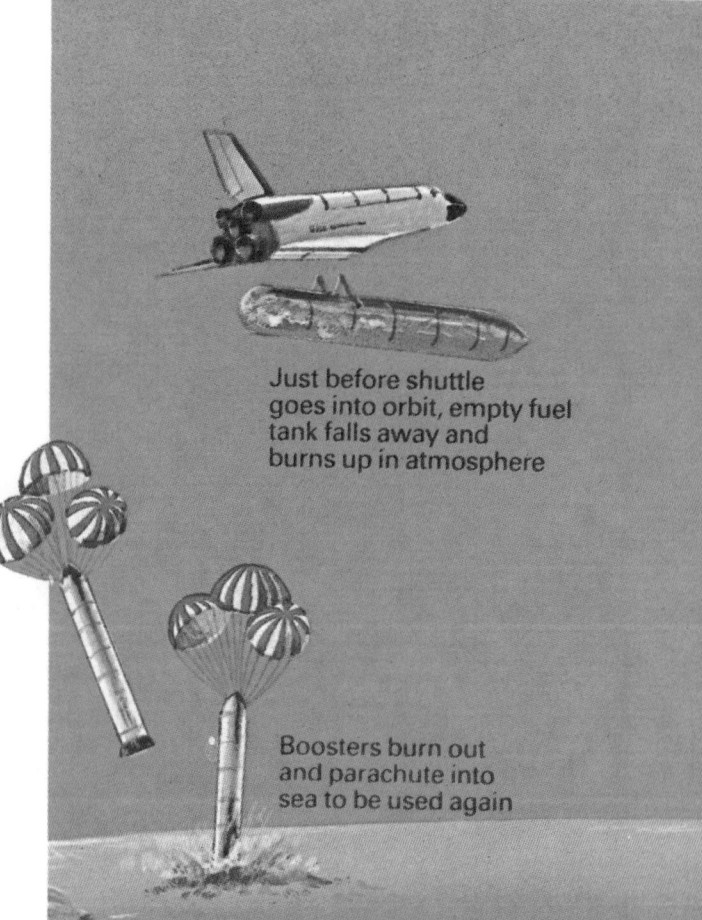

Just before shuttle goes into orbit, empty fuel tank falls away and burns up in atmosphere

Boosters burn out and parachute into sea to be used again

that is essentially what she is. She can manoeuvre in space, releasing satellites from her roomy hold or picking up old satellites from their orbits, and she is a flying laboratory herself (below). Re-entering the atmosphere, she is protected from the enormous heat generated by the friction of the atmosphere by special heat-proof tiles. She lands on a runway like an aeroplane, using a parachute as a brake.

In space travel, enormous power is needed for the actual launch (left); once in orbit, you need only a tiny fraction of the power it took to get you there. For take off, *Columbia* is attached to a massive fuel tank and two great booster rockets. The boosters do most of the hard work of launching, and when they burn out they are released and parachute into the ocean to be picked up and used again. The giant tank, the only part which cannot be reused, falls away close to orbit altitude and burns up as it descends.

Are an oliphant and an elephant related?

An oliphant is a type of musical horn which was used in Europe in the Middle Ages. It probably came originally from Byzantium (now Istanbul). The oliphant was made from a section of an elephant's tusk, and the ivory was often beautifully carved, as above. Being such a beautiful object in itself, it became a symbol of royalty.

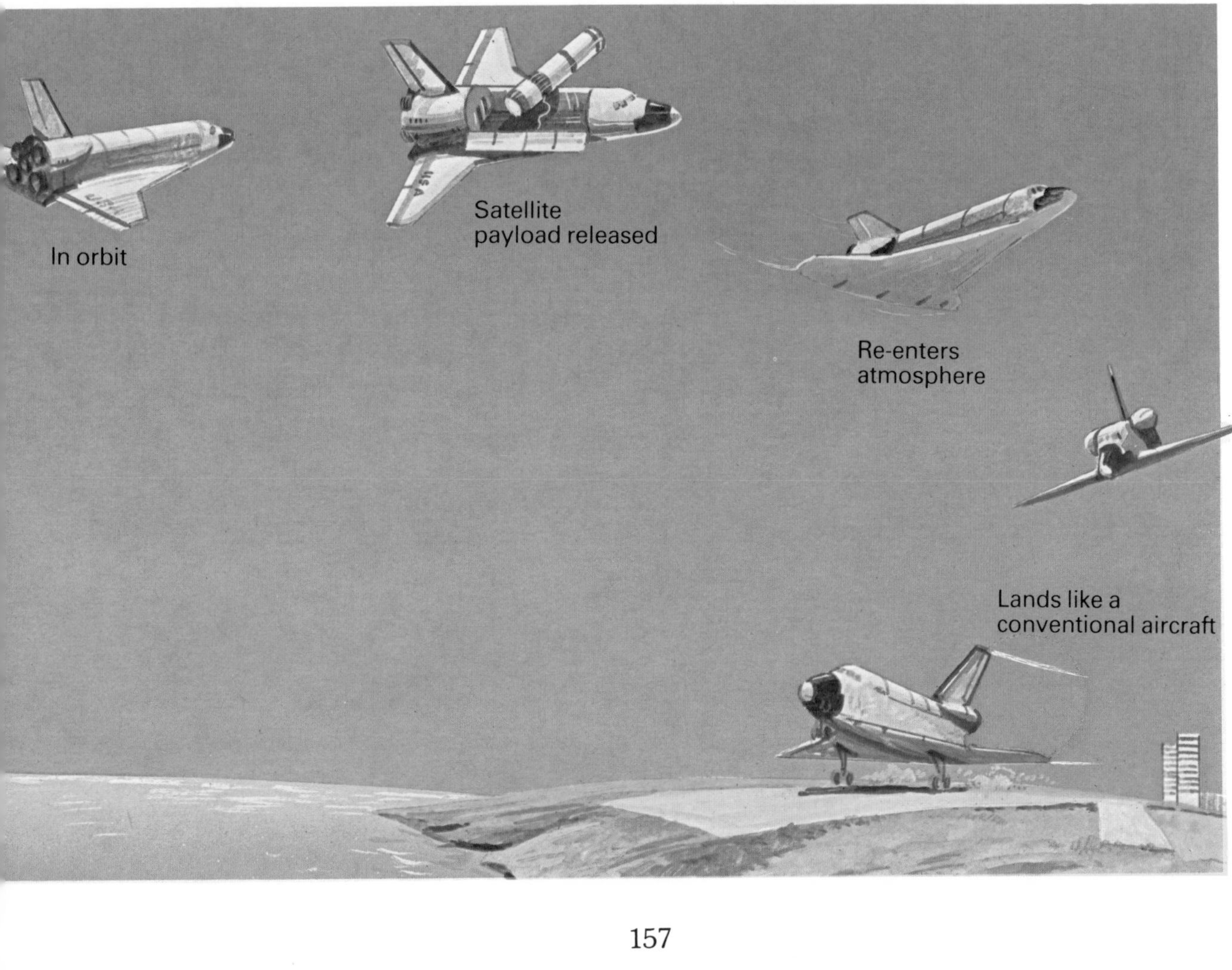

In orbit

Satellite payload released

Re-enters atmosphere

Lands like a conventional aircraft

Where would you eat breakfast twice?

Concorde (below) travels at a speed faster than the Earth turns. This means that if you fly from east to west the time gets 'earlier'. Local time in New York is five hours behind London time, but as Concorde takes less than five hours to fly from London to New York, you will arrive earlier than you left. You may have eaten breakfast before you left London, but the New Yorkers won't have started squeezing the oranges or scrambling the eggs when you arrive.

Concorde was designed and built by British and French engineers working together. The project began in 1962 but the first flight with fare-paying passengers did not take place until 1976. It carries 100 passengers and is powered by four Rolls Royce (Bristol) Snecma Olympus engines. Its wing shape is known as a 'slender delta'. Unfortunately, it is not only the fastest, but it is also the noisiest and most expensive airliner in the world. While the Europeans were developing a supersonic airliner, the Americans were building the jumbo (Boeing 747) – large, quiet, cheap and far more profitable. The real justification for Concorde was that it kept the French and British aircraft industries busy, and gave them experience which may be important in future developments in aeronautical engineering.

What makes lightning?

Many people are frightened by thunder and lightning today, and it is not hard to imagine how terrifying a thunderstorm must have seemed to our ancestors, who knew nothing about its cause.

Lightning is an electrical discharge, produced in the turbulent conditions of a thundercloud. The heat of the flash creates a sudden increase in pressure which results in the bang of thunder. As light travels faster than sound, you see the lightning before you hear the thunder. Lightning usually appears as a jagged line, often with several branches (left). When the whole sky seems to light up for a brief instant, it is called sheet lightning.

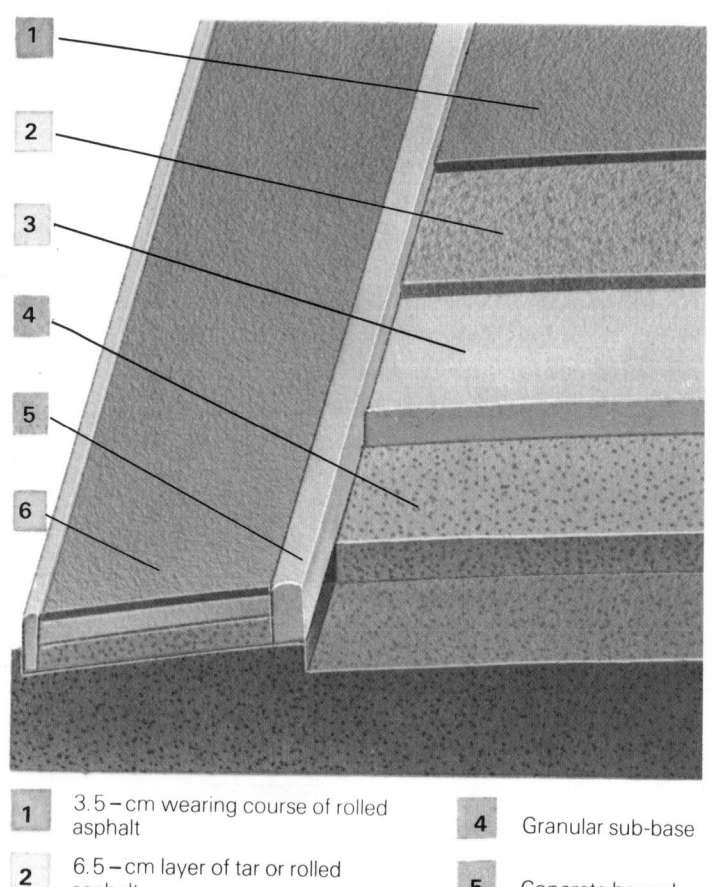

1	3.5–cm wearing course of rolled asphalt
2	6.5–cm layer of tar or rolled asphalt
3	25–cm base layer of lean concrete
4	Granular sub-base
5	Concrete haunch
6	Hard shoulder

How are roads made?

Roads don't look very exciting, but there is a lot more to them than you might think. Modern roads are built to stand constant wear from motor vehicles (including lorries weighing over 30 tonnes) running on rubber tyres inflated with air. They are quite different from the roads of 100 years ago, which were designed for horses' hooves and iron-rimmed carriage wheels. Modern roads usually have at least four layers (above) of different material on an earth base which has been compacted by a heavy roller (sometimes dry cement is injected and water poured on to make a harder base). Then the different layers are laid, with coarse material at the bottom, and smooth, rolled asphalt at the top. Sometimes roads are paved with concrete slabs instead of asphalt.

Were these animals dangerous?

Below are two *Triceratops*, a species of horned dinosaur of the Cretaceous Period. It was a huge creature – an adult male could be over 11 m (37 ft) long – with a pair of long horns on its forehead and a smaller horn over the nose. But in spite of its great size and formidable weapons, it was a harmless creature which ate only plants. The horns were for defence only, and the heavy, bony frill protected its neck. Large herds of *Triceratops* once roamed the plains of North America. Their size and numbers protected them from powerful, meat-eating enemies, like *Tyrannosaurus* (see page 99). The horned dinosaurs increased five times in length and nine times in weight during the course of their evolution, making them very much harder for predators to kill.

Quick Quiz

What are the following?
(1) Appian Way, (2) Watling Street, (3) the M1, (4) the Pan-American Highway, (5) Massachusetts Turnpike.

Answer: They are all major roads.

What kind of collection might include the following?
(1) Nautilus, (2) Conch, (3) Abalone, (4) Cockle, (5) Periwinkle.

Answer: Seashells.

What is the world's largest seashell?

The false trumpet shell, found in the Pacific region, is the world's largest gastropod, the most numerous class of molluscs to which nearly all shellfish belong. You can see how big it is above – the Australian Aborigine is using one as a water jug. There are some molluscs with bigger shells, such as the giant clam – there is one in the American Museum of Natural History which weighs 263 kg (580 lb). All seashells were, of course, once 'inhabited', though when you look at a collection of these pretty objects it is hard to imagine the living creatures.

What was the Hay Wain?

In the art of painting, the British have no great tradition to compare with their neighbours in France and the Low Countries. But in the 18th and 19th centuries they produced several masters of landscape painting. Below, John Constable (1776–1837), perhaps the greatest, makes a sketch for his famous painting, *The Hay Wain* (a wain is a wagon).

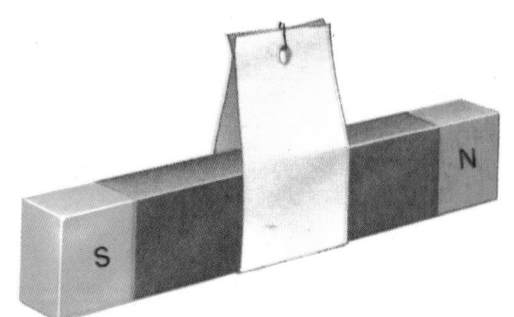

Why do magnets point north?

The Earth is like a giant magnet, with magnetic poles at the north and south, just like a small metal magnet. Allowed to swing freely, the north pole of a bar magnet like the one above will point towards the Earth's magnetic north pole. That's how a compass works.

Who are the Japanese?

The Japanese are an island nation on the edge of a continent (Asia). The islands of Japan are crowded, a problem which is made even worse because the land is mostly mountainous. Farm land is scarce so the Japanese grow heavy crops in limited space and they eat more fish than meat.

They are an extremely successful manufactur-

Hokkaido

• Sapporo

Sea of Japan

H o n s h u

• Sendai

PACIFIC OCEAN

■ **Tokyo**
Fujiyama ▲ • Yokohama

Kyoto
Kobe •• • Hamamatsu
Osaka

Hiroshima •

Kitakyushu •

Shikoku

Nagasaki •

Kyushu

0 ———————— 300 kilometres
0 ———————— 200 miles

ing nation, especially of cars and electronic goods. Japanese civilization is very old, and their current success derives from their fierce pride in their nation, their loyalty to their rulers and their hard work.

Though their industry is so up-to-date, the Japanese are proud of their old traditions, and you can still see plenty of evidence of their rich national history. The couple above are wearing the traditional costume of the northern island of Hokkaido.

Who was Nefertiti?

Above is a famous bust (sculptured head) of Queen Nefertiti, who lived in Egypt about 3400 years ago. It is probably the best-known work of all ancient Egyptian art. Nearly 50 cm (20 in) high and made of painted plaster and limestone, it is now in the state museum in Berlin, Germany. It was made during a period in Egyptian art called the Amarna period (after the city of El Amarna), and it is even more realistic than most works of that time.

She was the wife of the pharaoh (king) Amenhotep IV, who reigned at an eventful time in Egyptian history. Amenhotep hated the traditional religion in which the most important god was Amen and he resented the power that the priests had over the pharaohs. He encouraged a new religion, devoted to worship of one god alone, Aton, the sun god. He changed his own name from Amenhotep, which was formed from the hated 'Amen' to Akhenaton, 'the instrument of Aton'. He also introduced the first real civil service in Egypt. Nefertiti was renowned for her beauty and had great influence on her husband's new ideas, but his reign was short and his revolution did not last under his successor Tutankhamun (see page 111).

What was the Crystal Palace?

The idea of holding a great exhibition of science, arts and industry was taken up by Prince Albert (1819–61), the husband of Queen Victoria. Although similar exhibitions had been held

before, notably in France, this was to be bigger and grander than any of them. The site was Hyde Park, which was the largest open space in central London. With great daring the organizers chose an exhibition hall made of glass on an iron frame, designed by Joseph Paxton. It had the great advantage that it could be taken down and moved elsewhere after the exhibition.

Paxton, who had begun as a gardener and built greenhouses, submitted the design unasked.

The show, in 1851, was a great success – a visible sign of British leadership in science and industry. Besides all the machinery and manufactures, there were some odd exhibits, like a garden seat made of coal and 'champagne' made from rhubarb.

The Crystal Palace itself, seen below with the Queen and Prince Albert on opening day, was not only the first large glass building, it was the first prefabricated building, that is, built in sections and assembled on the site. When the exhibition was over, it was taken apart and put up again at Sydenham, south-east London. It was destroyed by fire in 1936.

Kikuyu

Masai

Kamba

Masai

Who lives in East Africa?

Above are members of some of the peoples of East Africa in traditional costume. In former times the Masai (the largest group when related groups are included) were herdsmen who despised settled farming as practised by the Kikuyu and the less numerous Kamba. Traditional herding still goes on in some parts.

What are antlers?

The antlers of deer are different from horns because they are shed each winter and grow anew every year. At first they have a blood supply and are covered with a kind of velvet; as they grow harder and more bony, the blood supply stops and the 'velvet' is rubbed off on trees. Usually, only males have antlers. They vary in size: the roe buck's (below) are small.

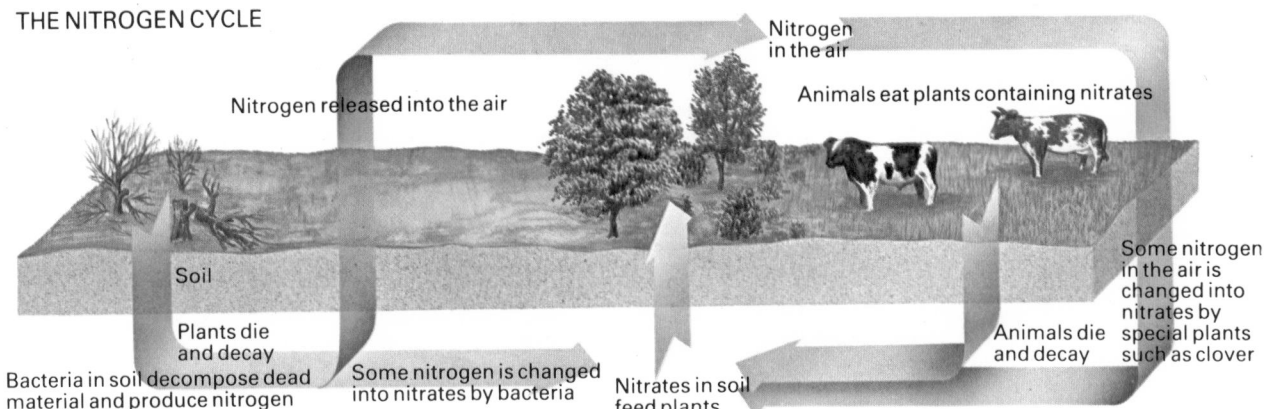

THE NITROGEN CYCLE

Nitrogen in the air

Nitrogen released into the air

Animals eat plants containing nitrates

Soil

Some nitrogen in the air is changed into nitrates by special plants such as clover

Plants die and decay

Bacteria in soil decompose dead material and produce nitrogen

Some nitrogen is changed into nitrates by bacteria

Nitrates in soil feed plants

Animals die and decay

Why do we need nitrogen?

Most of the air we breathe is made up of the gas nitrogen. However, it is of no use to us; we need oxygen. But some nitrogen compounds are vital in nature, particularly for plants. Modern farming depends on nitrate fertilizers.

The nitrogen cycle is a series of chemical reactions which change the nitrogen of the air into compounds, make it part of plant and animal proteins, and eventually decompose the compounds to make nitrogen in the air again.

Who built St Paul's?

St Paul's is the cathedral church of the City of London (Westminster Abbey is a national church). The huge medieval cathedral which once stood here was burnt down in the Great Fire (1666) and its replacement (below) was built between 1673 and 1711 to a design by Sir Christopher Wren (below left), one of England's finest architects. Against opposition from the clergy, he insisted on a dome instead of the usual spire.

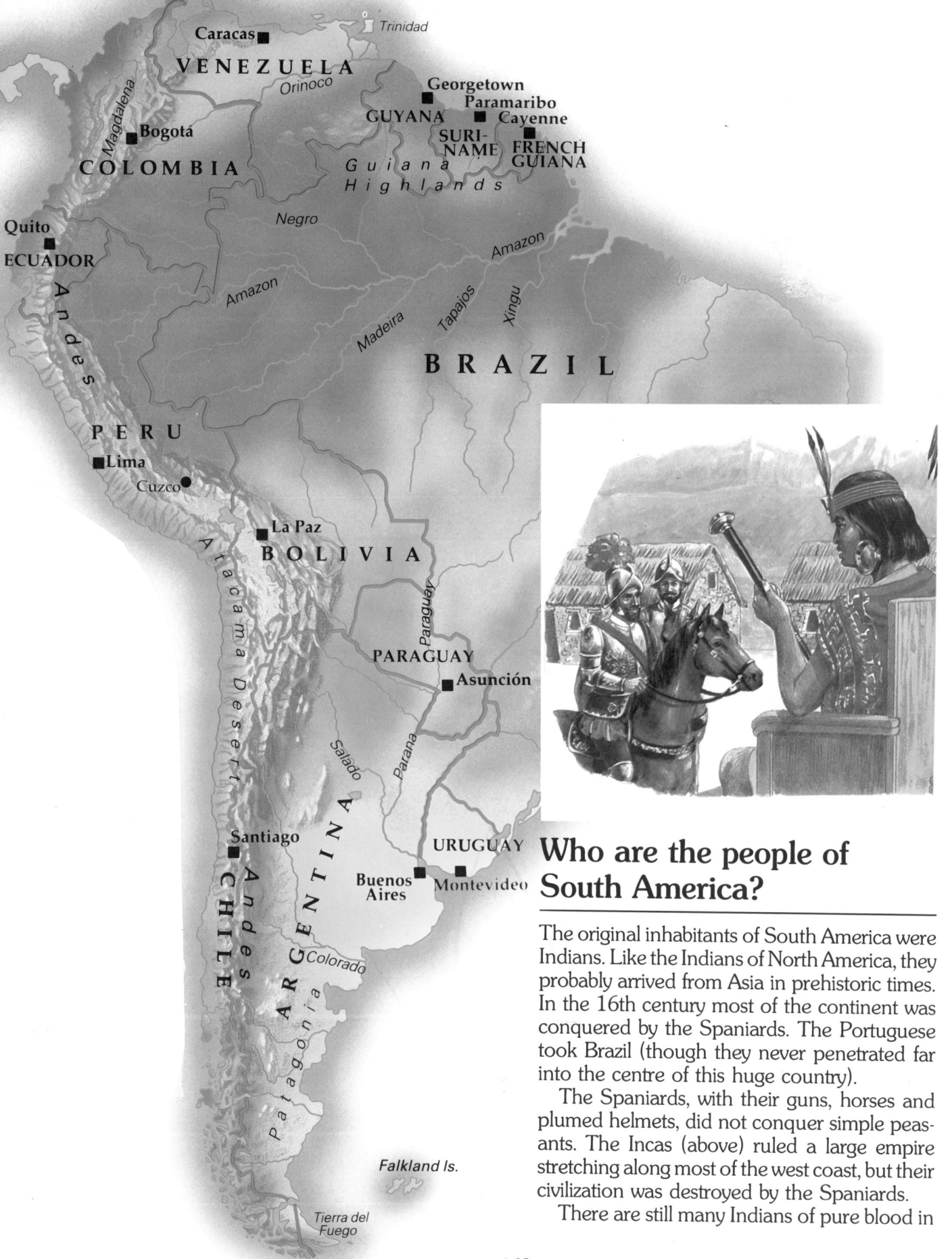

Caracas ■
Trinidad

VENEZUELA

Orinoco

Georgetown ■
Paramaribo
GUYANA ■ Cayenne ■
SURI-
NAME FRENCH
GUIANA

Magdalena

■ Bogotá

COLOMBIA

*Guiana
Highlands*

Quito ■
ECUADOR

Negro

Amazon

Amazon

A
n
d
e
s

Amazon

Madeira *Tapajos* *Xingu*

B R A Z I L

P E R U

■ Lima

Cuzco ■

■ La Paz

B O L I V I A

Paraguay

PARAGUAY

■ Asunción

Salado

Parana

A
t
a
c
a
m
a

D
e
s
e
r
t

Santiago ■

A
R
G
E
N
T
I
N
A

URUGUAY

Buenos
Aires ■ Montevideo ■

C
H
I
L
E

A
n
d
e
s

Colorado

*P
a
t
a
g
o
n
i
a*

Falkland Is.

*Tierra del
Fuego*

Cape Horn

168

Who are the people of South America?

The original inhabitants of South America were Indians. Like the Indians of North America, they probably arrived from Asia in prehistoric times. In the 16th century most of the continent was conquered by the Spaniards. The Portuguese took Brazil (though they never penetrated far into the centre of this huge country).

The Spaniards, with their guns, horses and plumed helmets, did not conquer simple peasants. The Incas (above) ruled a large empire stretching along most of the west coast, but their civilization was destroyed by the Spaniards.

There are still many Indians of pure blood in

South America, like the Peruvian woman (below) from the Andes mountains. A greater number, like the Argentinian *gaucho* (cowboy, below right) and the Brazilian girl (right) in beads and turban are of mixed descent – Indian and European (not only Spanish and Portuguese but also British, German, Italian, etc). A much smaller number, which includes many recent immigrants, have no Indian blood.

Who was Hitler?

Adolf Hitler (1889–1945) was born in Austria and served in the German army in the First World War, rising no higher than corporal. By 1933 he was dictator of Germany.

In the 1920s Hitler became the leader of the National Socialist (nicknamed 'Nazi') Party thanks to his electrifying speech-making. The party gained support because of the bitterness of many Germans after their defeat in the First World War and their fear of communism. Hitler talked of a 'greater Germany' and believed that the Germans were a superior race; he had a particular hatred of Jews, as well as other races he considered inferior.

After other governments had failed, he was appointed chancellor (prime minister) in 1933 and swiftly turned democratic Germany into a totalitarian state. He began to expand German power in Europe, taking over Austria and part of Czechoslovakia. At home, the Nazi government depended on secret police, violence, torture, and concentration camps to eliminate opposition. The Nazi empire was destroyed in the Second World War. Hitler is pictured below making a speech.

How old is a fossil?

Fossils are the remains of living creatures preserved in rocks. It is through the evidence of fossils that we know something (though not as much as we would like) about the plants and animals that lived on Earth in earlier ages. For example, in this book there are several pictures of dinosaurs (see pages 99, 110 and 160–61). Thanks to fossil remains, scientists have been able to build up detailed pictures of what some dinosaurs looked like.

Creatures with hard shells or bones are the most likely to become fossils; softer parts like skin and flesh are more often rotted or eaten before they can be fossilized. Bones will only be fossilized if they are buried in mud or sand, preventing their decay or destruction. If the mud or sand is compressed and hardened into rock, the bones will be permanently encased. Thus fossils are most often found in rocks, like chalk, which were formed from compressed mud or sand. Some examples of fossils are shown on the left.

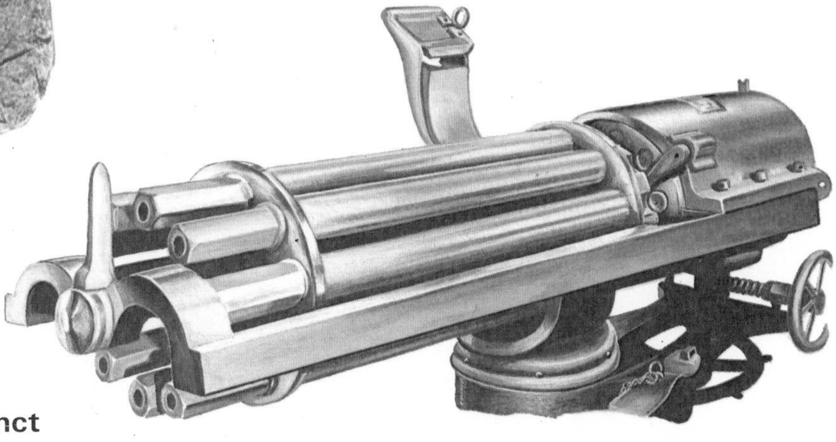

Insect in amber

Trilobite (extinct crustacean)

Sea urchin

Starfish

Coal-measure plant

Ammonite (extinct mollusc)

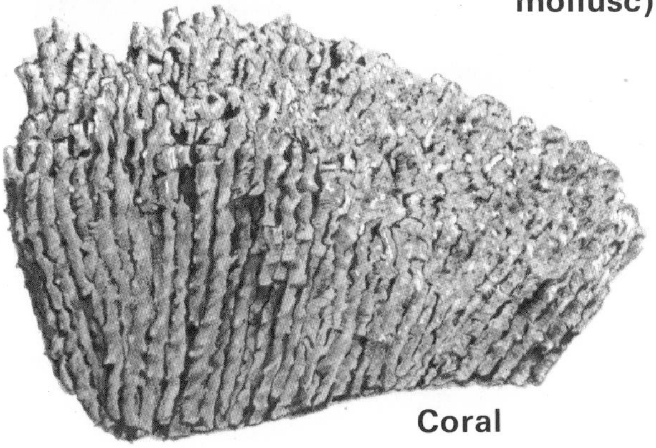

Coral

What was a Gatling gun?

The Gatling gun (above), named after its inventor, was an early type of machine gun. There were many versions, but the most widely used had 10 barrels, fired in turn by rotating them with a hand crank. First used in the American Civil War, its high rate of fire was devastatingly effective, eventually causing soldiers to fight from trenches.

What lives in ponds and rivers?

A pond or a stream, with its banks and margins, is one of the most fascinating natural environments. Many plants and animals are specially adapted to live in or near the water and cannot be found anywhere else. If the ground roundabout is wet and marshy, there may be tall banks of reeds looking like a larger form of grass, or clumps of bulrushes with their velvety spikes. Some trees, like the willow and alder, prefer to grow near the water, and there is a huge variety of wildflowers which like to sink their roots in nice wet mud. Some plants, like the wild water lily, grow *in* the water, their roots anchored on the bottom and their flowers blooming on the surface. Others, like duckweed, float on top with no roots to keep them in place.

Such plants require still water (a fast current would wash them away) and it is in ponds, lakes and canals that you find the most plants. Providing the water does not become overgrown and stagnant, lacking oxygen, the rich plant life allows many small animals to live here.

heron

moorhen

water vole

water spider

pike

dragonfly

dragonfly larva

tench

Tiny plants – too small to see – float in the water, to be eaten by animals not much larger, like the water flea about the size of a pinhead. They in turn provide food for the smaller fish and other animals, including birds.

mallard (drake)

coot

water shrew

mallard

water vole

roach

water beetles

minnows

Animals of ponds and rivers

The animals pictured in and around the water on the two preceding pages are not drawn to scale.

Birds

Among the many kinds of birds you are likely to see around the water, one of the largest and most distinctive is the heron. All the same, the heron is not easy to spot because, like any good fisherman, it keeps very still. It will stand in shallow water on its long legs without moving, waiting for a fish to swim within range of its long, stabbing beak. Frogs and other small animals are also at risk. The heron has a comb-like middle claw which it uses when grooming with a powder produced among its breast feathers.

The mallard is the most common species of wild duck. The drake (male) has a brilliant green head, but the duck (female) is less handsome. In the picture her brownish head can just be seen as she feeds on pond weed. Mallards are surface feeders, which dabble rather than dive. They are also fast and powerful flyers.

The coot is another dabbler, a black bird easily recognized by its white beak and forehead. Its extremely large feet give it a slightly comical look when it walks about on land, as it often does. It makes its large and rather untidy nest in the reeds and can be quite aggressive towards intruders, despite its gentle name and appearance. It needs a long 'runway' when taking off, pattering along the surface of the water to get up speed.

The moorhen or waterhen is a similar bird to the coot but it is smaller, with distinctive white bands under the tail and along the sides, and its beak and forehead are vivid red. It has long toes but its feet, unlike the coot's, are not webbed. Its smart appearance and bustling behaviour make it one of the most attractive water birds. The name moorhen sounds wrong, as it is not a bird of the moors. The original name, however, was 'mere-hen', a mere being a lake.

otter

Mammals

At the edges of lakes and rivers some interesting mammals make their home. That most loveable creature, the otter, is now unfortunately rare, and many other animals are endangered by pollution – the greatest menace to pond and river life today.

Many people first learn about otters through Henry Williamson's book, *Tarka the Otter*, just as water rats make us think of Kenneth Grahame's *The Wind in the Willows*. Actually, the water rat's proper name is water vole; it has the typical blunt head (not pointed like a rat's) of the vole family. It makes long tunnels in the banks, sometimes with an underwater entrance. Unlike many small rodents, the water vole is active by day, so you have a fair chance of spotting one.

The smaller water shrew has a double row of stiff hairs along its tail which acts like a kind of keel. It is almost black on top, whiteish below, and when swimming it looks silvery because of the air bubbles trapped in its fur. One of the first people to study water shrews was the great Austrian naturalist, Konrad Lorenz, and they are the subject of a chapter in his *King Solomon's Ring*, one of the finest animal books ever written.

grey heron

moorhen

dragonfly

Insects

There are many different species of dragonfly, some of them very colourful – brilliant blue, or yellow, or red and green – with huge eyes. They dart about so quickly that the human eye can hardly follow, but they will sometimes hover like a helicopter. They are some of many fascinating and little-known insects which live double lives in water and air. The eggs are laid in the water and hatch into larvae, or nymphs. The nymph is an underwater hunter, armed with pincers. After a time it climbs a plant stem into the air. There its skin splits and a mature dragonfly emerges.

The large water beetle is another fierce hunter, both as a larva and as a mature beetle, swimming after other water insects or even small fish, and carrying its own air supply under its wing cases.

The water spider is still more remarkable. It fetches bubbles of air from the surface; they stick to its hairy body, and it stores them under a bell-shaped web, spun between plant stems. In this little tent of air the water spider lives, darting out to catch its prey which it brings back to the tent to eat.

Fish

Wherever there is water, you expect to find fish, and it is amazing what small ponds some fish will live in.

Minnows are colourful little fish which seldom grow to more than 10 cm (4 in) in length. Although they can be found in ponds and canals, they really prefer clear, flowing water where the bottom is sand or gravel. They seem to have become less common in the past 20 years or so, and if that is true the reason is probably pollution. They are very curious, which is why they can be caught (with patience) in a net.

minnow

The tench is a fish of still waters; it likes a muddy bottom where it can forage for food. A stout, greenish-gold fish, it may reach a weight of 3.5 kg (8 lb) or more. Like the carp, another bottom-feeder, tench can live for some time out of water, and they have been known to survive in the mud during a dry summer when the pond has dried up.

tench

Roach and bream may be found in shoals in all but the quickest rivers, though bream especially prefer slow currents: their slab-like bodies are not well designed for fast water. Roach may grow up to 2 kg (4 lb), though any fisherman who catches a 1-kg (2-lb) roach thinks himself lucky – or clever. Bream grow much larger, up to 4 kg (10 lb) or more. Until a few years ago, experts believed that there were two species of bream, but we know now that the small silver bream grows up to be a common bream.

The pike is the great hunter of fresh water; it

pike

has a savage look. Female pike may grow very large: specimens over 20 kg (50 lb) are known in Ireland. Pike are solitary fish which lie unmoving, often among reeds or weedbeds, until they decide to attack, when they flash into action like an underwater rocket. They mainly eat smaller fish, though they will take anything that moves – water voles, frogs, ducklings, even (according to legend) a milkmaid's foot or the nose of a drinking horse.

What makes a train go?

Until about 1950 nearly all trains were pulled by steam locomotives. A few still are, but in most countries different types of locomotive have taken over.

There were two main choices for a railway which decided to give up steam: to use either electric- or diesel-powered locomotives. Some electric trains already existed, and so did a few diesel locomotives. Many railways decided to choose diesel locomotives for most long-distance routes. Diesel oil was cheap, and electricity was expensive. Unfortunately oil is no longer cheap, and railways are now converting more main lines to electricity.

Modern high-speed electric trains like the one above pick up the current from overhead wires. Suburban and city rail systems use a third rail running along the track to supply the electric power.

What happens in a planetarium?

A planetarium is a building with a domed ceiling on to which images of the Sun, Moon and stars are projected. The audience sees a perfect replica of the night sky. The various heavenly bodies move in the same way as the real ones seem to move in the sky, and it is possible to arrange an eclipse of the Sun or the passage of a comet. The instrument on the left is the projector in the planetarium at Jena, Germany. Planetariums enable people to learn about the stars and planets in an easy way.

Are horses useful?

Horses once performed many vital jobs now done by machines. Before the railways, about 150 years ago, the horse was the fastest method of transport, and powerful horses like the shires below did the heavy work on farms. The horse-drawn cab (bottom right) provided local transport until the arrival of the motor car. You could see cabs waiting outside railway stations as recently as the 1920s.

We still have some uses for the horse. The police (bottom left) find them the best means of controlling crowds, and in a few places they deliver beer to pubs. More importantly, they are used for a number of popular sports, racing, polo and show jumping to name but three.

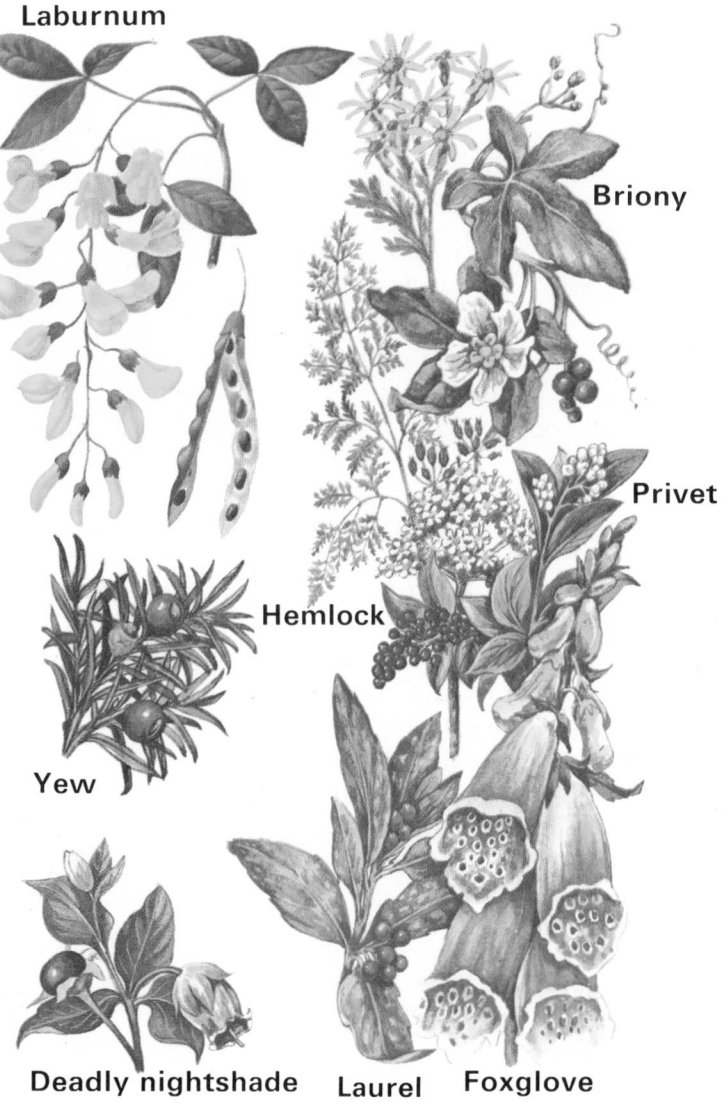

Laburnum

Briony

Privet

Hemlock

Yew

Deadly nightshade

Laurel

Foxglove

Can plants be dangerous?

Everyone knows that some kinds of fungi, or toadstools, are highly poisonous, but many common wild plants, like those above, are poisonous too. They can be dangerous to plant-eating pets and to small children, especially as the poisonous parts (like orange ivy berries) often look tasty. It is often only one part that is poisonous. We eat the stalks of rhubarb in safety, but the leaves are poisonous. Other plants may be poisonous when raw, but harmless when cooked, or the other way around. Stinging nettles are poisonous to the skin, though they make a nice soup.

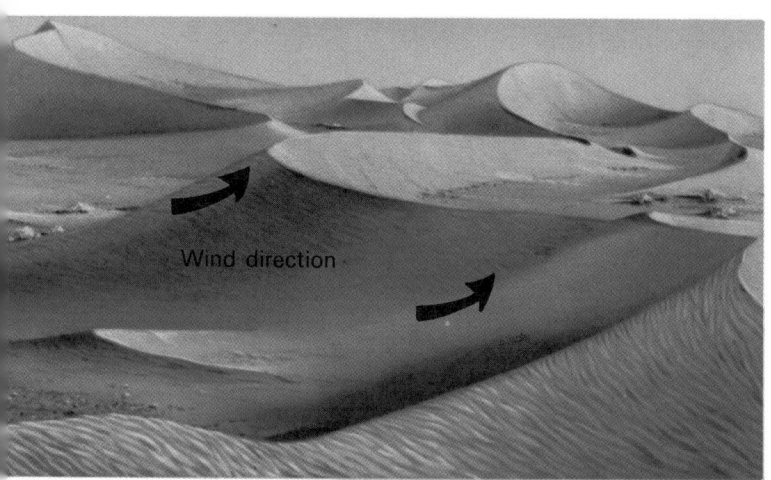
Wind direction

Who are the Zulu?

The Zulu people were a small tribal group in Natal in southern Africa who became a fierce conquering nation, under their chief Shaka (died 1828), in the early 19th century. In the time of Shaka's successors they came into conflict with Europeans: first the Boers, descendants of Dutch colonists seeking land in Natal; second the British, the chief imperial power in southern Africa. In 1843 the British became masters of Natal and the Zulu settled peacefully in Zululand.

How is sand made?

Sand is simply masses of very tiny pieces of rock. The sand on the beach is made by the sea, which grinds the rocks to very fine powder. In deserts, rocks are broken into sand by their expansion and contraction as a result of high temperatures in the day and freezing temperatures at night. The wind helps, and also blows the sand into dunes – shifting hills of sand.

Who will save the panda?

Human beings are very prejudiced about animals. To us, the giant panda (below) is one of the most attractive of all animals – we like its looks and we approve of its general behaviour. If it were a dingy brown meat-eater, it would not be so popular.

The giant panda looks like a smallish bear but is actually a member of the raccoon family. It lives in remote bamboo forests in western China and will eat little except bamboo shoots. It is solitary, though mothers may be accompanied by their young, and was unknown to Europeans until 1869. There are now several giant pandas in European and American zoos. Its nearest relative is the lesser or red panda which lives high in the Himalayas.

It is a very rare animal – there are probably only a few hundred giant pandas living in the wild. Because their lifestyle is so specialized, and because they do not seem to breed easily, there is a danger that pandas will become extinct. However, they are carefully protected by the Chinese authorities, and some have been bred in captivity.

The rise of another warrior-king, Cetewayo, caused growing tension with white settlers and British administrators. A special commission was appointed to look into quarrels over land. It reached a judgement in favour of the Zulu, but the British High Commissioner, without orders from London, attempted to force conditions on Cetewayo which would have destroyed his military power. The result was the Zulu War of 1879.

It began with a Zulu victory at Isandhlwana, followed by a famous action at Rorke's Drift, when 110 men held off a large Zulu army (above). Eventual defeat for the Zulu was certain, as they were not equipped for modern war. The British took over Zululand and, after a brief rebellion in 1888, the Zulu accepted British rule. They were less satisfied when they were put under the colonial government of South Africa in 1897. The last great Zulu revolt took place in 1905–06.

How does a helicopter fly?

Leonardo da Vinci designed a helicopter of a sort in the 15th century though, even if it had been built, it would not have been able to fly. In fact, helicopters are a recent development. They were practically unknown until the Second World War and have only become common since the 1950s. One early form of rotary-wing aircraft was the autogiro, invented by a Spanish engineer in the 1920s. In an autogiro, however, the main rotary blades are turned by the air as the aircraft is driven forwards by a propeller.

The aircraft below is a typical modern helicopter based on the system devised by the Soviet-born American engineer, Igor Sikorsky. A single engine drives the main rotary blades and the tail rotor. The purpose of the tail rotor is to stop the

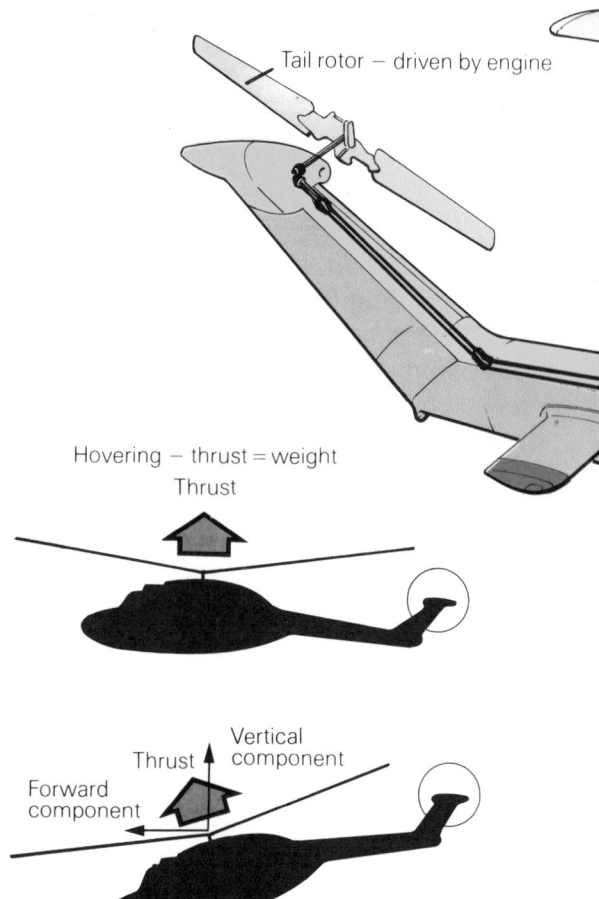

Tail rotor — driven by engine

Hovering — thrust = weight
Thrust

Forward component
Thrust
Vertical component
Forward flight

Can you name these cats?

There is a world of difference between a pet tabby curled up by the fire and a leopard stalking its prey in an African forest, but they are both members of the cat family. Most cats can be tamed, even large ones (eastern kings used to hunt with tame cheetahs), and pet cats, valued as rat-killers, have been kept since prehistoric times. The ancient Egyptians were especially devoted to cats (see page 89). The various breeds of domestic cat have developed over hundreds of years.

Much of the human fascination with cats must lie in their being skilful hunters. Most cats hunt by stealth, creeping up on their prey unobserved, and then rapidly pouncing on their victims.

The three members of the cat family above are the ocelot of South and Central America (bottom left), the rare snow leopard or ounce of the Himalayas (stretching), and the cascal or Persian lynx of south-west Asia and Africa (right).

whole aircraft being spun round by the main blades. When the helicopter is hovering, the upward thrust of the rotating rotor blades just balances the weight of the machine. To move upwards the pilot operates the collective pitch lever which increases the pitch (or angle of twist) of all the rotor blades, and hence the lift. More lift requires more power from the engine. The cyclic pitch control changes the direction of the rotor's thrust, giving it a horizontal component as well as a vertical one, enabling the helicopter to manoeuvre in any direction. To turn, the pilot uses the rudder pedals to control the tail rotor.

On the right are helicopters at work: a US Army helicopter delivering supplies in a container which forms part of its body (top); a US Marines helicopter lifting a Mercury astronaut and his space capsule from the sea; and a military helicopter transporting a field gun (far right).

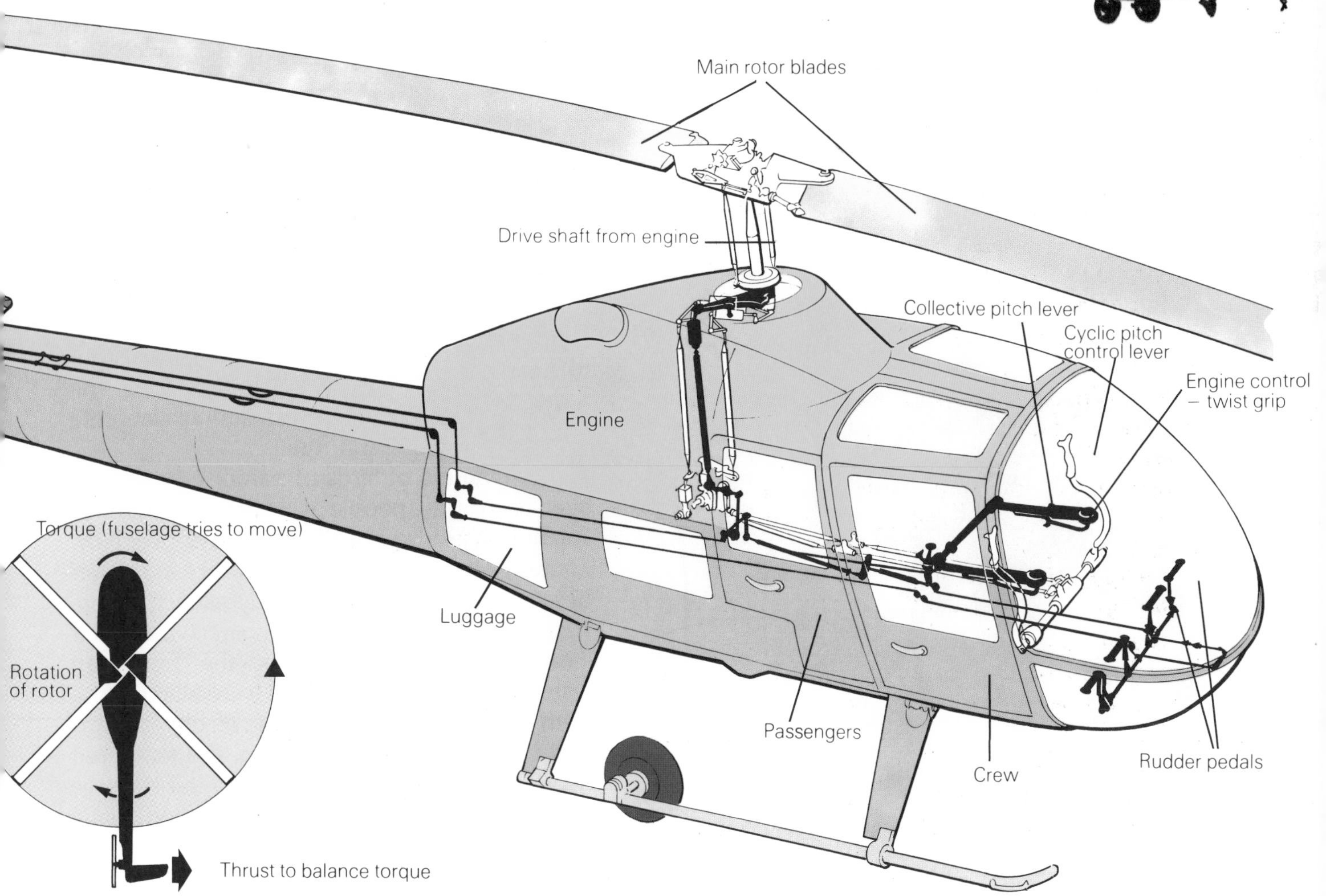

Main rotor blades

Drive shaft from engine

Collective pitch lever

Cyclic pitch control lever

Engine control – twist grip

Engine

Torque (fuselage tries to move)

Rotation of rotor

Luggage

Passengers

Crew

Rudder pedals

Thrust to balance torque

Balancing the torque

181

Where are the birds of paradise?

There are about 350 different species of birds of paradise, all of which live in the forested mountains of New Guinea. They gained their name because, when their skins began to arrive in Europe, someone said that creatures so beautiful must come from paradise. These early specimens had no legs. Some people thought the birds spent their whole lives in the air and therefore did not need feet! The absence of legs,

however, was simply due to the method of preparing bird skins in New Guinea. Most species have stocky bodies, rounded wings, short legs, a squarish tail and vary in length between 5 and 40 in (12.5 to 100 cm). The males' plumes become erect during elaborate courtship displays and rituals.

The feathers of birds of paradise have long been used by the people of New Guinea to make splendid headdresses like the one above. Now many species of birds of paradise are in danger of extinction (some are already extinct). However, the birds were only endangered when their feathers were demanded by the European fashion trade. Huge numbers were killed in the 19th century for the well-dressed ladies of Paris and New York. By comparison, the feathered headdresses of the New Guinea tribes have some importance. They play a part in many traditional ceremonies.

Who built the world's longest wall?

The Great Wall of China was built to keep out the fierce, nomadic tribes who found China's settled civilization such a tempting target for raids. Begun in the 3rd century BC and enlarged at various times during the next 16 centuries, it is the largest single structure ever built. The total length is about 2500 km (1550 miles), with about 25 000 towers. In some sections the road along the top is 5 m (16 ft) wide. It is the only man-made structure on Earth which can be seen from the Moon.

Who dug the Grand Canyon?

The Grand Canyon in Arizona, USA (below), is one of Nature's most spectacular creations. It is a gorge cut over many millions of years by the Colorado river, and the height from top to bottom is about 1800 m (5900 ft) at its deepest point. On the same day you could be shivering in a fur coat at the top or sweltering in a T-shirt at the bottom. It is 450 km (280 miles) long and varies from 6 km (4 miles) to 18 km (11 miles) in width. With gigantic rock mounds, spires and turrets banded in many colours, the Grand Canyon's scenery is stunning.

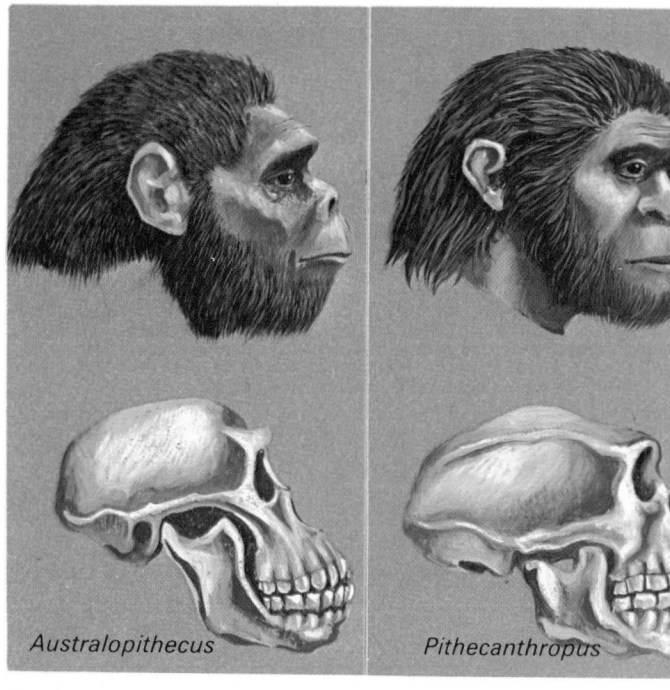

Australopithecus   *Pithecanthropus*

What did our ancestors look like?

The Grand Canyon was already old (though not so deep) when the hominids, or man-like creatures, above were alive. The whole question of the origins of mankind is today a matter of argument, but these examples show the development from an ape-like creature to someone quite like Dad.

Australopithecus means 'southern ape-man' and it was one of the first hominids to walk upright, over three million years ago. It lived in Africa and was originally thought to be an ape. However, its erect position, hip bone structure and teeth led to its reclassification as a hominid. The brain was the size of that of a gorilla but the body was smaller. *Pithecanthropus* lived about half a million years ago. Neanderthal man appeared about 70 000 years ago and gave way to Cro-Magnon man about 30 000 years ago.

As one type succeeded another the top of the skull grew larger, making room for a larger brain. When meat was eaten cooked instead of raw, the powerful jaws and teeth became unnecessary. The jaw retreated and the bony ridge of the brow, which had supported strong jaw muscles, disappeared.

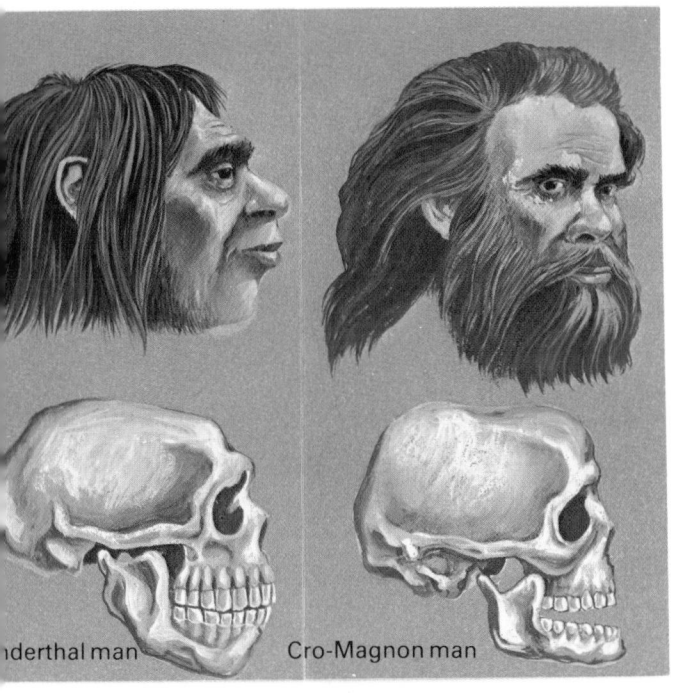

Neanderthal man   Cro-Magnon man

Who is studying the iguanas?

The English naturalist Charles Darwin's ideas about evolution were stimulated by a visit to the remote Galapagos Islands (below), off South America, during his voyage on the ship *Beagle* (1831–36). He observed that many animals there were similar to the animals on the mainland, yet they were not exactly the same. They had evolved into different species. He explained this by his theory of natural selection. Individuals of any species are more likely to survive – and reproduce – if they are better suited to life in their environment than other individuals. These slight individual differences are inherited and thus, over a long time, the species evolves, or changes. He published this theory in *On the Origin of Species* (1859).

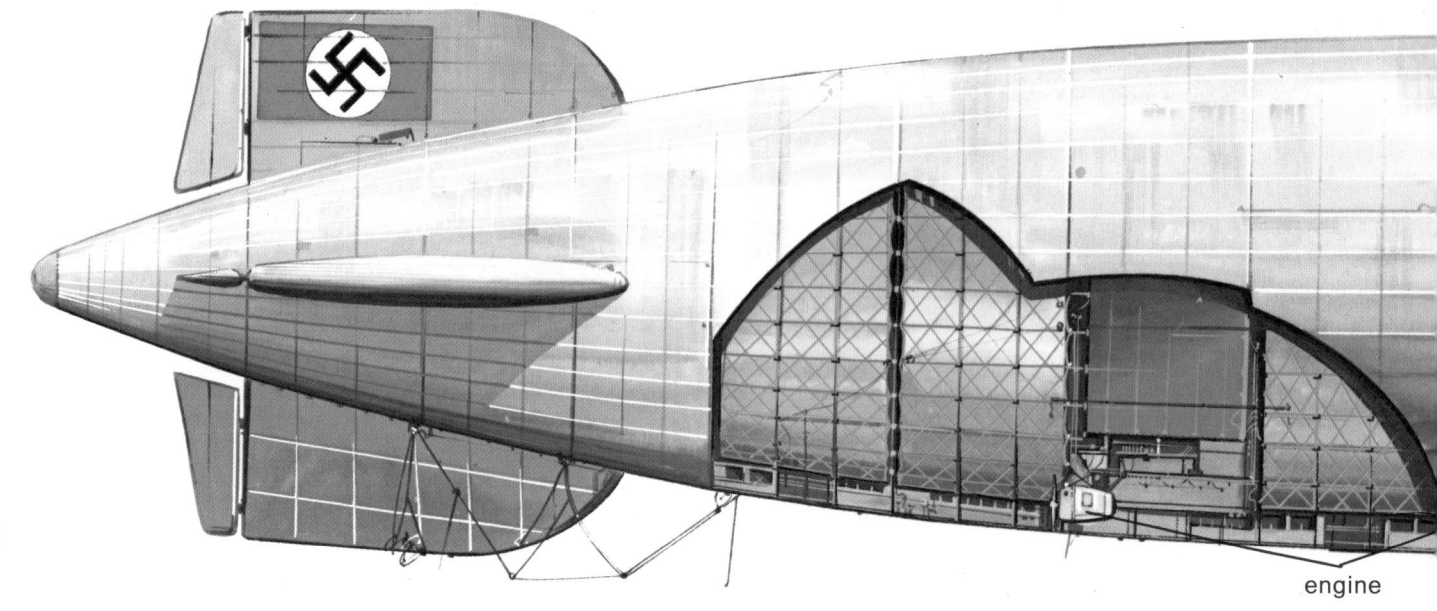

engine

Has the airship a future?

Almost as soon as balloons were invented, about 200 years ago, people began to dream of a balloon that could be moved and directed. In the late 19th century the invention of electric and petrol engines made the dirigible (manoeuvrable airship) a possibility. Several non-rigid airships – true, soft balloons with a basket containing the engine (and everything else) slung underneath – made short but successful flights.

The German Zeppelins (named after their inventor) were rigid airships, with bags of gas inside a framework covered with fabric. They began carrying passengers in 1910 and were used in the First World War. The British R34, which crossed the Atlantic in both directions in 1919, was a similar design, and by the 1930s huge airships were making Atlantic passenger flights regularly. That came to an end when the *Hindenburg* (above) burst into flames on landing in New York in 1937, killing 30 people.

Non-rigid airships (blimps) are still used for pleasure trips, as airborne advertisements, and for carrying TV cameras. Much better rigid airships could be built today and some people believe they might make useful cargo transporters.

Who was Nehru?

Jawaharlal Nehru (1889–1964), above, was the father of the republic of India. He came from an upper-class family and studied in England before returning to India in 1912. He became a close associate of Gandhi in the National Congress party which was devoted to gaining

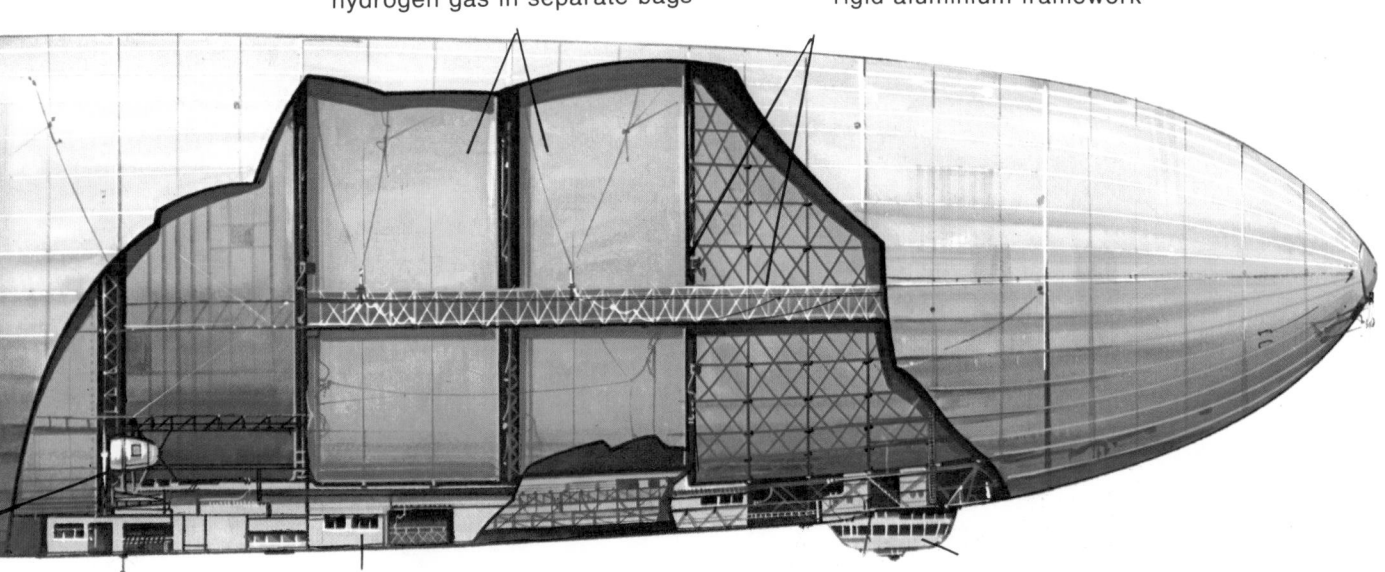

hydrogen gas in separate bags   rigid aluminium framework

passenger accommodation   control car

independence from Britain. Pandit (a title meaning 'learned man') Nehru, however, believed that socialism and industrialization should be India's aims rather than the rural programme of Gandhi. Nehru was prime minister of India from independence in 1947 until his death. He was a world statesman and leader of the non-aligned nations (not closely linked to the Soviet Union or the USA), who was loved in his own country and respected throughout the world. His daughter, Mrs Indira Gandhi, was to fill her father's position after his death.

Quick Quiz

With what countries are the following people associated?
(1) Washington, (2) Lenin, (3) Mussolini, (4) Napoleon, (5) Cromwell, (6) Nehru, (7) Hitler, (8) Nasser, (9) Kublai Khan, (10) De Valera.

Answers: (1) USA, (2) Soviet Union, (3) Italy, (4) France, (5) England, (6) India, (7) Germany, (8) Egypt, (9) China, (10) Ireland.

Why build an observatory on a mountain?

The Earth's atmosphere creates difficulties for astronomers: even when it's not cloudy, dust in the atmosphere obscures the view of the stars. At the Pic du Midi observatory below, nearly 3000 m (10 000 ft) up in the Pyrenees, the atmosphere is thinner, and therefore clearer.

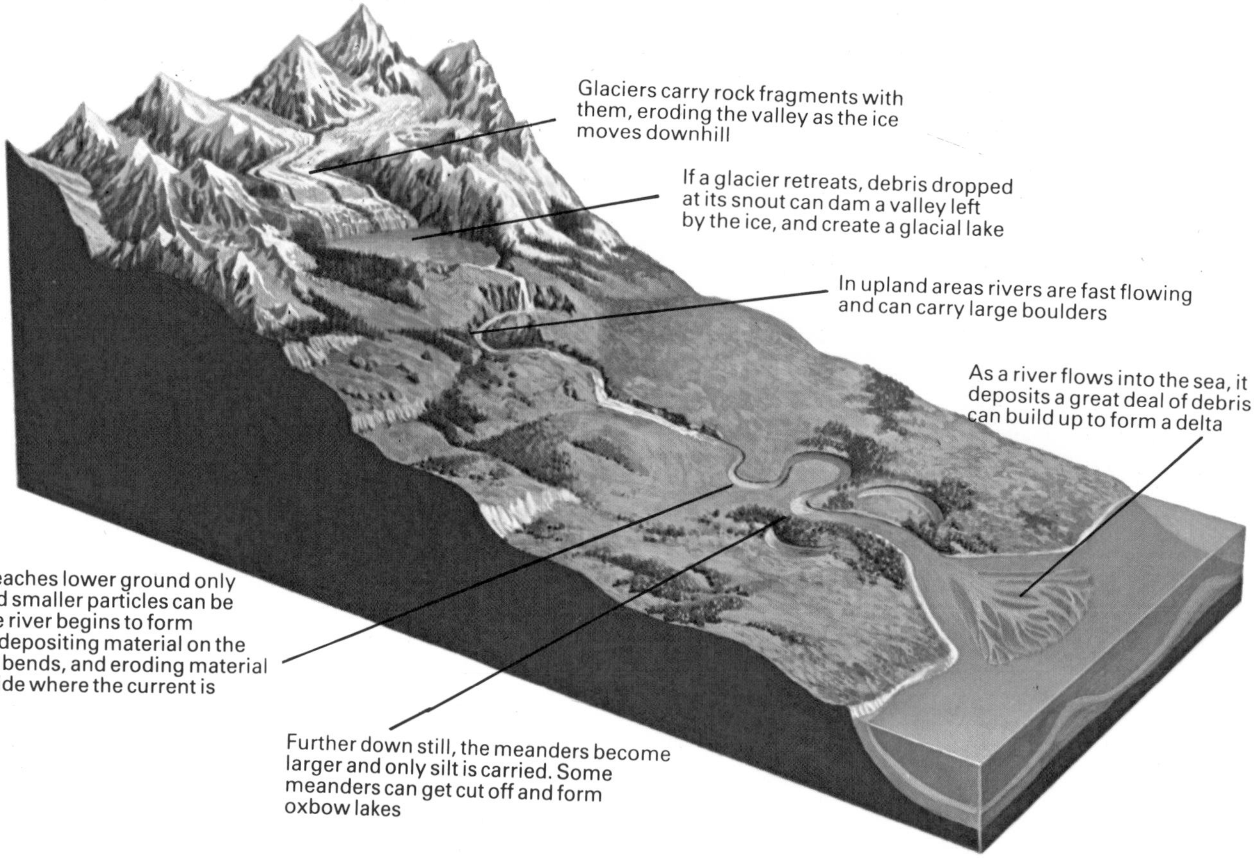

Glaciers carry rock fragments with them, eroding the valley as the ice moves downhill

If a glacier retreats, debris dropped at its snout can dam a valley left by the ice, and create a glacial lake

In upland areas rivers are fast flowing and can carry large boulders

As a river flows into the sea, it deposits a great deal of debris which can build up to form a delta

As a river reaches lower ground only pebbles and smaller particles can be carried. The river begins to form meanders, depositing material on the inside of its bends, and eroding material on the outside where the current is stronger

Further down still, the meanders become larger and only silt is carried. Some meanders can get cut off and form oxbow lakes

Can the Earth be shaped by water?

bay with beach

cave

cliff

arch

stack

wave-cut platform

Water is a very important agent for shaping the landscape. In fact, much of the surface of the Earth owes its form to the action of water. Rivers can both erode, or wear away, the land, and deposit large masses of material to build up the land (above). Both these actions occur over very long periods of time. Where rivers flow quickly, as in mountains, they pick up much soil and stones (a river in flood always looks dirty because it carries a lot of mud), but when they slow down, as in flatter country, they leave the debris behind.

The seas and oceans also have enormous effects on the land, creating a great variety of coastal features (left). The action of waves on the land will erode it, but depending on the type of rock, it will erode in different ways and at different rates. If soft rock occurs next to hard rock on the same coast the soft rock will wear away faster than the land, creating bays and headlands. Waves and currents can also move material along coastlines, and spits and sandbanks can be formed in this way.

Do cats eat cabbage?

Unfortunately, cats prefer to eat birds, yet in a sense they *do* eat cabbage. The picture below illustrates a simple food chain: aphid eats cabbage leaf, bird eats aphid, cat eats bird. You can easily imagine hundreds of such food chains, but they all begin with green plants.

Plants contain chlorophyll, a substance which enables them to trap the energy in sunlight (it is also what makes them green). This is the source of all energy. As all living things, plant or animal, need energy to stay alive, the Sun can be seen as the source of life. Animals do not have chlorophyll and therefore cannot tap the Sun's energy themselves. They do so by eating plants, or by eating an animal which eats plants, or by eating an animal which eats an animal which eats plants.

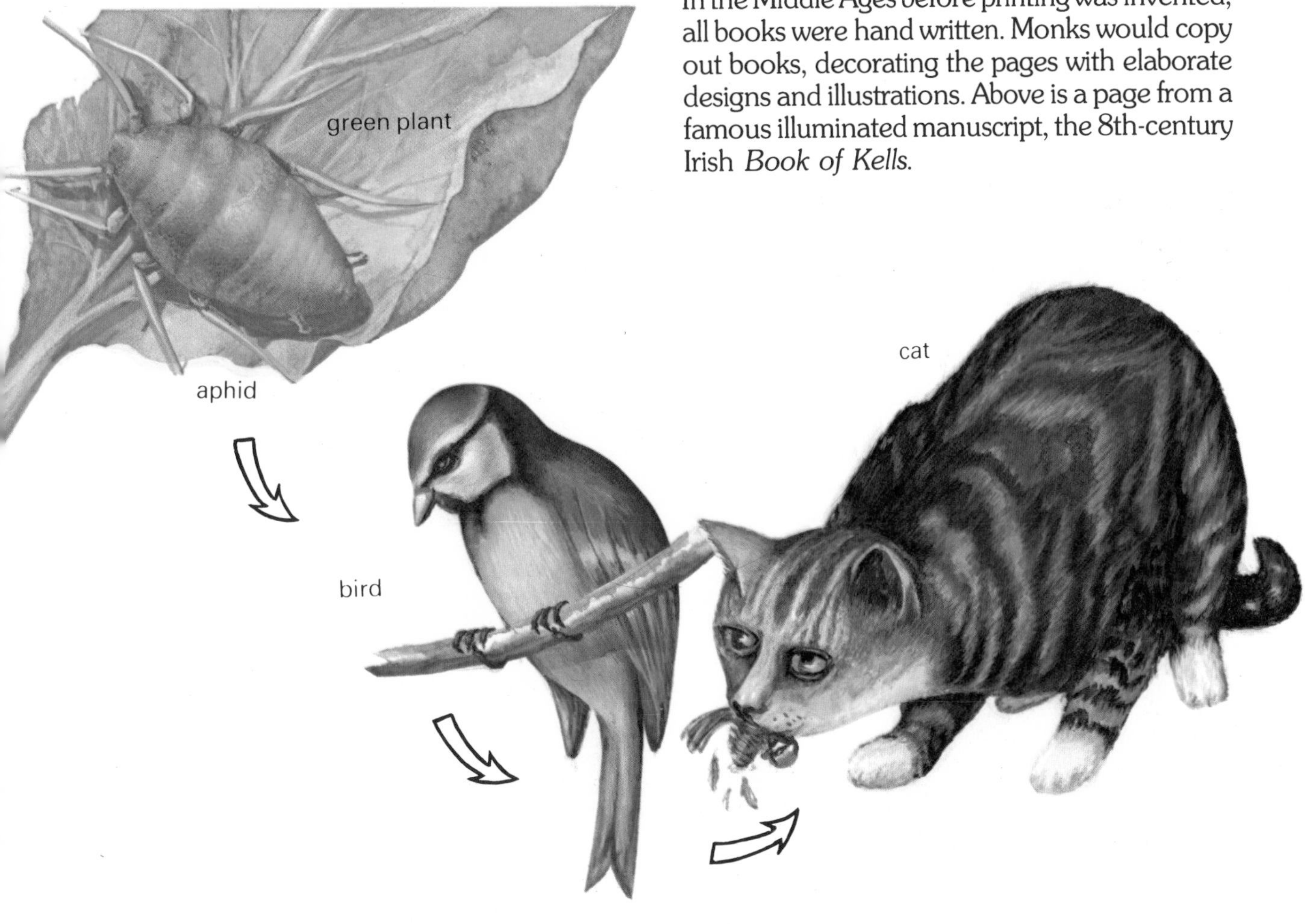

What is an illuminated manuscript?

In the Middle Ages before printing was invented, all books were hand written. Monks would copy out books, decorating the pages with elaborate designs and illustrations. Above is a page from a famous illuminated manuscript, the 8th-century Irish *Book of Kells*.

green plant

aphid

bird

cat

Who lived in castles?

In the Middle Ages few places were completely peaceful for very long, and kings and rulers lived in castles which could not be easily captured by an enemy. In England the greatest castle-builders were the Normans. Having conquered the country in 1066, they were determined to keep it!

In a Norman castle the central building was the keep (below). It was where the lord and his family lived, along with many of his soldiers and servants. It often had dungeons below it, and the castle was surrounded by a wall and moat.

Can lemurs fly?

Lemurs are rare animals which come mainly from the large island of Madagascar. They are primates, like monkeys and apes, with fox-like muzzles and large staring eyes. There are 10 species, but the flying lemur, or colugo (above left), which comes from South-east Asia, is not a true lemur at all. In fact, it seems to be quite unique, and is classified in an order of its own. It has loose folds of skin between its four feet and neck and, with limbs outstretched, it is the shape of a kite. It can glide quite a distance, though it cannot actually fly. The 'wings' also help to make a useful cradle for a baby when it hangs upside down. Although the flying lemur can glide and crawl along branches, often hanging upside down, it cannot walk. If it gets stranded on the ground it has to drag itself along to the nearest tree.

It is not the only mammal built like a glider. There are several species of squirrel which have similar flaps of skin to help them from one tree to the next. The giant flying squirrels are almost 1 m (3 ft 3 in) in length, and can glide for over 450 m (490 yards).

Have you ever seen an armadillo?

The armadillos (above right) – there are about 20 different species – come from Central and South America and are related to ant-eaters. They have an unusual defence against predators – armour plating. The bony scales of the armour are closely linked by tough and flexible skin, so the armadillo can move quite freely in spite of its teeth-proof layer (the flesh of the armadillo is said to be tasty). Some can roll themselves into a tight ball, protecting the soft underparts as well. They have strong claws which they use to dig for food – mainly insects and grubs – and most of them are good burrowers, spending the day asleep underground. The fairy armadillo in fact spends most of its life in the earth, like a mole. This tiny creature is only just over 1 cm (0.4 in) long, but its largest relation, the giant armadillo, is nearly 2 m (6 ft) and can weigh as much as 50 kg (110 lb). Armadillos, sloths and anteaters belong to the order (group of families) Edentata, which means 'without teeth'. However, only the anteaters lack teeth and the giant armadillo actually has more teeth than most mammals.

191

How did Blériot win £1000?

On 25 July 1909 Louis Blériot (1872–1936) flew his aircraft (below), which he designed himself, across the English Channel from Calais to Dover. It was the first flight – except in balloons – over the Channel (or any other sea) and won him a prize of £1000 offered by the *Daily Mail*, a London newspaper. Blériot's 37-minute cross-channel flight created so much interest in his aircraft that he soon had orders for 100 of his Blériot XI model. It was a monoplane, whereas most aircraft of its time were biplanes.

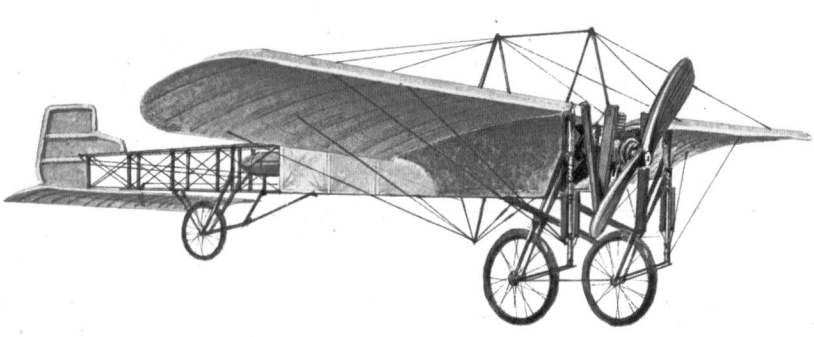

What are pitcher plants?

Although many animals eat plants, plants that eat animals are rather unusual. Among those that do are the pitcher plants (below). A pitcher is a kind of jug, and pitcher plants have leaves which form a container and are lined with bristles. Insects are attracted by nectar and are trapped. They die and decompose, and their bodies are absorbed as nutrients by the plant. There are many different pitcher plants. Most of them grow in wet, tropical regions.

What was the 'Blitz'?

For a period early in the Second World War, Germany had only one active enemy in Europe. That enemy was Great Britain.

Hitler, the German leader, decided to overcome the British by a campaign of bombing by night. 'Blitz' is the English name for this campaign, but it is not a good one. *Blitzkrieg* means 'lightning war', but the Blitz was a slow process

which was meant to grind down the spirit of the British. It failed. In fact, it had the opposite effect. When people speak about 'the spirit of the Blitz', they are referring to the comradeship and patriotism shown by the British people at that time.

London was the first target. It was bombed every night from 7 September to 2 November 1940. Then the attack was switched to other big industrial cities; Coventry was the worst hit. The

Blitz lasted until May 1941. After that, air raids continued, but not on the same massive scale.

Although the Blitz was a total failure for the Germans, it did cause great destruction. Over 3.5 million houses were damaged or destroyed, and so were many famous buildings, including the House of Commons. About 30 000 people were killed, more than half of them in London. A far larger number were made homeless.

Can an aeroplane flap its wings?

An aeroplane needs *lift* to keep it in the air, and wings are designed to give as much lift as possible, especially when the aeroplane takes off. A wing gives more lift if the curve of its top surface is increased, so wing flaps (above) are designed to do this. As they also increase *drag* (the force holding the aircraft back), they are retracted during flight, when the aeroplane has reached its cruising speed and altitude.

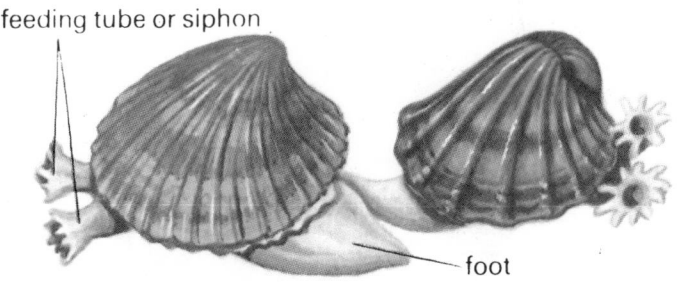

feeding tube or siphon

foot

What creatures have only one foot?

The class of molluscs (animals with shells) called gastropods, which includes cockles (above) and snails, have a single 'foot' extending from their shell which enables them to move about – slowly.

What kind of weapon was the longbow?

Tradition says that the longbow was a Welsh invention. Certainly it was much used in Britain. The bowman below is waxing the string of his bow, which is nearly 2 m (6.5 ft) long and made of yew wood. A good archer could shoot up to 12 arrows a minute to a range of nearly 300 m (328 yds). At close range certain arrows could pierce armour. The pointed stakes protected archers from charging cavalry.

outer case

silvered surface

double-walled glass container

vacuum

contents

Why does a vacuum flask keep drinks hot?

The vacuum (a space with no air) between the walls of the flask (above) will not carry heat, thus keeping the contents warm.

arrows with selection of heads

Were North American Indians a single nation?

Although the total population of North American Indians when the Europeans arrived was quite small (probably less than 1.5 million), they were divided into a bewildering number of nations and tribes. Many different languages were spoken, some quite unrelated to their neighbours, and two Indian nations like (for example) the Apache and the Cherokee were no more closely related than Scots and Italians. We may think of American Indians as nomadic, horse-riding people, but there were no horses in the Americas before the Europeans, and many of the larger groups lived a settled life in villages. The Plains Indians may have hunted buffalo, but the various tribes of the Algonkin group in the east were mainly farmers and fishermen.

Chief Sitting Bull (below) was one of the most famous leaders of the Sioux in the 19th century. The map shows the the territories of some of the Indians.

What is a totem pole?

Only the Indians of the North-West, from Vancouver to Alaska, made totem poles (above). They are large wooden pillars, carved with symbols, or totems. Some of them represented events in the history of the tribe, some were like coats of arms, and some were simply memorials to the dead. The art of carving totem poles flourished in the 19th century, when steel tools were available, but it has almost disappeared today.

What lives in cold lands?

The cold lands of the world, where the temperature seldom rises above freezing during the long dark winters, and where the summers are very short (though often quite hot in daytime), are nearly all in the northern hemisphere. The only cold land in the southern hemisphere is Antarctica, and there it is so cold that very few animals or plants can survive.

A great forest of pine and fir trees stretches across the northern hemisphere, from Alaska and northern Canada, through Scandinavia and most of the northern Soviet Union. These trees can survive the intense winter cold, and provide our largest supply of softwood, besides supporting a varied population of animals.

Farther north, where no trees grow, the land is under snow for most of the year, and a few inches below the surface the soil may be permanently frozen. These cold plains are called tundra. In the short summer mosses, lichens and flowering plants appear. There are about a thousand different species of wild flower which bloom north of the Arctic Circle.

squirrel

crossbill

elk

wolves

brown bear

fox

beavers

weasel

South of the Antarctic Circle, only two wildflowers have been found. The reason the Antarctic is so much colder than the Arctic is that it is land – mountainous land at that – while the Arctic is mostly ocean. The sea holds heat better than land, and temperatures are higher at sea level than on high, windy mountains. Even the Arctic Ocean is more or less covered by ice, but its waters support many fish and other animals, as do the waters of the Antarctic. The animals of cold lands are described in more detail on the next two pages.

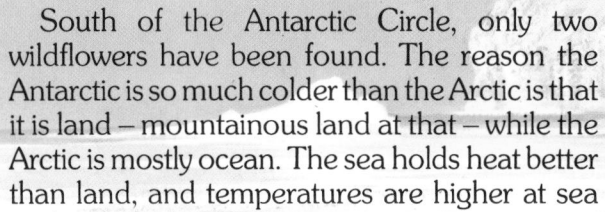

polar bear

blue whale

emperor penguin

leopard seals

reindeer

arctic fox

ermine
(stoat in winter coat)

ptarmigan

lemmings

arctic hare

Animals of cold lands

Some of the animals in the illustration on the previous two pages only live in the northern or the southern hemispheres, so would never meet. For example, the emperor penguin and the leopard seal are inhabitants of Antarctica, but the polar bear is found only in Arctic regions.

Small mammals

The red squirrel ranges right across northern Europe and Siberia, feeding on cones and storing up a supply to last through the winter.

The red fox, like many other animals in the far north, changes its coat according to the season, growing thicker fur for the cold winter months.

Other animals also change the colour of their coat. The ermine discards its white fur in the summer along with the melting snow, and adopts an attractive colour scheme of brown and pale gold. Also called the short-tailed weasel, it is in fact very closely related to the stoat.

The common European weasel is one of several other members of the weasel family to live in the northern pine forests. It is one of the smallest meat-eaters, and lives mainly on mice and voles.

The beaver was once quite common throughout North America south of the Arctic and in northern Europe and Asia. This remarkable

animal is now found mainly in far northern forests because it has been exterminated in other parts. It has a broad tail which acts as a rudder when swimming and large, webbed hind feet. Beavers build a 'lodge' out of sticks plastered with mud. This is sited in the middle of a pond which the beavers make by damming a stream. When the mud freezes, no predator can get in, as the entrance is underwater.

The lemming is a small rodent which has become famous through one peculiar habit. Like many small Arctic animals, its population varies enormously. When a 'population explosion' occurs, roughly every four years, they leave their underground burrows and migrate in vast numbers. In the case of the Norway lemming, they often reach the sea – and keep right on going, until they become exhausted and drown.

Arctic hares remain snow-white all year round in the high Arctic, but those living farther south turn brown or grey in summer. They usually live in large groups, wandering over the tundra. Their fur is soft and warm, and greatly valued by the Inuit (Eskimo). But catching an Arctic hare is not easy. They are practically invisible against a snow background.

The Arctic fox is slightly smaller than the red fox and its ears are not so pointed. It has the thickest fur of any polar animal of its size. Unlike the Arctic hare, it is white only in winter, and those in more southern areas never turn white at all. It will sometimes follow a polar bear, feeding on the scraps it leaves.

Large Mammals

The greatest predator of the cold forests is the wolf. These social animals, living in packs, lead a complex life and we are only just beginning to understand them. The colour of the grey or timber wolf varies according to where it lives. In the high Arctic they are almost white; farther south, they are nearly black. They prey on the huge herds of reindeer, picking off sick or old

lemmings

bear

animals, but they probably eat more small animals, like voles.

Many bears live in the far north. The brown bear, or Kodiak bear, lives mostly in the forest region of Alaska. They are the largest of the land bears, larger even than the grizzly, but they are by no means as fierce as their reputation. Although, like most bears, they enjoy meat (to say nothing of fresh salmon), they are largely vegetarian.

The polar bear, a true Arctic animal, can be more of a menace to humans (though not so much as humans are a menace to it), not because they are aggressive but because they are inquisitive and fearless. Arctic explorers used to complain that there was no way to stop a polar bear pillaging their stores except to shoot it.

Two of the largest members of the deer family live in the cold northern lands. They have different names in Europe and America: the elk is called a moose in America (some zoologists think they are separate species) and the reindeer is called a caribou.

The elk prefers the forested regions, sometimes moving north on to the plains in summer. It has wide, scoop-shaped antlers and a broad, drooping muzzle, with a loose 'bell' of skin under its chin.

Reindeer are unusual animals in several ways. They are the only species of deer in which both males and females grow antlers, and they are the only species that can be tamed. They migrate across the tundra in enormous herds. The hairs in their coat are hollow, which helps to keep them warm and assists them when swimming.

Animals of cold oceans

Many northern coasts are crowded with seals, but the leopard seal is an animal of the Antarctic. It is the fiercest of seals, having powerful teeth and growing to a length of 4 m (13 ft). Besides fish, it eats great numbers of penguins.

Whales, including the gigantic blue whale, roam both the far northern and southern oceans. Most large species are baleen whales, which have no teeth but a whalebone (baleen) filter for catching plankton. One exception is the sperm whale. Many of the larger whales have been hunted almost to extinction, though recent internationally-agreed limits to the numbers killed have – we hope – made them safe.

Penguins live in the Antarctic. The emperor penguin is the largest and most fascinating. It breeds in, of all places, the freezing cold and darkness of the Antarctic continent in winter. The female lays a single egg and the male looks after it, placing it on top of his feet, so it does not touch the ice, and covering it with a special fold of his skin, like an egg cosy. He keeps it for about two months, until it hatches, and cannot feed during that time.

Birds

The colourful crossbill, a specialist cone-eater, is a type of finch whose bill, crossing at the tips, is ideal for prying apart pine cones to get at the seeds inside. The red crossbill is found throughout coniferous forests in North America, Europe and Asia.

Farther north live two species of ptarmigan, which will burrow into snow drifts to keep warm in very cold weather. They are white in winter, but a speckled brown in summer.

crossbill

199

Who was 'John Company'?

The English East India Company was founded in 1601 by a group of London merchants trading with the East Indies. Driven out of the islands by the Dutch, the Company concentrated on India. According to its royal charter, it had the right to build fortresses, raise armies, issue money and sign treaties with rulers in the territories where it traded. As its rivals – the Dutch, Portuguese, French and other British companies – were driven out, it became more and more a political organization, ruling most of India.

The nickname 'John Company' echoed the nickname of England itself – 'John Bull'. After several corruption scandals the British government decided to bring the Company under some control, and in 1773 a governor-general who had to answer to Parliament was appointed to India. After the outbreak known as the Indian Mutiny (1857), all the Company's powers were taken over by the government. Below, an East India Company ship unloads at the port of London in the 18th century.

200

How can you get through a mangrove swamp?

The answer any African explorer would give is, 'With great difficulty'! The mangrove tree is able to live in salty tidal swamps along tropical coasts around the world by growing roots that arch through the air before they descend into the mud. The roots may be thicker than your arm, and they make a formidable tangle which justifies the description of mangrove swamps as 'impenetrable'. Mangroves help to reclaim land from the sea by trapping sediment which accumulates to form mud banks.

Quick Quiz

What are the following?
(1) Mango, (2) Mangle, (3) Mangle-wurzel, (4) Mangrove, (5) Manganese, (6) Mange.

Answers: (1) tropical fruit, (2) a machine for rolling wet clothes, (3) a type of beet, (4) a tree or shrub growing in swamps, (5) a metal, (6) a skin disease, of cats especially.

Why is the Moon like a golf ball?

From the Earth the Moon may look like a golf ball in the sky. From closer up it has another feature like a golf ball: it is covered with dents. The craters of the Moon (above), or most of them, were caused by meteorites striking the surface. As the Moon has no atmosphere, it takes a tremendous battering from these flying chunks of space rock. On Earth, most of them burn up in the atmosphere as a result of the heat of friction.

However, some Moon craters may have been caused by volcanic explosions, as much of the surface is made up of volcanic lava. There is no volcanic activity on the Moon now and probably has not been for a very long time. The Moon rocks brought back by the astronauts who landed there were extremely old – at least three thousand million years. The dark patches on the Moon's face that form the 'man-in-the-Moon' shape, are lowland plains composed of dark, volcanic lava that once spilled out from inside the Moon. They are called maria, from the Latin for sea.

Who discovered America?

Christopher Columbus discovered America in 1492, but his ships were not the first from Europe to reach North American coasts. It is possible that Irish monks, or a Welsh prince, had crossed the Atlantic centuries before. Their voyages, if they ever took place at all, had been forgotten, and so had the voyages of the Vikings, who had settled first in Iceland, then in Greenland and finally in Newfoundland in the 10th century. Although Columbus was not the first European to reach America, his discovery is the important one.

The Viking colony in North America did not survive long. They were too few and the Indians remained hostile. The Viking ships had no cabins, though the sail would make a tent (below) and they slept in leather bags, three men to one bag for extra warmth.

What food do we get from plants?

Human beings are omnivores – they eat both animals and plants. However, you can have a healthy diet without eating meat at all. Many people do, either by choice (they are called vegetarians) or because they cannot afford meat. It would be more difficult to live on a diet of meat alone.

We eat a great variety of plant products. Some of them, especially fruits such as apples, cherries or tomatoes, can be eaten just as Nature (with help from the farmer) supplies them. Many vegetables can also be eaten raw, though most are more pleasant cooked (have you ever tried a raw potato?). Other plant products are normally processed before we eat them. The grain of wheat, which in Europe is probably the most important plant food, is milled into flour. From the flour we get bread, cakes and pastry, as well as such foods as spaghetti and noodles.

How a poppy makes its seeds

poppy flower

the petals die

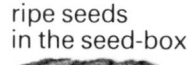

ripe seeds
in the seed-box

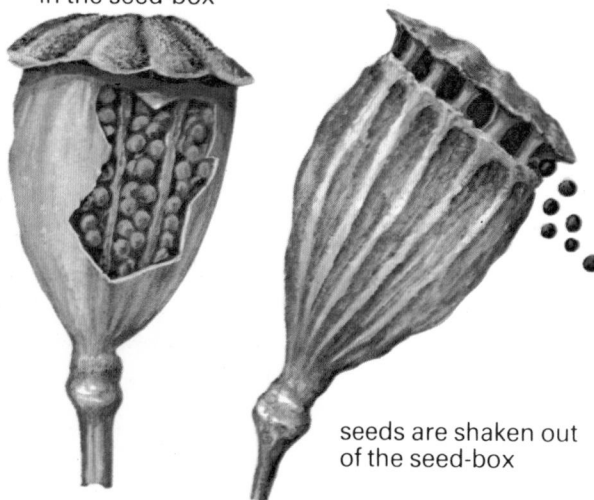

seeds are shaken out
of the seed-box

How does a plant make its seeds?

Plants which produce seeds can be divided into two groups according to the way they bear the seeds. In one group, called angiosperms, the seeds are enclosed in some kind of fruit. All flowering plants (like the poppy above) are angiosperms. In the other group, gymnosperms, the seeds are 'naked', that is, they are not encased in a fruit. Cone-bearing trees are an example. Seeds are made up of an embryo – a future plant – and a protective coating called the testa. Most also contain a food-storing tissue which is called the endosperm.

left to right, a herdsman from Afghanistan, a young woman with a water jar in Pakistan, and a well-armed Arab from Jordan. In a hot climate loose clothes are much more comfortable than European dress.

What is the fastest creature on four legs?

The cheetah is an odd cat. It has long legs, does not climb and its claws do not retract. It hunts gazelles and antelopes in Africa and Asia by rushing at them with great speed – up to 100 km/h (60 mph) – and pouncing.

Where do these people come from?

Although businessmen the world over may wear the same kind of suit, in many parts of the world, and in Islamic countries especially, traditional costumes are still common. These people are,

Who's been to Mars?

Above is a US Viking satellite which reached Mars in 1976. The bottom half stayed in orbit and the top landed on the surface. It sent back much information but found no signs of life.

What makes a car go?

In the future, people looking at a car in a museum will probably say, 'What a crude machine!' The engine may seem to run smoothly, but what makes it go is a series of explosions.

This typical modern car uses petrol as fuel. The petrol is pumped from the fuel tank into the carburettor (1), where it is mixed with air and becomes vapour. The petrol vapour enters the cylinders (6), where the power is created. As the piston moves down, the vapour enters the cylinder through a valve (a). The valve closes and the vapour is compressed by the piston moving up (b). A spark from the spark plug ignites the vapour: this is the explosion, which forces the piston down again (c). The exhaust valve opens as the piston moves up to force out the exhaust gases (d). This happens many times a second.

The pistons (usually four in a small or medium-sized car) turn a crankshaft which provides the rotary movement to turn the

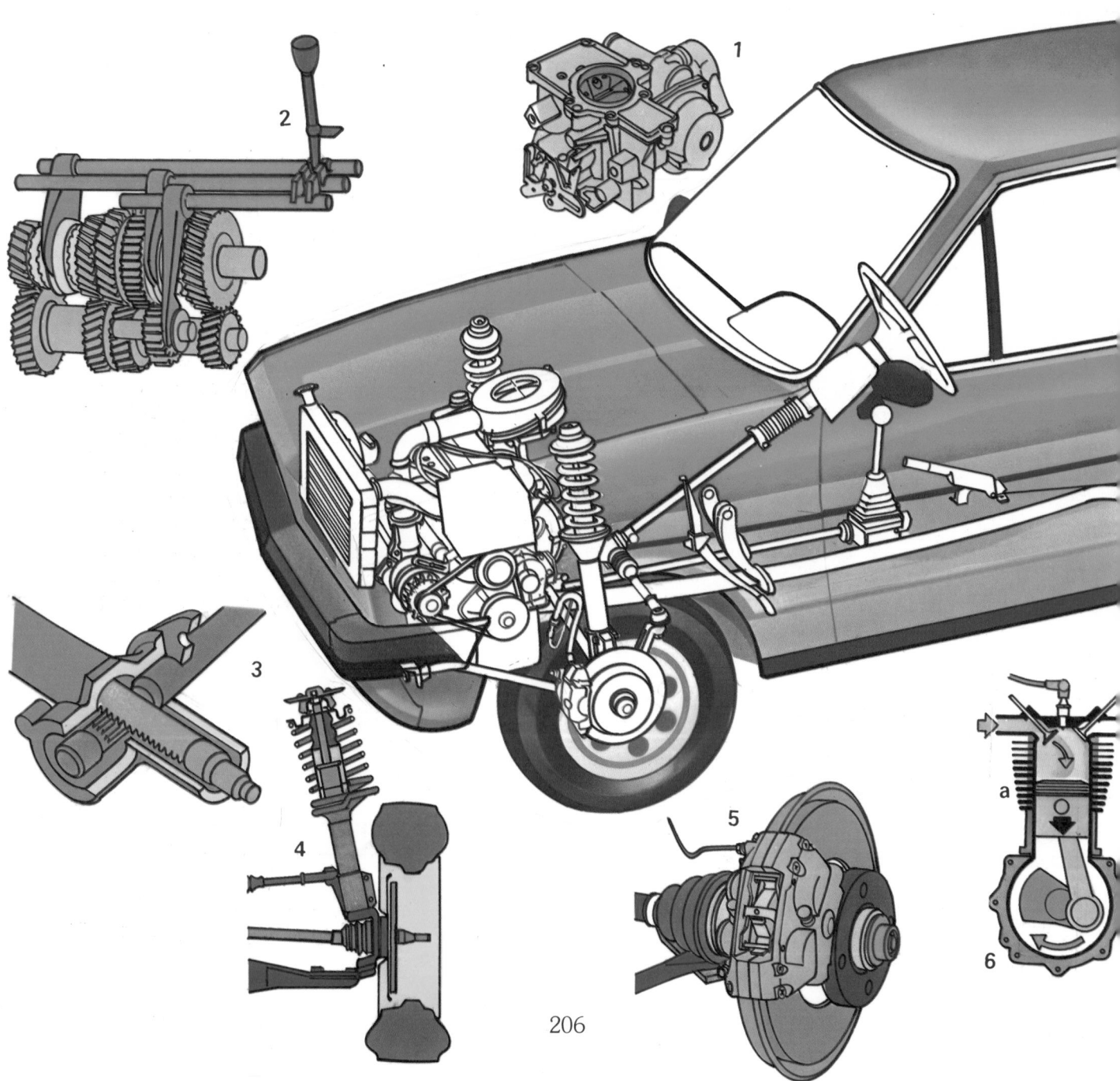

wheels. First, the crankshaft turns the gears in the gearbox (2). The different gears alter the speed of the engine in relation to the wheels, according to the power needed. The car is steered by a 'rack-and-pinion', which moves the front wheels when the driver turns the steering wheel (3). The suspension (4) absorbs bumps so the car 'rides' smoothly. Most cars have disc brakes (5) in which, when the driver presses the brake pedal, pads are clamped against an iron disc fixed to the wheel.

Why is the lion the king of beasts?

The lion's reputation as 'lord of the jungle' may be due to his fierce and splendid appearance, or to the fact that he has no real enemies – except humans. But perhaps his most regal characteristic is his ability to live a comfortable, well-fed existence without doing very much himself. Lionesses do most of the hunting, and members of a pride will spend as much as 18 hours a day asleep. They are the only truly social cat, and prides normally consist of one or more adult males, a large number of females and their cubs.

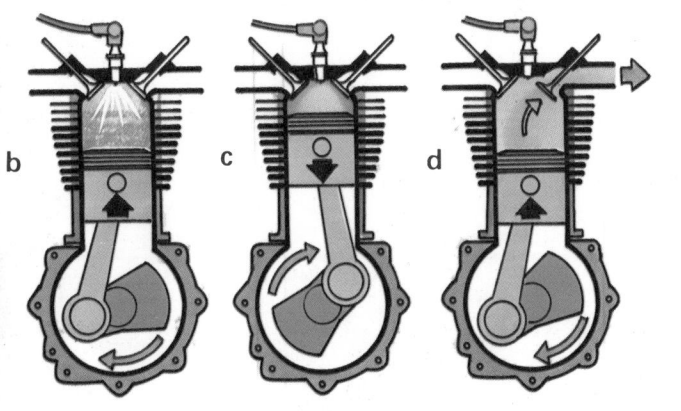

Quick Quiz

What countries use or have used the following coins?
(1) Yen, (2) Doubloon, (3) Rupee,
(4) Guinea, (5) Louis d'or, (6) Drachma.

Answers: (1) Japan, (2) Spain, (3) India, (4) Britain, (5) France, (6) Greece.

207

Who was the founder of modern China?

Probably the most important figure in modern Chinese history is Mao Tse-tung (1893–1976). Mao (shown on the right as a young man) began organizing Communist groups in 1920. Fighting between Mao's Communists and Chiang Kai-shek's Nationalists started in 1927 and continued until 1949 (though they did unite against the Japanese invaders in 1937).

After the Nationalist forces had fled to Taiwan in 1949, the establishment of the People's Republic of China was proclaimed with Mao Tse-tung as its leader. The new government transferred the land from the landowners to the peasants and established heavy industries. In the late 1950s communes were established to co-ordinate planning in agriculture, industry, defence and education. Mao remained the driving force behind the development of China until his death.

Why are earthquakes a danger in California?

The San Andreas Fault (below), which runs through California, caused the San Francisco earthquake of 1906, when much of the city was destroyed. It marks the division between two of the gigantic 'plates' which make up the Earth's crust, and which are pushing in opposite directions.

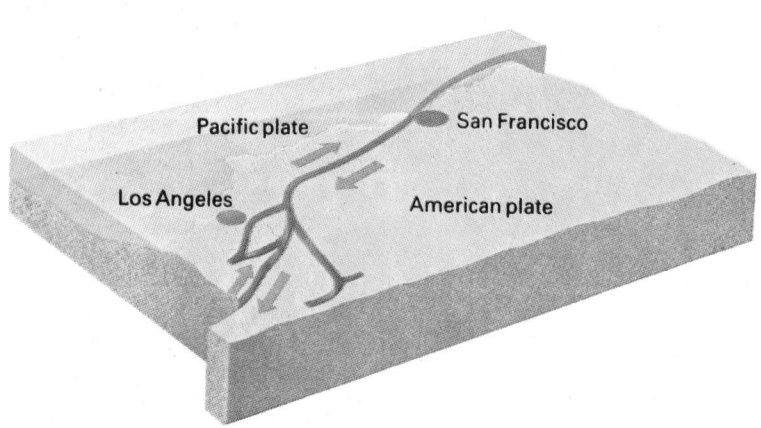

Where is Hadrian's Wall?

All great conquerors have run into the same problem: where do you stop? After the successful Roman invasion of Britain in AD 43, there seemed to be no alternative except to conquer the whole island, then made up of many small kingdoms. Most of England was soon under control, but farther north and west Roman rule was less secure, and the Roman legions never did manage to subdue the fierce Caledonian tribes of Scotland. Eventually the Emperor

Hadrian admitted defeat by constructing a permanent frontier in AD 122–128. The stone wall named after him ran between the Roman forts at Carlisle and Corbridge, a distance of about 200 km (125 miles), and was later expanded farther east. Forts and signal towers were built at regular intervals. The wall was about 3 m (7 ft) thick and 5 m (16.5 ft) high, with a deep ditch in front of it. Parts of it can still be seen today.

Who fought for Rome?

Beginning as a small republic in central Italy, by the 4th century Rome had grown into an empire which stretched from Scotland to the Red Sea, from Portugal to Persia. Although not all parts of the Roman empire were peaceful, and the Romans often had to face rebellions or attacks from tribes outside the empire, the Roman armies were almost invincible.

The soldiers who fought in those armies were not, of course, all Romans. They came from many different provinces of the empire, but Roman training, which could last up to five years, and Roman discipline made them effective troops. In time some of them earned the honour of Roman citizenship.

Roman soldiers (below) wore metal helmets, light body armour and metal-studded sandals. They carried javelins and slings for hurling lead missiles, as well as a short sword and shield. A soldier on the march, however, had to carry much more: 17 days' ration of grain, metal dish, water bottle and cook-pot (all wrapped in a bundle on a forked stick, seen opposite), a saw, pickaxe and perhaps a pair of sharpened wooden stakes for defending temporary camps. The total weight of this was 36 kg (80 lb).

On the move the legions (armies of 3000 to 6000 soldiers, or legionaries) were followed by a baggage train which might include giant catapults and other siege engines to attack fortified settlements. Another kind of 'legion' also tagged along: women, children, beggars, tradesmen – a motley following of civilians, some pushing barrows, some in carts, and a noisy rabble of goats, chickens and other domestic animals.

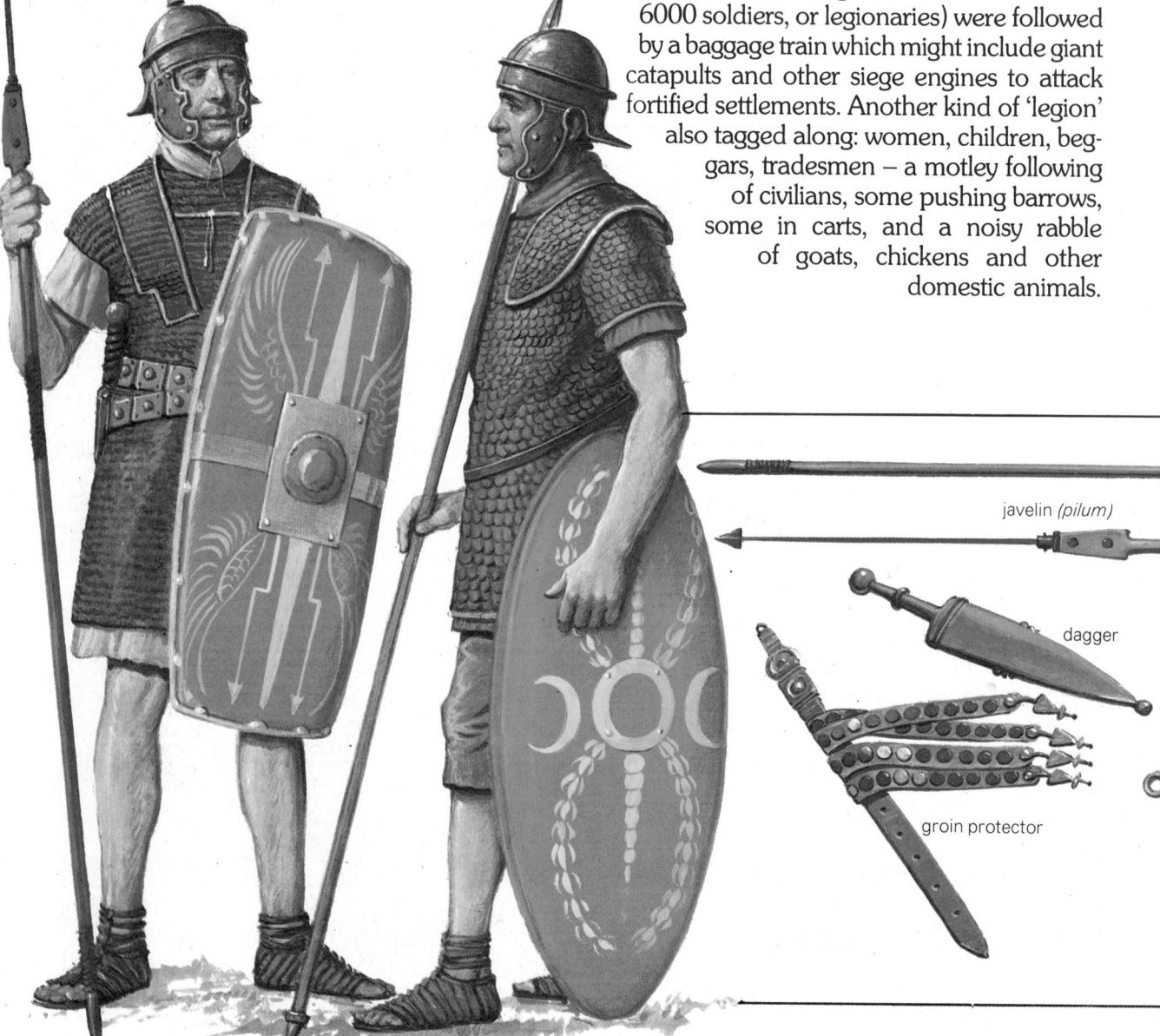

javelin *(pilum)*

dagger

groin protector

What was the Model T?

The early motor cars were expensive, hand-made vehicles which only rich and enthusiastic drivers could afford. The American engineer and businessman Henry Ford (1863–1947) changed all that when he set up the Ford Motor Company in Detroit, USA in 1903. Ford planned to produce cars for ordinary working people. His factory operated on the latest mass-production methods, with the cars produced on an assembly line, using standardized parts which could be made in large quantities. The Model T, first produced in 1909, was small, simple, and cheap but – for its day – reliable and easy to maintain. By 1922 a new Model T was leaving the assembly line every 15 seconds. The price then was US $295.

javelin (*pilum*)

sword (*gladius*)

waist belt

sling with lead shot (*glandes*)

How were the first radio programmes heard?

The British Broadcasting Corporation was set up in 1922 and its early broadcasts were received on crystal sets like the one these people are using. Crystal sets, ancestors of today's transistors, were very simple and the signal they received could only be heard through sensitive earphones. By the 1930s, radio sets using loudspeakers were more common.

Why did Gandhi fast?

Gandhi (1869–1948), known as Mahatma meaning 'great soul', is regarded as the father of India. From 1919 he led the country's campaign for independence from the British, which was eventually granted in 1947. He was committed to non-violent action, such as refusing to pay taxes, strikes, and non-cooperation with the British, believing that independence could not be achieved by force. When he became dissatisfied with the progress of the negotiations in the 1930s, he began fasting to death (left). He would refuse to touch any food for many weeks in an effort to influence the British and to gain attention and support among Indians for the campaign.

Can you eat herbs?

The word 'herb' really means a plant which dies down after flowering, but in cookbooks it refers to the leaves of plants used to flavour food. The wild herbs below are examples.

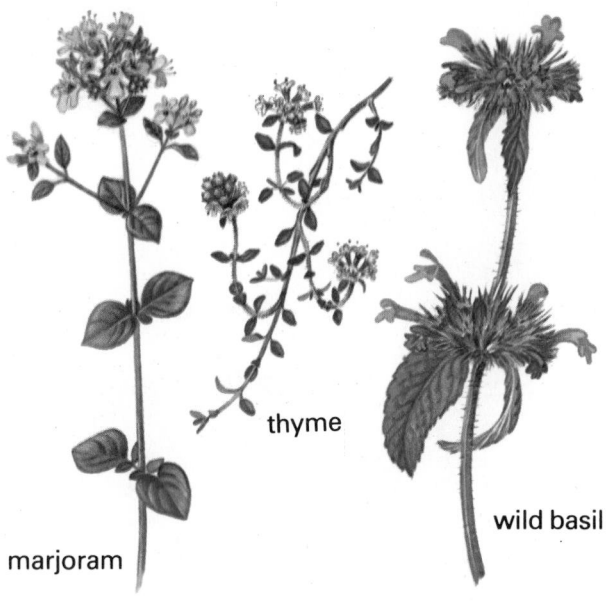

marjoram

thyme

wild basil

Is this a trap?

The Venus fly trap (below) is an insect-eating plant. The spiny leaves are about to clamp shut, and the fly will become food for the plant.

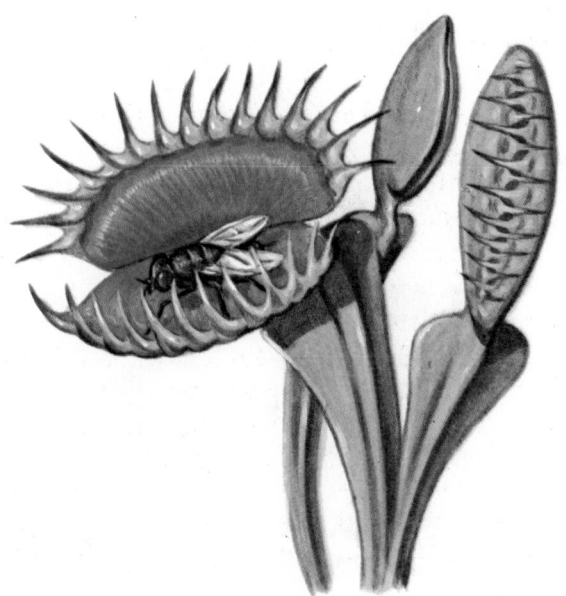

Does a rocket run on rails?

The locomotive above, which can still be seen in the Science Museum in London, is the *Rocket*, the first successful steam-driven locomotive to operate on a public railway line.

The Manchester and Liverpool Railway, the first public passenger line, hired as its engineer George Stephenson, who had designed several steam locomotives for mines. At this time, in the 1820s, steam engines were not yet recognized as the transport of the future. People considered them dangerous, and most of the directors of the Manchester and Liverpool company thought stationary engines, pulling the train by cable, would be better. Stephenson persuaded them otherwise, and a trial was held on a section of the unfinished line in 1829 to decide which type of locomotive should be chosen. The contest was won by the *Rocket*, built by Stephenson and his son Robert. It reached a maximum speed of 48 km/h (30 mph) and, unlike the other contestants, it did not break down. The railway opened in 1830 and the Railway Age was underway.

For the next century steam locomotives pulled nearly all the trains on the world's railways. By the 1930s they had grown enormously in size, power and speed, becoming the biggest land vehicles in history. It was another British locomotive, *Mallard*, which in 1938 set the world's steam speed record at 203 km/h (126 mph) pulling a seven-coach train.

213

Why build a flying boat?

In the years between the two World Wars an aircraft which could land and take off on water had many advantages. Airfields were then far fewer, especially in regions of low population, and in large cities there was little space to build long runways. Flying boats, however, could land on any convenient stretch of water.

In a flying boat, the bottom of the fuselage is formed like the hull of a ship and the aircraft lands on its 'stomach' (the floats near the wing tips prevent it dipping sideways). Flying boats were usually large aircraft, intended for long-distance passenger flights. Smaller aircraft with a normal fuselage and a float attached by struts are called 'floatplanes'. Today, floats are more common on helicopters.

The 'double-decker' flying boat on the right was a British attempt to overcome the refuelling problem on long-distance flights. The 'mother' plane took off and released her 'child' after reaching the right altitude and speed (a system like that now used for rocket-launched spacecraft). This scheme never went into regular operation, but the floatplane *Mercury*, launched by *Maia*, made a 10 000-km (6000-mile) non-stop flight from Scotland to South Africa in 1938.

How does a tank go to war?

It was obvious to the Allies in 1940 that tanks would be a major force in freeing Europe from the Germans, but this meant that large numbers of tanks had to be shifted across the English Channel from Britain to German-occupied land. The answer to this problem was the tank landing craft, which ferried the weighty monsters across the sea. On the left is a later (1953) and bigger US tank landing ship. The huge door in the bows opens downwards so tanks or other vehicles can drive on and off, once the ship has nosed onto a beach.

Quick Quiz

In what wars did the following people take part?
(1) the Roundheads, (2) the ANZACs, (3) the Desert Rats, (4) the Boers, (5) the Confederates, (6) the Black and Tans.

Answers: (1) English Civil War (2) First World War, (3) Second World War, (4) South African War, (5) American Civil War, (6) Irish Civil War.

215

Index